After War, Is Faith Possible?

After War, Is Faith Possible?

*The Life and Message
of Geoffrey "Woodbine Willie"
Studdert Kennedy*

G. A. Studdert Kennedy

Edited with an introduction by **Kerry Walters**

CASCADE *Books* • Eugene, Oregon

AFTER WAR, IS FAITH POSSIBLE?
The Life and Message of Geoffrey "Woodbine Willie" Studdert Kennedy

Copyright © 2008 Kerry Walters. All rights reserved. Except for brief quotations in critical publications or reviews, no part of this book may be reproduced in any manner without prior written permission from the publisher. Write: Permissions, Wipf & Stock, 199 W. 8th Ave., Eugene, OR 97401.

www.wipfandstock.com

Cascade Books
A Division of Wipf and Stock Publishers
199 W. 8th Ave., Suite 3
Eugene, OR 97401

ISBN 13: 978-1-55635-379-6

Cataloging-in-Publication data:

Studdert Kennedy, Geoffrey Anketell

    After war, is faith possible? : the life and message of Geoffrey "Woodbine Willie" Studdert Kennedy / Geoffrey Anketell Studdert Kennedy. Edited with an introduction by Kerry Walters.

    xii + 226 p.; 23 cm.

    Eugene, Ore.: Cascade Books

    ISBN 13: 978-1-55635-379-6

    1. World War, 1914–1918—Religious aspects. 2. World War, 1914–1918—Poetry. I. Title

PR6037.T93 2008

Manufactured in the U.S.A.

For Desmond Tutu

WOODBINE WILLIE

They gave me this name like their nature,
    Compacted of laughter and tears,
   A sweet that was born of the bitter,
   A joke that was torn from the years

Of their travail and torture, Christ's fools,
    Atoning my sins with their blood,
   Who grinned in their agony sharing
    The glorious madness of God.

Their name! Let me hear it—the symbol
    Of unpaid—unpayable debt,
For the men to whom I owed God's Peace,
    I put off with a cigarette.

Contents

Preface xi
Introduction—Woodbine Willie: The Man and His Message 1

part one **Broken Dreams**

What Is God Like? 34
What's God Up To? 36
Mad Misery 39
In a Shell Hole 40
Glory of War 41
Preserve Thy Body 43
Burying the Dead 44
Running 46
W-A-R 47
Fed Up 48
Facing Facts 49
Waste 50
A Song of the Desert 51
The Sniper 52
The Pensioner 53

part two **A Suffering and Triumphant God**

Christ Crucified Everywhere 58
After War, Is Faith Possible? 59
Why Does God Permit War? 65
God Is Powerful But Not Almighty 73

God Suffers But Overcomes 81
The Messianic Passion 83
In God's Heart 93
Facing Up to Suffering 94
The Sorrow of God 107
Indifference 113

part three **The Plain Bread of Religion**

Four Great Certainties 116
Master Passion and Neighbor Love 132
The Three Temptations 136
Sin Is No Private Matter 152
Community, Suggestion, and Salvation 155
A Sin-Bearing Community 162
Faith 169
I Lost My Lord 173

part four **Getting Christ Out of the Churches**

Herd Churches 177
Community Christians 178
Bread, Work, and Love 186
False Charity 192
Connecting Sacrament and Society 195
Making the World Less Mad, Bad, Inhuman, and Unkind 197
Force Is Weakness, Love Is Power 204
What Can *I* Do to Save? 207
The Spirit of Prayer Can Overcome War 210
This Good Samaritan Business 213
Work 217
If I Had a Million Pounds 218
It's Hard to Be a Carpenter 219

Sources 221
Select Bibliography 223

Preface

Desmond Tutu is responsible for this book, because it was while reading Tutu's *No Future Without Forgiveness* nearly a decade ago that I ran across a reference to "Geoffrey Studdert Kennedy, a chaplain who lived during the horror of the First World War [and] reflected on God's suffering over human behavior." I'd never heard of Studdert Kennedy, but was immediately intrigued and began to do a bit of spadework to find out more about this battlefield padre. It was hard going—Studdert Kennedy's books aren't that easy to find anymore—but the more I dug, the more convinced I was that I'd struck gold.

Studdert Kennedy, who earned the nickname "Woodbine Willie" during The Great War, was one of the most tireless and influential Christian pacifists and social reformers of the early twentieth century. Christian discipleship for him meant getting Christ out of the safe confines of churches and taking him where he was most needed: to sweatshops and factories that exploit workers, mansions where the privileged indulge in conspicuous consumption, political chambers where oppressive laws are written, and, most of all, on battlefields to stand between opposing armies and say *No!*

The prophetic witness of Studdert Kennedy rang a chord with his contemporaries. Thousands of demobilized and disillusioned veterans of World War I, factory and blue collar workers, miners, "navvys" or day laborers, students, clerical workers: all of them eagerly read his books and flocked to hear his sermons. They adored "Woodbine Willie," even as many members of the upper classes—including not a few high-placed Churchmen—deplored him as an ill-bred and troublesome radical.

Studdert Kennedy *was* a radical—a radical Christian who, in the truest sense of the word "radical," sought to rescue the fundamental roots of Christian discipleship from the layers of complacency, compromise, and distortion that have covered them over. Revealing the radical message of Christ is always liberating to those who are oppressed, even as it threatens those who do the oppressing or who benefit from it. That's the way it was in Studdert Kennedy's day, and so it remains in ours. In offering these selections from his works—selections which convey the heart of his message—my hope is that Studdert Kennedy's voice can inspire and guide this generation of Christians—and others—who yearn, as he did, for the coming of the beloved community.

A few words of gratitude are in order. Thanks to Charlie Collier, my editor at Wipf & Stock, for his enthusiasm and good guidance. Professor Michael Studdert Kennedy, Geoffrey's youngest son, encouraged me when I was at the beginning of this project and kindly lent me some important materials. My students in Peace and Justice Studies helped me refine my appreciation not only of Studdert Kennedy, but of Christian pacifism in general. One of them, Sara Harenchar, cheerfully and expertly aided me in the final preparation of this book. Jonah and Kim good-naturedly endured my bringing Studdert Kennedy into many dinner table conversations. And Jim Edwards, Jim Gardner, Robin Jarrell, John Jobson, Mark McCullough, and Karl Mattson sustain me with their friendship and their faithful witness to what Studdert Kennedy called the "law of love."

And, of course, "radical" thanks to Bishop Desmond Tutu.

Introduction

Woodbine Willie: The Man and His Message

It's easy to despair when one looks at the state the world is in. Climate change, partly (perhaps largely) the consequence of human irresponsibility, threatens the stability of the earth's ecosystem. Poverty, disease, and illiteracy still burden a frighteningly large percentage of the globe's population. Worldwide, national military budgets are on the increase, the production and peddling of weapons are flourishing, "terrorism" has become one of the most common words in the English language, and wars and rumors of wars abound. Add to these systemic evils the personal miseries endured by all humans—the grave illness of a child, the breakup of a relationship, the bondage of addiction, and so on—and the world can seem a pretty bleak place.

For the Christian, all this sooner or later provokes—or at least *ought* to provoke—uncomfortable questions about God and God's intentions. Why must humans suffer in the horrible ways we do? If God is loving and all-powerful, why does God allow evil to flourish? How can we continue to trust in a God seemingly indifferent to our fate?

These sorts of questions, born of the existential burden of being human, demand to be asked. They can't be adequately answered with religious platitudes that provide immediate comfort but little genuine satisfaction, much less with abstract theological defenses that try to take God off the hook. Sophisticated theodicies are as little use here as popular pietisms. Nor is despair an option. When confronted with suffering that calls our faith into question, what we need above all else is honesty: a forthright facing of the problem that refuses to retreat into sophistry, feel-good denial, or bleak despair, an honest response to the problem that takes full notice of the world's evil without allowing it the final say. Anything less than this sells short both human suffering and God.

One of the modern period's most honest and insightful Christian attempts to wrestle with the problem of evil comes from an Anglican priest, poet, and prophet named Geoffrey Anketell Studdert Kennedy. Studdert Kennedy was a World War I frontline padre, nicknamed "Woodbine Willie" by the troops to whom he ministered, whose battlefield experiences forced him to confront depths of evil and human suffering that few of us ever see. He went into the war with a relatively comfortable religious faith and a safely bookish understanding of evil. By war's end, he knew with the certainty born of the trenches that evil, especially the evil of war, is palpably real, and that its reality forever gives the lie to comfortable Christianity and abstract theologizing. His challenge was to find a way around and beyond despair.

Studdert Kennedy survived the war by a mere decade. But during his final ten years, he became one of the best-known Christian pacifists and social reformers of the day. A tireless author and lecturer, Studdert Kennedy traveled the length and breadth of the United Kingdom, as well as a fair amount of the U.S., proclaiming that faith in God is, indeed, possible after war, but only if the faith is a sober one which recognizes that our usual pious ways of conceiving God's power, majesty, purpose, and love need to be re-examined. What also needs re-thinking, Studdert Kennedy insisted, is human responsibility in light of the values taught and modeled by Jesus Christ. Translated into more concrete terms, fidelity today to Christ's message means advocacy of disarmament, pacifism, economic justice, and political freedom. Christ, as Studdert Kennedy was fond of saying, is so dangerous that most Christians want to keep Him safely bottled up in church. Let loose upon the world, His message is transformative.

Most of Studdert Kennedy's books are out of print, and his voice has been largely forgotten in the eight decades since his death.[1] This is a shame. William Temple, Archbishop of Canterbury during World War II, accurately said that there were two core questions around which all of Studdert Kennedy's thought revolves: "How to believe in and love God in

---

1. Although, a wide variety of theologians, including Desmond Tutu, Jürgen Moltmann, Eugene Peterson, John Stott, Alan Jones, and Samuel T. Lloyd, still cite him admiringly.

spite of evil; and how to get rid of it. He saw that these two questions are at root the same. For if it cannot be got rid of, that argues some fatal defect in the Creator. But if it can, then the process of getting rid of it will be the means of revealing the perfected glory of God."[2] Studdert Kennedy's struggle to arrive at honest answers has a great deal to offer those of us today who also find ourselves wishing to make the world a better place and wondering if we can hang onto our faith in the process.

The Man

Early Years

Judged by his day's standards, Studdert Kennedy was born on the wrong side of the tracks. In the first place, he had an almost unseemly number of siblings. Geoffrey, born on June 27, 1883, was one of nine children belonging to the Rev. William Studdert Kennedy and his wife Joan. When added to the children from William's first marriage, the Studdert Kennedy household bulged at the seams with fourteen youngsters.

In the second place, William and Joan were Irish-born, and their kids grew up speaking with an Irish brogue sugared with a West Yorkshire burr. Geoffrey never lost his, nor his fondness of the Irish "Paddy" stories he sprinkled throughout his sermons.

Finally, the family was poor. Although himself the son of a prominent churchman, William Studdert Kennedy shepherded one of the poorest parishes in Leeds. His church, St. Mary's at Quarry Hill, shared a sooty and squalid part of the city with a workhouse, a quarry, a tavern, and rows of tenement houses. Quarry Hill was notorious for being one of the worst slums in northern England.

From a very early age, Geoffrey displayed two characteristics that remained with him all his life: ill health and a talent for intense concentration. He suffered his first asthma attack when he was six or seven years old; growing up in polluted Quarry Hill most likely damaged his underdeveloped lungs even more. Many children "grow out of" asthma. Geoffrey never did. Exacerbated by exposure to mustard gas in the trenches during World War I and copious numbers of cigarettes, his asthmatic lungs frequently laid him up in his adult years, and they eventually killed him.

2. Temple, "Studdert Kennedy," 219.

Geoffrey learned to read while still quite young, and soon amazed his family by his prodigious consumption of books, while also amusing and sometimes irritating them by his growing absent-mindedness. Maurice Studdert Kennedy remembered his brother's "capacity for becoming entirely lost and absorbed in any and every sort of book or other written matter . . . , and emerging from it with a far-away look in his eyes . . . . He read *literally* everything that was put before him."[3] Moreover, he remembered whatever he read and was more than eager, to the occasional groans of his siblings, to lecture anyone he could corner on his latest bookish discovery. Even as a youngster, Geoffrey was a talker who delighted in sharing his ideas with others.

As Geoffrey's bookishness grew, so did his absent-mindedness. When caught out, his usual response was "I must've been thinking of something entirely different." This refrain soon became so familiar in the Studdert Kennedy household that it earned the status of a family joke, and was shouted out gustily by Geoffrey's siblings at appropriate moments. One of these, for example, was Geoffrey's returning home from the grocers with two stones of strawberries and one pound of potatoes, when he'd been sent for two pounds of strawberries and one stone of potatoes.[4]

His dreaminess also contributed to a certain insouciance when it came to his personal appearance. He frequently appeared in mismatched clothing, and was notorious for borrowing apparel from his brothers—a tie from this one, a jacket from that one—none of which really fit or suited him. "On one famous occasion," recalls a sibling, "he appeared before us almost faultlessly attired, and the one solitary article of attire he had on that belonged to him was a pair of old brown shoes, and these were so utterly down at heel that they spoilt the whole thing."[5]

In later life, Studdert Kennedy's absent-mindedness would occasion dozens of stories fondly passed around by friends and family. He frequently missed train stops and connections because he was absorbed in a book. As a young curate, on his way to a graveside committal following a funeral, he got into a conversation with a passer-by and completely forgot about the service. During the war, he regularly lost his toilet kit

---

3. Quoted in Mozley, "Home Life," 33.
4. Purcell, *Woodbine Willie*, 28.
5. Mozley, "Home Life," 36.

and assorted bits of uniform. After the war, when he'd been appointed Chaplain to the King, he showed up to conduct services for the royal family wearing rugby shorts under his cassock because he'd forgotten to change into long pants. Once, dashing from hotel room to taxi to make a speaking engagement, he forgot his false teeth, and had to send someone back to the hotel for them.

Two other characteristics of Geoffrey's childhood that stayed with him as an adult are worth mentioning. He developed a loud, braying laugh that always startled anyone hearing it for the first time. Combined with his homely face, over-sized ears, and large, puppy eyes, his extraordinary laugh was unforgettable and in later years delighted the huge audiences that came to hear him preach. More significantly, Geoffrey also developed at an early age the passion for social justice and the personal selflessness that everyone who knew him as a man associated with him. "One thing that impressed itself constantly upon one," writes his brother Maurice, " . . . was his gentle, forgiving, loving nature. He would blaze with fierce indignation at anything nasty, mean, unmanly, treacherous or unkind—any wrong or injustice done to another; but always took with a good-natured smile—or with a patient sad forgiveness—any unkindness or injustice to himself."[6]

Geoffrey's formal education was unusual. After attending a private school for a few years, he enrolled at Leeds Grammar School when he was fourteen. At the same time, he was admitted to Dublin's Trinity College. Although too young actually to attend Trinity, he remained a matriculated student *in absentia* and was allowed to take examinations at the end of each term. So until he was eighteen, Geoffrey was a student at both Leeds and Trinity, acquiring college credits even as he completed his formal secondary education. After graduating from Leeds, he moved to Trinity as a full-time student and in 1904 took a First in Classics and Divinity, winning a silver medal for academic achievement.

Slum Priest

The beginning of 1905 saw Studdert Kennedy at Caldey Grange Grammar School in Lancashire, where he taught a variety of subjects for the next two and a half years. During that time he continued his voracious read-

---

6. Quoted in Mozley, "Home Life," 36–37.

ing, diving especially into Freud and Havelock Ellis. He also read a great deal of Tolstoy. All this came to fruition in future years, when Studdert Kennedy became one of the few clergymen of his day to write frankly about sexual morality *and* embrace pacifism.[7]

Although he enjoyed teaching, Studdert Kennedy eventually felt called, like his father and grandfather before him, to the ministry. In October 1907 he left Caldey Grange to prepare for ordination at Ripon Clergy College. He was ordained deacon in June 1908 (clerical preparation was more fast-paced in those days!), and eventually priested in 1910.

Studdert Kennedy's first curacy was at Rugby Parish Church. Rugby was home to the posh public school made famous in *Tom Brown's School Days*, but it was also host to a growing number of industrial factories and their attendant slums. Studdert Kennedy soon became a familiar figure to Rugby's slum dwellers. He eventually convinced his rector, A. V. Ballie, to buy an abandoned nonconformist chapel in the middle of the slums as a center for his work with the poor. Dressed in a cassock that more often than not showed signs of wear and tear, he made it his habit to wander in and out of local pubs to chat with—*not* preach at—the men gathered there. His generosity was indiscriminate and sometimes irritating to people who knew him. Baillie remembered that whatever his young curate "had in his pocket he gave away, until his landlady took charge of his money and rationed him with it. It was the same with his clothes. He gave them all away and walked about almost in rags, wearing a cassock to conceal the fact."[8] The same landlady mentioned by Baillie, pitying her threadbare tenant, once bought Studdert Kennedy an overcoat, which he promptly—to her intense annoyance—gave away.

While at Rugby parish, Studdert Kennedy developed the oratorical skills that in just a few years' time would make him one of the best-known and -loved British preachers of his day. His easy eloquence in the pulpit didn't always please all his parishioners, however. As one of them told him soon after he arrived, "I want to thank you for your sermon; of

---

7. Two of Studdert Kennedy's books, *The Woman, the Warrior, and the Christ* (1928) and *I Pronounce Them* (1927), his only novel, deal with sexual matters, focusing on issues of birth control, desire, and fidelity. Neither of them is a particularly good book, but each is noteworthy for its willingness to publicly take on issues usually avoided by clergymen of Studdert Kennedy's generation.

8. Purcell, *Woodbine Willie*, 58.

course most people thought it very bad, but it was a great help to me."[9] In one sermon, for example, he startled some in his congregation by declaring that he found the Epistle of Jude the most repulsive document in the entire New Testament. On another occasion, he offended others by insisting that sometimes he wished he could smash the church's stained glass windows and celebrate the Eucharist outside with a cup and platter.[10] Even Baillie, who recognized and nurtured Studdert Kennedy's genius, sometimes found his sermons over the top. "In his earlier days," Baillie recalled,

> he preached a sermon in the heat of the moment in which I felt he had gone more than a little too far. After church I took him for a walk in the Rectory garden and, with apparent gravity, I said 'You know, I think you exaggerated when you said there had been no one between yourself and St. Paul who had understood the Gospel.' At once he burst into a shout of uproarious laughter. He had learnt his lesson. I always told him he must not come to me with more than one heresy a week, as after that it became a bore.[11]

Studdert Kennedy found the Rugby years fulfilling. But in 1912 he returned to Leeds. His father, still vicar of St. Mary's, was eighty-seven years old, frail, widowed, and badly in need of help. Studdert Kennedy got himself reassigned to St. Mary's, where he assisted until his father died two years later. The poverty and squalor of the Quarry Hill parish was even worse than when he had lived there as a lad, and once again he threw himself into service to his congregation.

His father's passing in early 1914 marked a new chapter in Studdert Kennedy's life. He married Emily Catlow in April of that year, and the next month accepted a call to St. Paul's Parish in Worcester. He'd had offers from two other parishes. True to form, though, he leaned toward the least impressive of them. "St. Paul's has the smallest income and the poorest people," he told his new wife. "Go and look at the house, and if you think you can manage it I will accept the offer." She thought she could manage, and the couple moved to Worcester. Studdert Kennedy's new

---

9. Mozley, "Home Life," 59. Studdert Kennedy loved to tell this anecdote.
10. Purcell, *Woodbine Willie*, 62
11. Ibid., 57–58.

Introduction · 7

parish was home to nearly 4,000 souls, and his salary something less than a pound a day.

St. Paul's was Anglo-Catholic in its liturgy, and this perfectly fitted the new rector's own preference for ornate services. But although his liturgical tastes ran towards High Church, Studdert Kennedy was evangelical in his willingness to go to the everyday world of his parishioners instead of demanding that they come to his. He continued his habit of visiting local pubs. He spoke to people there and wherever else he saw an opportunity—in organized outdoor services or extemporaneously in the streets. He tirelessly visited homes and he was just as generous—some would say, profligate—with funds and possessions in Worcester as he'd been in Rugby and Leeds. One famous story of his generosity is told by one of his friends, W. Moore Ede, Dean of Worcester Cathedral:

> [F]inding an aged invalid lying on a comfortless couch he brought a pillow from the vicarage, then a pair of sheets, and when his wife came home she found he had taken a whole bedstead, the several parts of which he had carried to the sick man's house himself. She herself helped him to take the mattress which he had left behind.[12]

Ede is silent about Emily Studdert Kennedy's response to all this.[13]

Studdert Kennedy's first three months at St. Paul's strengthened his conviction, already formed in Rugby and Leeds, that economic poverty was both morally unjust and contrary to Christianity. The grinding penury endured by many of his parishioners, who for the most part worked twelve-hour shifts in Worcester's Fownes glove factory or Hardy and Padmore's foundry for weekly wages of twenty shillings, broke his heart. He exhausted himself organizing soup kitchens, boot and clothing drives, and children's clubs (something like today's after-school childcare centers), and became persuaded that charity wasn't enough to battle the chronic evil of economic injustice. What was needed was an overhauling of the entire economic system to put it more in line with Gospel values of love, servanthood, compassion, and reconciliation. Geoffrey would de-

---

12. Ede, "Studdert Kennedy," 92.

13. It's worth mentioning that Emily was devoted to Studdert Kennedy, and remained so after his death. When she died in 1964, her last words were "Geoffrey is here! Geoffrey is here!" (Grundy, *A Fiery Glow*, 86).

vote his last years to just such an overhauling. But for now it had to wait, because there was a more immediate battle to fight. The First World War erupted in August 1914. It changed his life forever.

Frontline Padre

It's astounding that the Anglican priest who would become famous as the foremost Christian pacifist of his day was initially a patriotic defender of Britain's participation in the Great War. One month after its outbreak, Studdert Kennedy admonished the men of his parish: "I cannot say too strongly that I believe every able-bodied man ought to volunteer for service anywhere. There ought to be no shirking of that duty. Those who cannot volunteer for military service can pray." He followed his own urging by immediately applying for a commission as a wartime chaplain. But he discovered that things were more complicated than he'd imagined. Priests seeking to enlist had first to receive their bishops' release, arrange for someone to take over their parish duties for the duration of their military service, and pass an interview with officials in the Royal Army Chaplain's Department, which meant at least one visit to London.

While wading through these bureaucratic waters, Studdert Kennedy began preaching to the recruits gathering in Worcester, designated an Army training center by the War Department. On Sunday mornings, more than 2000 men marched to Worcester Cathedral to hear him. According to Dean Ede, whenever Studdert Kennedy preached to the troops, he held them "spellbound—not a cough, no shuffling of feet. What he said became the main topic of conversation during the ensuing week."[14] There are no records of what Studdert Kennedy's sermon topics were, but it's safe to assume they conveyed an enthusiastic for-God-and-country message.

Studdert Kennedy sat on the sidelines for the first fifteen months of the war. But in November 1915 his paperwork was finally in order. He was appointed Temporary Chaplain to the Forces on December 21, and with dizzying speed found himself four days later conducting a field Christmas service during a freezing downpour in France. "There were not many [communicants]," he wrote in a letter to his family and parishioners, "but they meant it. No lights, no ritual, nothing to help but the

---

14. Ede, "Studdert Kennedy," 100.

rain and the far-off roll of guns, and Christ was born in a cattle-shed on Christmas Day."[15]

By New Year's Day he was in Rouen, a staging post on the way to the Front. Day and night, a steady flow of soldiers in route to the front line detrained at the post for a quick cup of tea at the makeshift canteen. Studdert Kennedy would be waiting with a few encouraging words, an offer to write letters home for them, and perhaps a song or two. As the men loaded back on the trains, he would pace up and down the platform handing out New Testaments and packets of cigarettes—Woodbines. It was only a matter of time before the grateful troops affectionately christened him "Woodbine Willie," and the nickname stuck for the rest of his life. During his funeral procession fifteen years later, veterans of the Great War tossed packets of Woodbines on his coffin as it passed by.

Studdert Kennedy remained at Rouen through Lent of 1916. His main duty was at the railroad station, but he was also ordered to give a series of inspirational talks to British troops during the season of Lent. Reworked, these lectures became the basis of his first prose book, *Rough Talks of a Padre* (1918). In later years, the book's jingoistic support of the war embarrassed Studdert Kennedy. One of the book's most painful (but not unrepresentative) claims was that the Tommy was morally superior to the Hun because of the British "sporting tradition [which], at its best, is the highest form of the Christian spirit attainable by men at our present stage of development." Germany's "crime" is the "denial of this sporting spirit and its universal application." In fairness to Studdert Kennedy, though, his "sporting tradition" howler was a stab at answering the question that, even at this early stage of his war experience, was starting to haunt him: "How can I reconcile the spirit of those who live to kill, with the Spirit of Him who died to save?"[16]

This question took on even more urgency when Studdert Kennedy was posted for his first frontline duty in June 1916, just in time for the Somme Offensive. It was at this time that he was gassed—"I have been up the line again," he wrote his wife. "We got deluged with gas shells and had a very terrible time. I got a bit of gas, which makes me feel very miserable"[17]—and his chronic asthma grew even worse. Before war's end, he

15. Quoted in Purcell, *Woodbine Willie*, 98.
16. Kennedy, *Rough Talks by a Padre*, 26–28.
17. Quoted in Purcell, *Woodbine Willie*, 121.

would serve two more tours of frontline duty: in 1917 during the attack on Messines Ridge, and in 1918 during the final advance. At Messines Ridge, Studdert Kennedy tended to the wounded under such heavy shelling that he was awarded a ten-day leave and the Military Cross, the third highest medal for courage under fire awarded by Britain. The official record cited Studdert Kennedy "for conspicuous gallantry and devotion to duty. He showed the greatest courage and disregard for his own safety in attending to the wounded under heavy fire. He searched shell holes for our own, and enemy wounded, assisting them to the Dressing Station."[18] Studdert Kennedy more modestly insisted that he rushed out of the bunker during the shelling because he "had the wind up"—that is, panicked—fearing it would collapse under the bombardment.

A number of ailments—the ever-present asthma, trench fever, exhaustion, and general debility—laid Studdert Kennedy up for weeks at a time during his war service, and even when he was relatively well he was often unsuited for frontline service. So much of his time was spent in the rear. He served as chaplain to three different infantry schools, where his eccentricities—absent-mindedness, unmilitary bearing (at one point he showed up wearing oversized and upside-down spurs on his boots; no one ever quite figured out how he got his hands on them)—as well as his talent for speaking to soldiers on their colloquial level, earned him the love of his uniformed flocks. He was also attached at one point to a School for Physical and Bayonet Training, an extraordinary, almost surreal morale-boosting outfit that included a couple of boxers and a sergeant whose claim to fame was eighteen kills with the bayonet. The school had many of the elements of a traveling circus. Studdert Kennedy warmed up troops before preaching by asthmatically sparring with one of the boxers. It was embarrassing and it was crude. But it was also a way of reaching the troops, and Studdert Kennedy wasn't too proud to take it.

In 1916, Studdert Kennedy became part of a less clownish effort to reach the troops: the newly-launched National Mission for Repentance and Hope. Initially he resisted the posting, wanting to remain at the front. But when he protested to the Deputy Chaplain General, he was told that his "gift of the gab" was from the Almighty, and that he could do more good with the NMRH than at the front.[19]

---

18. *London Gazette*, 16 August 1917 quoted in Carey, "Studdert Kennedy," 143.
19. Carey, "Studdert Kennedy," 130.

Sponsored by the Church of England, the NMRH aimed to revitalize the flagging religious sensibilities of troops by pressing home what the Church of England saw as the larger context of the war: that the current conflict was symbolic of the battle to enthrone Christ in the hearts of all persons, and that British soldiers, when they returned to civilian life after the war, should be prepared to make of Britain a New Jerusalem—a just, fair land where poverty, privilege, and oppression have been banished. The campaign itself wasn't terribly successful—just staying alive left little energy for dreaming about the New Jerusalem—but Studdert Kennedy's preaching was. In fact, it was a hit.

There were a number of reasons for its popularity. When Studdert Kennedy preached, he used the vernacular without lapsing into condescension. He cracked jokes, laughed at them, sat on the ledge of the speaking platform with his legs dangling, and used salty language. (A typical opening line that always brought laughter and applause was: "I know what you're thinking: here comes the bloody parson!" Words like "bloody" are considered tame enough today. But in Studdert Kennedy's time, they weren't used in polite company, and certainly not by gentlemen-priests in sermons.) After his first few months of war experience, he never tried to romanticize or glamorize the brutal, mucky, day-to-day task of soldiering. He was honest without being cynical, sympathetic without being sentimental.

Above all, Studdert Kennedy's preaching reflected his utter devotion to the men in his spiritual charge. That devotion was captured in a piece of advice he gave a new chaplain:

> Live with the men, go where they go; make up your mind that you will share all their risks, and more, if you can do any good. You can take it that the best place for a padre (provided that he does not interfere with military operations) is where there is most danger of death. Our first job is to go beyond the men in self-sacrifice and reckless devotion. Don't be bamboozled into believing that your proper place is behind the line; it isn't. If you stay behind you might as well come down: you won't do a ha'p'orth of good. Your place is in front. The line is the key to the whole business; work in the very front, and they will listen to you when they come out to rest, but if you only preach and teach behind you are wasting time: the men won't pay the slightest attention to you. The men

will forgive you anything but lack of courage and devotion—without that you are useless.[20]

As preacher to thousands of troops, many of whom were asking battlefield-prompted questions about God's existence, the nature of good and evil, and the role of organized religion, Studdert Kennedy constantly searched for a way to explain theological complexities in ordinary language. He didn't try to provide the usual canned responses expected of clergy. His own battlefield experiences by this time had convinced him that those responses were totally inadequate. But he did legitimize the asking of questions by taking them seriously and acknowledging that they were worth asking. One way in which he tried to do this was by "having a go at the poetry stunt" and writing a series of dialect poems. The poems were reminiscent of Kipling's barracks ballads. The speakers in them were soldiers, grieving mothers, or wives of invalided veterans. Through their voices, Studdert Kennedy tried to do justice to the fears, doubts, anger, and questions about God and life he heard from the troops whom he served. They make for touching, sometimes haunting, and only occasionally mawkish reading even today. First collected in *Rough Rhymes* (1918), the poems went through numerous editions, were widely anthologized, and are still occasionally quoted in sermons and lectures. They made "Woodbine Willie" a household name in Britain. Characteristically, Studdert Kennedy donated all the royalties from the book to St. Dunstan's, a charity for the blind.

The same year that Studdert Kennedy published his first collection of poems also saw the appearance of his second prose book. *The Hardest Part* (1918), unlike his earlier *Rough Talks of a Padre*, was a sober, nonjingoistic examination of the question that had become uppermost in Studdert Kennedy's mind: given the insanity and brutality of war, what must the God who allows it be like? Through a series of autobiographical and theological reflections, Studdert Kennedy eventually comes to an answer he'll continue refining for the rest of his life: God isn't sadistic or indifferent, neither is God "almighty" enough to prevent humans from harming one another. But what God can and does do is to suffer along

---

20. Quoted in ibid., 139–40. The advice was given to Theodore Hardy, the most decorated chaplain of the war. Hardy was already over fifty years old when he joined up in late 1916. His battlefield service in France earned him a Military Cross, the Distinguished Service Order, and the Victoria Cross. Hardy was killed in October 1918.

with humanity, because God is love, and to love necessarily means entering into the sorrows of the beloved.[21] Moreover, neither the suffering of humans nor God is futile, because both are birthing pains that herald renewal, rebirth, resurrection.

Studdert Kennedy returned to civilian life and the parish of St. Paul's in March 1919. In some respects, he was the same man who left Worchester for the front three years earlier. He was still absent-minded, careless in appearance, boisterous in laughter, tirelessly compassionate, and lovingly generous. In other respects, though, he was deeply changed. His time in uniform had undermined his fragile physical health. God only knows what it did to his emotional well-being; such things were rarely spoken of in those days. His frontline experiences as well as his ministry to wounded and dying soldiers behind the lines destroyed once and for all any complacency about faith or any naïve confidence that God's in heaven and all's right with the world he might've once had. As he told a fellow chaplain, "You know, this business has made me less cocksure of much of which I was cocksure before. On two points I am certain: Christ and His Sacrament; apart from those I am not sure I am certain of anything."[22]

But Studdert Kennedy sold himself short, because the business of war had convinced him of three, not two, points. He came out of the war trusting in Christ, the efficacy of the Eucharist, *and* the absolute moral stupidity of war. "When I went to the war," he wrote, "I believed that the war would end to the benefit of mankind. I believed that a better order was coming for the ordinary man, and, God help me, I believe it still. But it is not through war that this order will be brought about. There are no fruits of victory, no such thing as victory in modern war. War is a universal disaster, and as far as I am concerned I'm through."[23]

---

21. The book's title, in fact, was taken from one of Studdert Kennedy's own dialect poems, "The Sorrows of God," which focuses on the necessary relationship between love and suffering. The stanza from which the title comes is this:

> The sorrows of God must be 'ard to bear
> If 'e really 'as love in 'is 'eart.
> And the 'ardest part i' the world to play
> Must surely be God's part.

22. Carey, "Studdert Kennedy," 154.
23. Quoted in Ede, "Studdert Kennedy," 107.

When Studdert Kennedy returned to Worcester, the single most important question for him, as well as for tens of thousands of other demobilized veterans, was how faith in a loving, wise, and almighty God was possible after the hell of war. Why would a good God have allowed the misery of the past four years? Come to think of it, why would a good God have allowed the pre-war miseries of poverty, ignorance, and squalor? Doesn't God care about justice? Hasn't God compassion? Wouldn't it simply be better to throw over the idea of God and go it alone? What sort of a universe should an honest person believe in?

These weren't theoretical questions for Studdert Kennedy and his fellows. They carried colossal existential weight. The response to them determined not only whether he and they could pick up the pieces of their personal lives in a post-war world, but also whether they could muster the spiritual energy to believe in the possibility, much less help build, the New Jerusalem. After war, what did the future hold: bitterness, disillusionment, and cynicism or resolve, faith, and hope?

The Prophetic Years

The first post-war years were hard ones for Studdert Kennedy, as they were for thousands of demobilized vets who returned to civilian life only to be repulsed by what they perceived as its hypocrisy and dry-rot. The Church seemed indifferent to the gospel of justice and peace proclaimed by Jesus and afraid to confront the very real crisis of faith caused by the war. The government seemed reluctant to tackle very real problems such as class privilege and poverty. Businessmen who had profited from the war grew richer, and disabled veterans and war orphans and widows grew poorer. It was the same old world. Nothing had changed, even though the rhetoric of "fresh beginnings" and "war to end all wars" was thrown about everywhere. "We trusted that God would bring us out into a wealthy place, into a new world," Studdert Kennedy wrote,

> But it is no new world that we find ourselves in, but an old world grown older, a world of selfishness grown more selfish, of greed that has grown more greedy, and of folly that knows no limit to its foolishness. There has come upon us a great disillusionment. We thought that the great Peace Conference was travailing to the birth of Peace, and it has brought forth an abortive pandemo-

nium. Millions who gave up their all in a frenzy of self-sacrifice during the war are asking themselves bitterly what they gave it for. What's the good? and who's to gain? We are fed up.[24]

The situation maddened Studdert Kennedy. "This post-war world is black with lies," he wrote, "biting and buzzing round everything . . . There's a bad smell about—a very bad smell; it is like the smell of the Dead—it is the smell of dead souls."[25]

A lesser man might've shut down. But Studdert Kennedy embarked on a program to help the people of his generation come to terms with the roots of their malaise. He had emerged from the war a celebrity—Woodbine Willie. Unlike the tens of thousands of anonymous Tommies with whom he'd served, he had a national name and commanded national attention. He was an author, a holder of the Military Cross, and a red-cassocked King's Chaplain (appointed right after the Armistice). He felt that it was his duty to turn his fame to good end.

As far as Studdert Kennedy was concerned, the moral and political problems of his day were at bottom spiritual ones born of the existential vacuum created by the war: "the uselessness of life, the fatuous futility of our sufferings and pains, the boredom of energy expended to no purpose and with no clear end in view, the pure silliness of modern warfare."[26] Help people discover genuine purpose in life, help them to live their faith rather than indifferently mouth platitudinous caricatures of it, and the New Jerusalem Studdert Kennedy had preached during his tour of duty with the NMRH would come a little closer.

The first task was to diagnose with honesty and compassion. So for the first three years after the war, Studdert Kennedy spent many evenings and late nights after a full day of parish work writing a couple of books—*Lies!* (1919) and *Food for the Fed Up* (1921)—that examined the soul-rotting nihilism bred by the war. *Food for the Fed Up* is one of his best books. Ostensibly an examination of the Apostles Creed, it's actually an attempt to persuade readers that the phenomenon of war need not destroy religious faith. It contains in germ the ideas he would develop over the next decade about the suffering God, evolution and community, Christ, the role of the Church, pacifism, and the just society. *Lies!* is an

24. Studdert Kennedy, *Food for the Fed Up*, 7.
25. Studdert Kennedy, *Lies!*, ix.
26. Studdert Kennedy, *Food for the Fed Up*, 2.

exploration of the essential principles of Christ (as opposed, sometimes, to the dogma of the Church) and how they ought to be applied to social and economic problems. The writing of these two books helped Studdert Kennedy sort through his own thoughts, and they most likely also helped lay to rest some of the ghosts he brought back from the war.

For the next ten years, Studdert Kennedy produced a stream of books, pamphlets, articles, and poems, becoming one of Britain's most prolific religious authors. (Eventually, as a timesaver, he started dictating his books, pacing back and forth with great strides, his face screwed up in concentration, smoking nonstop.) But easy as the written word was for him, he was first and foremost a preacher. In 1922, Studdert Kennedy gave up his living at St. Paul's to become the chief missioner or "Messenger" of the recently formed Industrial Christian Fellowship. He stumped up and down the country, in all kinds of weather, visiting cities, towns, and villages to speak at ICF crusades in factories, cathedrals, street corners, town halls, theaters and chapels, until his death. Indeed, death would finally catch up with him while he was embarked on ICF business.

The Industrial Christian Fellowship was formed in 1919 through the merger of two separate agencies, the Christian Social Union and the Navvy's Mission.[27] The Christian Social Union, founded in 1889, took as its primary purpose the application of Christian moral principles to social and economic problems. The Navvy's Mission, founded in 1877, was an advocate for navvys, or casual laborers who drifted from town to town following work. The Mission aimed to promote the spiritual well-being of navvys, but also to make the Church mindful of the wretchedness of their living and working conditions. After the two older organizations incorporated to form the ICF, the new organization's mission was to proclaim Christ's supremacy to both employers and employees in the hope of encouraging just wages, hours, and working conditions. ICF missioners worked with priests and bishops around the country to offer crusades. Traditional evangelical crusades or revivals focused almost exclusively on emotional soul-searching and personal salvation. But ICF crusades, while not dismissing the importance of personal salvation, aimed primarily at encouraging listeners to understand their Christian faith as an alternative to materialistic socialism on the one hand and ruthlessly

---

27. Gerald Studdert Kennedy, Geoffrey's nephew, writes about the ICF's origins and history, as well as his uncle's role, in "'Woodbine Willie,'" and *Dog-Collar Democracy*.

competitive capitalism on the other when it came to healing social ills. Crusading missioners met working people on their own ground—factories and shops—spoke their plain language instead of lofty Churchspeak, and avoided condescension and feel-good-piety.

An ICF handbook drawn up for missioners—one that Studdert Kennedy doubtlessly consulted many times—clearly explains the purpose of the crusade:

> It is an endeavor to present the Christian religion to the people of a town or district as the solution of the problem of modern social life as they see and experience it . . . The appeal to the individual is made to him as a member of society. A Crusade endeavors to give this message to those whom the Church does not otherwise reach . . . It does not aim directly at getting people into the Church, though that has sometimes happened to a considerable extent; but it offers a magnificent opportunity for the removal of deep-seated misconceptions, and for putting truer ways of thinking before people who have hitherto left organized religion altogether out of account.[28]

His talent for preaching made Studdert Kennedy exactly the right person to serve as the ICF's chief missioner. He toned down the (mild by today's standards) swearing that he'd used in speaking to soldiers during the war, but he retained and improved on his ability to speak to large crowds in their own idiom. To his auditors, his sermons seemed spontaneous, their delivery fresh and inspired. In fact, Studdert Kennedy wrote out each of his sermons, carefully working and reworking them until he was satisfied. Then he memorized them, word-for-word. Literally tens of hours went into the making of each sermon.

Studdert Kennedy's stumping across the country for the ICF didn't interfere with his writing; in fact, his sermons frequently served as raw material for his books. In 1921, he published his most explicitly political book, *Democracy and the Dog Collar*. The only one of his books that hasn't aged well, *Democracy and the Dog Collar*, written as a rather stilted dialogue, explores the relationship between "organized labor" and "organized religions." *The Wicket Gate*, perhaps his single best book and cer-

---

28. ICF Handbook *Christ the Lord of All Life*, quoted in Purcell, *Woodbine Willie*, 203.

tainly most read one, appeared in 1923. It's a kind of catechism that takes readers through the fundamentals of Christian faith, using the Lord's Prayer as a vehicle. *The Word and the Work* (1925), a series of Lenten meditations based on the Prologue to John's Gospel, and two works on human sexuality, sublimation, and society, *I Pronounce Them* (1927) and *The Warrior, the Woman, and the Church* (1928), appeared in quick order. He also continued to write poetry, gradually moving away from the dialect verse he'd written during the war to more lyrical poems. A new edition of his poetry appeared in 1924 under the title *The Sorrows of God*, and he continued revising subsequent editions of it until his death. A few unfinished writings, anthologized as *The New Man in Christ* (1932), were published posthumously.

When Studdert Kennedy left St. Paul's, he was offered the parish of St. Edmund's in the middle of London's financial district. The living was given him to provide a steady income for his growing family (his third and last son was born in 1926) as well as some relief from his hectic schedule. Since St. Edmund's was in a section of London practically deserted on weekends, it was thought that there would be little pastoral work connected with it for Studdert Kennedy to perform. But his fame as a preacher and priest was so great that St. Edmund's soon attracted large crowds, and eventually Studdert Kennedy found himself preaching there at least two Sundays a month. He was also in great demand throughout Britain as a retreat leader. In fact, most of his posthumous *The New Man in Christ* are retreat outlines, sermons, and notes.

Although his pastoral duties added to his work load, Studdert Kennedy wouldn't have preferred things otherwise. He took his clerical role seriously. A candidate for ordination once asked him for his thoughts on the priesthood. Studdert Kennedy replied that a clergyperson should be prophet, pastor, and priest: proclaiming the social gospel to the world, caring for the souls in his charge, dispensing the sacraments, and "bearing upon himself the burden of the sins and sorrows of his people."[29] This last conviction, expressing as it does his ever-present compassion and fellow-feeling, is one of the reasons so many people sought him out as a spiritual counselor and confessor. A characteristic story comes from one of his parishioners at St. Edmund's:

---

29. Quoted in Kirk, "Studdert Kennedy," 185.

> The Rector would never press confession on anyone. I never heard him mention it in his sermons; but he would always hear confessions when asked. I want to mention a little incident in this connection which is very precious to me, and which shows the wonderful understanding he had. I went to the Rector for my first confession, and amongst all the sins I had to confess there was one which literally made me squirm with shame to have to mention. It was by no means so serious as some of the others, but somehow to admit it before a human being was frightfully hard. But it had to be done, of course. He saw how I felt, and as I finished, he said with infinite tenderness, "Yes, my dear, that's my great temptation, too!" Just imagine how that helped me![30]

Studdert Kennedy's travels for the ICF often separated him from his family, as did his duties at St. Edmund's (his family continued to live in Worcester). It was a lonely and exhausting life. Frequently he arrived at his next speaking engagement tired out and gasping for breath from an asthma attack. After mustering up enough energy to preach in his usual spellbinding style, he'd collapse later, on occasion sobbing out apologies to his hosts because he feared he'd "made a mess of it." He was burning the candle at both ends, and he knew it. "Worn out," he reassured concerned friends, "but not worked out!"[31]

It wasn't surprising that the end came when he was away from home and family. In March 1929, Studdert Kennedy left his home in Worchester to travel to Liverpool to give a series of Lenten addresses. His wife and children were down with the flu, and he was reluctant to leave them. But duty called, and he took a train to Liverpool. Shortly after his arrival, he too began to show symptoms of flu. His old enemy asthma set in, and his heart began to fail. A hasty telegram was sent to Worcester to summon his wife. Studdert Kennedy was in coma by the time she arrived, and died shortly afterward on March 8, 1929.

The next day, P. T. R. Kirk, head of the Industrial Christian Fellowship, proposed to the Dean of Westminster that Studdert Kennedy be buried in the Abbey. "What!" the Dean replied. "Studdert Kennedy? He was a socialist!" So Woodbine Willie was buried in Worcester, with

---

30. Ibid., 182.
31. Purcell, *Woodbine Willie*, 213.

a funeral service, attended by over 2,000 mourners, at his old parish, St. Paul's. Thousands of people lined the streets of Worcester during the funeral procession. Wreaths came from all over the country, including one from the King and Queen. Other wreaths carried notes saying "A token of respect on behalf of the Worcester unemployed," "from one of Worcester's poorest widows," "from a disabled Irishman," "from the little cripples of Newtown Hospital," and "from just an ordinary working girl from Liverpool."[32] A memorial plague erected in Worcester Cathedral said it all:

GEOFFREY ANKETELL

STUDDERT KENNEDY

A POET: A PROPHET: A PASSIONATE SEEKER AFTER

TRUTH: AN ARDENT ADVOCATE OF CHRISTIAN FELLOWSHIP

The Message

The Problem of Evil

"How to believe in and love God in spite of evil; and how to get rid of it": so William Temple characterized the heart of Studdert Kennedy's message. Temple was quite correct in his appraisal. There's no good substitute for Studdert Kennedy's own words, but a brief overview of how he wrestled with the problem of evil will provide the reader with a roadmap for the selections from his writing assembled in this volume.

Given his parish experiences of brutal poverty at Rugby, Leeds, and Worcester, it's possible that Studdert Kennedy would've found his way to the problem of evil even if World War I hadn't occurred. But there's no doubt that his participation in The Great War hurtled him with dynamite-force straight into it. For Studdert Kennedy, war *was* the problem of evil in "acute form,"[33] the test case for determining if Christianity can cope with evil. There are, he wrote, "no words foul and filthy enough" to describe war. It's so hideous that a theist—and especially a Christian—is faced with what looks like a bleak but necessary disjunction: "God is

---

32. Grundy, *A Fiery Glow*, 82.
33. Studdert Kennedy, "The Religious Difficulties of the Private Soldier," 380.

helpless to prevent war, or else He wills it and approves of it. There is your alternative. You pay your money and you take your alternatives."[34]

For the most part, Christians in the past have taken the second alternative, the thought of a less-than-omnipotent God seemingly more offensive to them the apparent inconsistency of an all-loving God who nonetheless wills and approves of war. But for Studdert Kennedy the pacifist, this conclusion is deadly. "If it is true, I go morally mad. Good and evil cease to have any meaning. If anything is evil, war is."[35] How, then, could God possibly will it? Yet wars obviously plague humanity. Why doesn't God prevent them?

In trying to address these questions, Studdert Kennedy takes as fundamental the claim that the primary attribute of God is love, and that God's power must be understood in terms of love rather than force. The belief that divine omnipotence means that God can do anything causes a great deal of mischief, not the least of which is human resentment and bewilderment when God apparently allows innocent suffering to take place. As a corrective, Studdert Kennedy insists that God's power must be thought of as capable of overcoming "humanly incomprehensible difficulties," but not of doing absolutely *anything*.[36] God's only real power is noncoercive love.

The primary function of love is to unite. In creating the natural order God "had to submit to limitations, due to the necessary nature of matter itself."[37] For example, God was constrained to create the natural order so that its constituents are united through intricate patterns of causal interdependence. But a necessary condition for love is freedom to choose love. So God also created humans who are both causally interdependent and capable of free choice. The combination of interdependence and freedom is obviously risky, but it's a risk a loving God had to take. Interdependence and freedom mean that humans can voluntarily cooperate with one another to make for themselves a good, just, and rewarding community. But it also necessarily means that they can choose to savage one another in a struggle for resources, space, and power, destroying themselves and

---

34. Studdert Kennedy, *The Hardest Part*, 34.

35. Ibid., 35. In *Lies!* (p. 6), Studdert Kennedy is even more emphatic: "If God wills War, then I am an atheist, an anti-theist. I am against God. I hate Him."

36. Studdert Kennedy, "The Religious Difficulties of the Private Soldier," 382.

37. Studdert Kennedy, *Lies!*, 153.

despoiling the environment. If they choose this second course, God cannot intervene without stepping on both causal interdependence and free will. God can't do anything. God is self-limiting.

But if God won't intervene to prevent war and other kinds of harm to innocents set in motion by human freedom and interdependence, what's the point of it all? How can humans bear the sheer weight of existence?

Studdert Kennedy responds by defending an evolution/eschatology in which divine love works itself throughout all creation, prodding the natural order ever forward toward greater cooperation, unity, concord, and reconciliation. This movement follows from his axiomatic claim that God is love: the loving Creator stamps the creation with His likeness. God has already laid down the necessary condition for the possibility of cooperation in the natural order by making all things interdependent. The "law of love," as Studdert Kennedy came to call it, quickens this interdependence and embeds within the entire evolutionary process an eschatological drive toward the emergence of the beloved community, that culmination of history in which God's vision of concord reaches fruition and war, injustice, and suffering are no more. Studdert Kennedy's beloved community is the New Jerusalem he preached while working for the wartime National Mission for Repentance and Hope.

It follows for Studdert Kennedy that neither nature nor history ought to be judged according to their frequently bloody past but instead according to the highest point they achieve, for the nature of something is revealed not in how it began but in what it becomes. The high point of all creation is the Christ, the embodiment of the law of love, the harbinger of the beloved community. Evolution is "not a descent but an ascension, not a mechanical and determined ascension, but a moral and spiritual progress which can only take place as men are in Christ, living their life in His Spirit, and basing their thought on His law—the law of Love."[38]

Human beings have the potential to grow ever more Christ-like in their love for God, one another, and all of creation. This is part of what it means to be made in God's likeness. But until they consciously embrace this potential and strive to actualize it in their lives, force rather than love will remain the dominant expression of power in society. Force is an uncreative, unimaginative power. It may strong-arm a certain degree of uniformity, but is forever incapable of achieving genuine unity. Under its

---

38. Studdert Kennedy, *Food for the Fed Up*, 289.

dominions, wars and the rumors of war will continue. So will economic and social systems that exploit the many for the sake of the few.

That's the bad news. God's omnipotence simply can't eliminate the evil of innocent suffering by "imposing" love, because not even God can perform such a contradictory act. Love must be freely given and accepted, not forced. But the good news is that the universe is an "unfinished movement" in which the underlying melody is love, and that all of creation is moving toward ever greater concord that will culminate in the beloved community.[39]

In the meantime, as we humans painfully and haltingly wean ourselves of the illusion that force rather than love is the universe's fuel, we suffer. We continue to assail one another, both systemically, with wars and unjust social and economic institutions, and personally, with hateful and uncompassionate behavior. And, insists Studdert Kennedy, God suffers along with us. Humanity is God's martyrdom.[40] To love is to take on the beloved's suffering for the sake of love. This God willingly does. For Studdert Kennedy, the classical claim that God is impassable, incapable of experiencing pain, is contrary to both human experience of the Divine and the testimony of Scripture. God isn't an aloof, untouched observer. God suffers along with us, groans and travails with the creation, and longs, as do we, for the coming of the beloved community.

But as affirmed by the Passion, Death, and Resurrection of Christ, God's suffering—and, Studdert Kennedy claims, humanity's as well—isn't the final word. The good news of Christianity isn't just that Christ was crucified, but that he is not dead. Loveless power, the violence of war, exploitation, the agents of suffering and death: these are all forms of sin which God takes upon himself in order to lead the world to love. As Studdert Kennedy wrote, speaking specifically of war,

> War is just sin in a million forms, in a million of God's gifts misused. God cannot deal with war in any other way than that by which He deals with sin. He cannot save us from war except by saving us from sin. How does God deal with sin? By what way does He conquer it? By the way of the Cross, the way of love. He suffers for it; He takes it upon Himself, and He calls on us

---

39. Ibid., 195.
40. Ibid., 187.

to share His burden, to partake of His suffering . . . , that by [His and our] suffering the power of evil may be broken and the world redeemed.[41]

In part because of his eschatological faith that love is the driving force in creation, in part because of his own compassionate temperament, Studdert Kennedy placed more emphasis in both his writings and pastoral work on explaining and alleviating suffering than condemning those who inflicted it or bemoaning the world's cruelty. In spite of the chaos of the war and the blight of poverty, Studdert Kennedy had no patience for dour, world-hating Christianity, and thought it stupid and cruel of the Church to preach that God's creation is fallen.[42] He was also wary of those who saw humanity as hopelessly depraved. Most sin, he asserted, isn't outright willful rebellion so much as ignorance.[43] Even Christ suggested as much when he pled with the Father to "forgive them, for they know not what they do." Humans, made in God's likeness, are no more irretrievably fallen than creation is. But they live in a culture that encourages moral stupidity. Teach them the truth about power and the suffering God; inspire them with the promise of the beloved community; instruct them in alternatives to war; offer them, in short, the countercultural vision preached and practiced by Christ, and the likeness of God which they carry within them will respond with gratitude and enthusiasm. Like speaks to like.

Getting Rid of Evil

Humans are called to collaborate actively in the eschatological/evolutionary movement from force to love. But in order to do this, they must become quite clear about their religious convictions, because the kind of God one worships—one's "master passion"—in turn determines how one looks at self, others, and the world.[44] It's the Church's business to help people honestly explore the basis of their faith and come to an appreciation of how its fundamental principles can and should influence

---

41. Studdert Kennedy, *The Hardest Part*, 114–15.
42. Studdert Kennedy, *Food for the Fed Up*, 177.
43. Ibid., 201.
44. Studdert Kennedy, *Lies!*, 111.

both private and social life. "A divorce between the secular and the sacred means the death of real religion."[45]

For Studdert Kennedy, getting clear about God, as we've seen, is recognizing that God is Love and that God suffers along with creation when the law of love is thwarted or violated. Four certainties, referred to by Studdert Kennedy as the "plain bread of religion," follow from this understanding of God. They're crucial for faithful obedience to Christ and cooperation with him in building the beloved community.

The first certainty is about self: as a child of God destined to grow into my Parent's likeness, my fundamental nature is love rather than aggression or competition. Violence and egoism are unnatural to me. When I behave violent or selfishly, I'm acting less than fully human. The second certainty is about others: since all persons share a common Parent and a common inherited nature, the fundamental identity of my fellow humans is loving as well. And since love is always a movement toward unity and concord, it follows that my well-being is bound up with the flourishing of all. "We do not live, unless we live in and through the beloved community."[46] The third certainty is about the natural world. As the creation of a loving God, it necessarily bears its Creator signature. Nature is orderly, reliable, sacramental, and sacrificial, shot through with divine beauty, truth, and goodness. The Creator has not thrust his beloved children into a hostile or indifferent physical environment. The universe is benign. The fourth certainty is about death. Death is inevitable, but is never the end. Things fall only to rise again. The Death and Resurrection of Christ is both prototype and guarantee of this cosmic parabola.

Studdert Kennedy's four certainties serve both to reassure and to exhort. They reassure us by arguing that the nature of God is such that those "facts" of existence which awaken in us our most primal fears and too often determine our behavior in the world—the aggression and rage we at times recognize in ourselves, the danger to our safety we think others pose, the hostility of the natural world's army of germs, viruses, earthquakes, and now global warming, and the final and insurmountable assault, death—aren't necessary facts at all. In part they're illusions that, because we confuse them for reality, become self-fulfilling. But mainly they're the consequences of our refusal, sometimes motivated by rebel-

---

45. Studdert Kennedy, "Salvation," 146.
46. Studdert Kennedy, *The Wicket Gate*, 42.

lion but more often by ignorance, to embrace the love from which we're fashioned and to which we're destined. And this, of course, points to the exhortatory function of the four certainties: if our interpretation of self, others, the natural world and death are illusions on which our fears have bestowed a pseudo-reality, our duty is to clarify our understanding of the world and its Creator so that the power of love supplants the power of force.[47]

Practically speaking, one of the ways all this translates is by redirecting religious and moral analyses to emphasize the social rather than primarily the personal or private aspect. If love is the principle characteristic of both Creator and creation, and if the purpose of love is to unify, it only stands to reason that the basic unit of reality should be thought of as relationship or community rather than as isolated individual. Certainly the early Church thought so, thinking of both sin and virtue as primarily corporate rather than personal. The humanism of the Renaissance and Enlightenment shifted the focus from the corporate to the personal in the modern era, and the Church followed the trend. But Studdert Kennedy is clear in his disagreement with it. "Indeed," he writes, the whole notion of an individual who exists and grows by communion with God apart from communion with man is, from a Christian point of view, nonsense."[48] One properly speaks of the "body," not the "individual," when referring to Christian morality and soteriology. It's not enough to focus on personal virtue or salvation. So as a member of the Body of Christ, the individual must also confess complicity in social evil and accept his or her role in the greater corporate responsibility to fix it.

As a visible sign of the unifying love that empowers creation, the Church must be united to the world and serve as a catalyst for the movement toward ever greater concord and community. The Church must embrace its identity as a sin-bearing community, acknowledging that the

---

47. It's interesting to note that Studdert Kennedy's insistence that our primal fears about self, others, nature, and death are illusory and born from the worship of unworthy gods is similar to Sigmund Freud's thesis in *The Future of an Illusion* that religious faith is the cultural artifact that helps humans cope with their primal fears of others, nature, and death. The difference of course is that Studdert Kennedy thinks the fears are for the most part unfounded because of the existence of a loving God, while Freud thinks that the fears point to quite real dangers and the religious faith that insulates us against them is illusory. Freud's book was published three years after Studdert Kennedy's treatment of the four certainties in *The Wicket Gate*.

48. Studdert Kennedy, *The Wicket Gate*, 181–82.

guilt of the world is also its guilt, shouldering the sins of all out of love for all.[49] Love bears the sins of others, and if the Church is to be authentic, it must so love the world that it bears the world's burdens instead of retreating into an isolated and other-worldly churchiness. This is the perennial temptation of the Church: to disassociate from the world, to rationalize the suffering in it as part of some grand and inscrutable plan, and to repress its nobler instincts to assuage suffering.[50] Had the Church accepted its responsibility to the world by denouncing the sins of militarism and nationalism, the First World War's slaughter of Europe's finest might have been avoided. Had the Church accepted its complicity in the sins of imperialism and greed, the slums of Leeds, Rugby, and Worcester—not to mention those of Delhi, Jakarta, and Nairobi—might never have blighted countless lives.

Once responsibility is confessed, genuine collaboration with God in the building of the beloved community can begin. The poverty that afflicts the majority of the world's inhabitants is a perverse sacrament, a diabolical inversion of God's plans, an "outward and visible sign of an inward and spiritual disgrace."[51] Christians should no more tolerate its continuation than they should tolerate more dramatic evils such as murder or rape. Poverty, no more than murder or rape, is either inevitable or natural. It violates the fundamental law of love. It is a perversion of the natural order.

But alleviating poverty isn't simply a matter of redistributing wealth (although some of this might be necessary), much less of simple charity (although in times of crisis charity is essential). The human ability—the human *opportunity*—to work is important. Society owes the poor meaningful, creative, and rewarding labor. Moreover, the rich should resist the urge to sit idly on their fortunes. Their wealth is a responsibility, not an entitlement. Contrary to the claims of Marxist interpretations on the one hand and capitalist ones on the other, work is best understood not in terms of class struggle or competition, but as a catalyst for the love that percolates through human history. "God's plan and purpose for the world are being wrought out through work."[52] Work encourages cooperation

49. Ibid., 183.
50. Studdert Kennedy, "Salvation," 142–46.
51. Ibid., 147.
52. Studdert Kennedy, "Bread, Work, and Love," 265.

and collaboration between people. It's one of the ways in which evolution progresses and eschatology unfolds, and the just society honors it as such. The Church's business, through preaching from the pulpit, hands-on service, and social agitation such as embodied by ICF crusades, is to remind society of this truth. Christians should emulate the Good Samaritan in tending to the immediate and urgent needs of those who suffer. But this isn't enough. Christians must also confront the unjust social structures that cause the suffering in the first place.

> You and I are part owners at any rate of these roads to Jericho that are infested by sharks and thieves, and it doesn't do for us to think that our duty ends in helping us to supply endless charitable funds, and financing innumerable societies to save the underdog. We cannot stop short of an earnest endeavor to clear out the thieves, and so to strengthen the travelers on the road that they may be able to defend themselves against those we cannot clear out.[53]

Studdert Kennedy insisted time after time that he was no theologian or intellectual. Although well-read in theology, he came to distrust its authenticity, seeing it as a continuously changing way of glossing over hard realities—such as the problem of evil—that seem incompatible with the Christian story. Echoing the fourth-century Hilary of Poitiers, Studdert Kennedy worried that theologians too often labored under an "irreligious solicitude for God" and tried to protect God's good name by contriving all sorts of face-saving but artificial abstractions.[54] But God has no need of our theological solicitude. The simple religion embraced by the working poor, the simple laborer, the self-sacrificing mother and wife, father and husband, are better tributes. Its essentials are few: God loves us enough to bear our burdens and suffer along with us; the destruction of war and the grinding poison of poverty will not have the final word, because Christ's example promises us resurrection from death; the beloved community, that spiritual state of affairs in which the law of love finally comes into its own, is the terminus point toward which hall history is directed; and that the beloved community's appearance, while inevitable, is hastened by our earnest steps to wean ourselves of force and embrace the power of love.

53. Studdert Kennedy, *The New Man in Christ*, 234.
54. Studdert Kennedy, "The Religious Difficulties of the Private Soldier," 285.

This is the heart of Studdert Kennedy's message. For him, it was the core of Christ's good news.

A Note on the Text

The writings collected here, prose as well as poetry, are organized into four thematic sections.

Part I, "Broken Dreams," offers some of Studdert Kennedy's rawest descriptions of the horror of war. Most of them are autobiographical. All of them chillingly express the despair, cynicism, and general feeling of being "fed up" Studdert Kennedy and thousands of other demobilized veterans carried with them from the war.

Part II, "A Suffering and Triumphant God," focuses on Studdert Kennedy's struggle to come to terms with the problem of evil as he explores the nature of divine power, the evolutionary/eschatological drive of love, and the fellow-suffering voluntarily shouldered by God. In many ways, the writings collected in this section are the heart of Studdert Kennedy's message.

Part III, "The Plain Bread of Religion," offers writings that explore Studdert Kennedy's assertion that our way of thinking about reality and treating our fellow humans follows from the sort of God we choose to worship. The community-centered nature of his understanding of Christianity is the central theme throughout them.

Part IV, "Getting Christ Out of the Churches," focuses on Studdert Kennedy's thoughts on specific ways to apply Christ's gospel to the world's problems, and especially his understanding of work as a prime facilitator of the law of love.

In a collection of this kind, a bit of repetition is unavoidable, especially since Studdert Kennedy tended to return to the same basic themes throughout most of his writing and public speaking. But when he *does* return to them, he almost always approaches them from angles different from earlier ones. The result is a variety of fresh perspectives on constant themes. I hope that whatever repetition the reader encounters in the texts anthologized here follow the same pattern.

I've changed nothing in the texts except Studdert Kennedy's British spelling. His use of upper case letters is a bit eccentric, and probably reflects his sensitive ear for the rhythm of the spoken word. Fearing that imposing an editorial uniformity on them would step on the intonations and inflections Studdert Kennedy wanted to get across, I've left them alone. Original publication dates are indicated at the end of each selection.

All footnotes and ellipses in the selections are mine. The former are explanatory or bibliographical, the latter signal an editorial omission on my part of words or passages in the original texts.

part one

Broken Dreams

The Christian Creed won't wash or wear. When you plunge it into the cold water of reason it shrinks until there is nothing left of it, nothing save this splendid but shadowy Figure who fades away into the mists of time, and leaves us alone with wars and workhouses, factory chimneys and squalid streets—alone in a modern mechanical, vulgar world of sordid realities. O my God, these tales of unbearable beauty that break the hearts of men because they are not true! I came out of Birmingham Cathedral, from the Burne-Jones window of the Ascension, into the twilight streets, and an amateur prostitute giggled. The oldest profession in the world—dreams and reality.

(1921)

What Is God Like?

When I had been in France as a chaplain about two months, before I had heard a gun fired or seen a trench, I went to see an officer in a base hospital who was slowly recovering from very serious wounds. The conversation turned on religion, and he seemed anxious to get at the truth. He asked me a tremendous question. "What I want to know, Padre," he said, "is, what is God like? I never thought much about it before the war. I took the world for granted. I was not religious, though I was confirmed and went to Communion sometimes with my wife. But now it all seems different. I realize that I am a member of the human race, and have a duty towards it, and that makes me want to know what God is like. When I am transferred into a new battalion I want to know what the Colonel is like. He bosses the show, and it makes a lot of difference to me what sort he is. Now I realize that I am in the battalion of humanity, and I want to know what the Colonel of the world is like. That is your real business, Padre; you ought to know."

 . . . I pointed to a crucifix which hung over the officer's bed, and said, "Yes, I think I can tell you. God is like that." I wondered if it would satisfy him. It did not. He was silent for a while, looking at the crucifix, and then he turned to me, and his face was full of doubt and disappointment. "What do you mean?" he said. "God cannot be like that. God is Almighty, Maker of heaven and earth, Monarch of the world, the King of kings, the Lord of lords, whose will sways all the world. That is a battered, wounded, bleeding figure, nailed to a cross and helpless, defeated by the world and broken in all but spirit. That is not God; it is part of God's plan: God's mysterious, repulsive, and apparently futile plan for saving the world from sin. I cannot understand the plan, and it appears to be a thoroughly bad one, because it has not saved the world from sin. It has been an accomplished fact now for nearly two thousand years, and we have sung hymns about God's victory, and yet the world is full of sin, and now there is this filthy war. I'm sick of this cant. You have not been up there, Padre, and you know nothing about it. I tell you that cross does not help me a bit; it makes things worse. I admire Jesus of Nazareth; I think He was splendid, as my friends at the front are splendid—splendid in their courage, patience, and unbroken spirit. But I asked you not what Jesus *was* like, but what God *is* like, God Who willed His death in agony upon the Cross, and Who apparently wills the wholesale slaughter in this war. Jesus Christ I know and admire, but what is God Almighty like? To me He is still the unknown God."

(1918)

What's God Up To?

June 7th, 1917. In the assembly trenches on the morning of the attack on the Whyschaete-Messines Ridge. The _____ division attacked first, and our men went through their lines to the last objective.

☙

It is God alone that matters. I am quite sure about that. I'm not sure that it is not the only thing I am sure about. It is not any Church of God, or priest of God; it is not even any act of God in the past like the Birth of Christ or His death upon the Cross. These may be revelations of what God is or means by which He works; but it is God Himself, acting here and now upon the souls of men; it is He alone that can save the world.

There is only one commandment really: Thou shalt love the Lord thy God with all thy heart, with all thy mind, with all thy strength—with the whole bag of tricks in fact. It's got to be a whole hog, go-ahead and damn the consequences kind of love—a complete and enthusiastic surrender of the whole man to the leadership of God. It is funny that the body isn't mentioned; it comes in here a bit, the giving of the body. It's about all some of these dear chaps know how to give, and they give like kings: better than many kings, God bless 'em. There is the whole of vital religion, and therefore the whole of life, in a nutshell—Love God all out, and then live with all your might. The other commandment is only a bit off the big one. You couldn't help loving your neighbor if you once loved God. You may love churches and services and hymns and things, and not love your neighbor; lots of people do, but that is not loving God. These things become ends in themselves, and then they are worse than useless. That's always been the bother with religion.

It's a difficult business. I suppose loving God means knowing God. You can't love a person unless you know him. How can a man know God? "By their fruits ye shall know them." I suppose that rule applies. By God's fruits ye shall know Him. That is the queerest yet. It fairly beats the band—God's fruits. Where do they begin, and where do they end?

☙

I suppose it must be getting on time now. Five minutes past three, I make it, and ten minutes past is zero. It will be the devil of a shindy when it starts. What a glorious morning! So still. Now the birds are just waking in English Wood. How soft the silver dawn light is, and this grey mist that hangs so low makes all the open meadowland just like a dim-lit sea, with clumps of trees for islands. In the east there is a flush of red—blood red. Blood . . . Beauty . . . God's fruits. I wonder what—

⁂

God Almighty! What's that? It's the Hill gone up. Lord, what a noise! And all the earth is shaking. It must be like that Korah, Dathan, and Abiram business in the Book of Numbers up there.[1] All the lot went down, women and children and all. I always thought it was hard luck on the children. It's like war though. War is just a mighty earthquake that swallows all before it. Now for it. Here come the guns. Listen to that big 12-inch. It sounds like the man with a loud voice and no brains in an argument. I thought I'd get the wind up, and here I am laughing. We're all laughing. We're enjoying it. That's the stuff to give 'em. It is a glorious sight, one silver sheet of leaping flame against the blackness of the trees. But it's damnable, it's a disgrace to civilization. It's murder—wholesale murder. We can't see the other end—ugh—damn all war! They have wives and kiddies like my Patrick, and they are being torn to bits and tortured. It's damnable. What's that, lad? Shout a bit louder. It is, you're *right*, it is the stuff to give 'em. They can't stand much of that; they'll have to quit.

⁂

How wonderful that sky is, golden red, and all the grass is diamond-spangled like the gorgeous robe that clothes a king. Solomon in all his glory. Look at that lark. Up he goes. He doesn't care a tuppeny dump for the guns. His song is drowned, but not his joy.

>God's in His heaven;
>All's right with the—

⁂

---

1. A reference to Numbers 16, which recounts the fate of Korah, Dathan, and Abiram, rebels against Moses during the Wilderness years. Along with their families and followers, they were swallowed up by a mighty earthquake as punishment for their transgression.

What awful nonsense! All's right with the world, and this ghastly, hideous—But, by George, it's a glorious barrage, and English girls made 'em. We're all in it—sweethearts, mothers, and wives. The hand that rocks the cradle wrecks the world. There are no non-combatants. We're all in it, and God, God Almighty, the loving Father Who takes count of every sparrow's fall, what is He doing? It is hard to fathom. God's fruits, singing birds and splendid beauty, flowers and fair summer skies, golden mists and—bloody slaughter! What is a man to make of it!

༄

"Almighty and everlasting God, we are taught by Thy holy word that the hearts of kings and governors are in Thy rule and governance, and that Thou dost dispose and turn them as it seemeth best to Thy godly wisdom."

I think that's right. It's in the Communion Service, anyhow. I suppose it includes the Kaiser. Anyhow, it is nonsense. What unspeakable blackguards some kings and governors have been, and what utter ruin they have caused! Why should we start a prayer with such a futile falsehood? Their hearts can't be in God's rule and governance when they are evil and base. There it is in the Communion Service. If it is true, what *is* God like?

(1918)

Mad Misery

Good Lord, what's that? A dead Boche. I kicked him hard, poor little devil. He looks like a tired child that has cried itself to sleep. He looks puzzled, as if he were asking, Why me? My God, my God, why me? What had he to do with it, anyhow? Not much great blond beast about him. He couldn't hurt a decent well-developed baby. That little chap is the very fly-blown incarnation of the filth of war. You can see all Europe asking questions in his weak blue eyes. War serves them all alike; good and bad, guilty and innocent, they all go down together in this muddy, bloody welter of mad misery. How can a man believe in an absolute Almighty God? What is He doing? "Peradventure he sleepeth." The God that answers by fire let Him be God. It is an odd thing God doesn't seem to work that way now. It would be a simple way of solving things, but Heaven makes no sign.

(1918)

In a Shell Hole

June 15th, 1917. In a shell hole near the pillbox which was battalion headquarters. The dawn of day after a battle. All night the evacuation of the wounded had gone on without a stop. There were many casualties.

☙

I don't believe I could carry another one to save my life. Lord, how my shoulders ache. I wish I were Sandow.[2] It's a good thing there are no more to carry. I wonder—will that last chap live? His thigh seemed all mash when we pulled him in. It was a beastly job. He cried for mercy and we had to drag on just the same. He is strong though, a splendid body all broken up. It's quiet now, only for those 5.9's[3] over on the right. They never stop. I'm glad to sit and think. How I do love quiet. What a perfect morning it is. All the sky burns red with the after blush of dawn, and here I seem surrounded by a soft gray sea of mist. What unutterable beauty there is in nature.

(1918)

---

2. Eugene Sandow (1867–1925), German-born Victorian strongman and bodybuilding celebrity.

3. Artillery guns.

Glory of War

In a German concrete shelter. Time, 2:30 a.m. All night we had been making unsuccessful attempts to bring down some wounded men from the line. We could not get them through the shelling. One was blown to pieces as he lay on his stretcher.

∽

I wonder how much this beastly shanty would stand. I guess it would come in on us with a direct hit, and it looks like getting one soon. Lord, that was near it. Here, somebody light that candle again. I wish we could have got those chaps down. It was murder to attempt it though. That poor lad, all blown to bits—I wonder who he was. God, it's awful. The glory of war, what utter blather it all is . . .

War is only glorious when you buy it in the *Daily Mail* and enjoy it at the breakfast table. It goes splendidly with bacon and eggs. Real war is the final limit of damnable brutality, and that's all there is in it. It's about the silliest, filthiest, most inhumanly fatuous thing that ever happened. It makes the whole universe seem like a mad muddle. One feels that all talk of order and meaning in life is insane sentimentality.

It's not as if this were the only war. It's not as if war were extraordinary or abnormal. It's as ordinary and as normal as man. In the days of peace before this war we had come to think of it as abnormal and extraordinary. We had read *The Great Illusion*,[4] and were all agreed that war was an anachronism in a civilized world. We had got past it. It was primitive, and would not, could not, come again on a large scale. It is "The Great Illusion" right enough, and it is an anachronism in a civilized world. We ought to have got past it; but we haven't. It has come again on a gigantic scale.

I say, keep that door shut; the light can be seen. I believe they are right on to this place. There was a German sausage[5] up all day just opposite, and they must have spotted movement hereabouts this morning.

---

4. Written by Norman Angell, *The Great Illusion* (1913) warned that a war between modern world powers would impoverish victors and vanquished alike. Jean Renoir's 1937 anti-war film *Grand Illusion* was influenced by Angell's title and thesis.

5. An observation Zeppelin.

There it goes again. Snakes, that's my foot you're standing on. Anybody hurt? Right-o, light the candle. It's no fun smoking in the dark.

Yes, war has come again all right. It's the rule with man, not the exception. The history of man is the history of war as far back as we can trace it. Christ made no difference to that. There never has been peace on earth. Christ could not conquer war.

(1918)

Preserve Thy Body

On the morning before the battle of June 7th, a large number of officers and men attended the Holy Communion. I noticed one corporal in particular whom I had never known to attend before. I remember thinking what a splendid young body his was as I said the words, "Preserve thy body and soul unto everlasting life." Three days later I buried his body, terribly mutilated, in a shell hole just behind the line.

(1918)

Burying the Dead

On the last Sunday in June 1917 the Advanced Dressing Station in which I was working was blown in, and everyone in it killed except the doctor, two stretcher cases, an R.A.M.C. sergeant, and myself. Among those killed was Roy Fergusson, my servant, a splendid lad of nineteen years, with whom I was great friends. He went out after the first shell had broken the end off the station to guide some walking wounded to a place of safety and was killed instantly. I found him leaning against a heap of sandbags, his head buried in his hands, and a great hole in his back.

○○

Poor old Roy. I thought I had saved his life when I sent him on that job. There seemed a decent chance of getting through, and it looked a dead certainty that we should all be killed within a few minutes. There must have been a chance. All the walking wounded apparently got through, and he alone was killed. He probably warned them and took it himself. It would be like him. He looks as if he were saying his prayers. I must get the body carried across to the cemetery near Railway Dugouts, and bury it at once. It will probably be unburied again before the morning if they start shelling again. That cemetery is an awful sight, with half its dead unburied; but it is the only place. I must give the body Christian burial somewhere, even if it is blown up again. His mother will surely want to know where he rests.

Mothers always want to know that first. I wonder why. Do they think that this same broken body will break the earth above its grave and rise again to become once more the temple of the spirit that has passed on? Do they think that it matters in the resurrection where the body lies, or is it just a natural longing, an echo of Mary's exceeding bitter cry beside the empty tomb, "They have taken away my Lord, and I know not where they have laid Him" (John 20:13).

The first Easter Day should have hushed that cry for ever and turned its sorrow into joy, but it has not done so for many who love and follow Christ. Still men and women seem to seek the living midst the dead, and to think of their dead as lying in their graves. They always want to know where the dead are buried. It may be natural sentiment, or it may be false religion. Anyway, that's not my business now. Sentiment or religion, the desire is there, and I must do my best to satisfy it. A Padre out here has got to be an amateur undertaker. So ghastly amateur, that is the worst of it. We cannot hope to bury half the dead. Many a mother's aching heart must go uncomforted because we know not where we have laid him. No one knows. Some are not buried, because there is nothing to bury but scraps of flesh and clothing. Some are buried, and then blown to pieces out of their graves. There is an enormous crater in the middle of the cemetery, and the bodies are not; that's all that can be said. But where Christian burial can be given, it must be given, if only for pity's sake.

I say, you chaps, this lad was my servant. Could you help me across with him to the cemetery? You'll have to lift him very carefully, he's so badly shattered. That's the way. Now we'll carry him across and have the service while the lull is on. There is a grave ready. Would you mind staying while I say the service over him?

No, you need not stay to fill in, boys, I'll do that. Thank ye very much. It only saddens them, and what's the use?

(1918)

Running

It was a common enough scene in those days, an advanced collecting post for wounded in the Ypres Salient, on the evening of June 15, 1917. Twenty men all smashed up and crammed together in a little concrete shelter which would have been full with ten in it. Outside the German barrage banging down all round us. The one guttering candle on the edge of a broken wire-bed going out every five minutes when a salvo of 5.9's from Pilkom Ridge shook the place to its foundations. A boy with a badly shattered thigh in a corner moaning and yelling by turns for "Somefing to stop the pain." So it had been for an hour or more. Between this Black Hole of Calcutta and Battalion H.Q. Death and Hell to go through. Hell inside and hell out, and the moaning of the boy in the corner like the moaning of a damned soul. "The pain—the pain—my Gawd—the pain. For Gawd's sake gimme somefing to stop the pain."

There was no morphia. That was the horror. Someone must go for it. I went. I went because the hell outside was less awful than the hell in. I didn't go to do an heroic deed or perform a Christian service; I went because I couldn't bear that moaning any longer. I ran . . . I ran, and cowered down in shell holes waiting for a chance to run again.

(1919)

W-A-R

History is so utterly merciless about War. We in Britain were accustomed to think of the nineteenth century as a time of progress, prosperity, and peace. That was a comfortable lie. The facts turn me sick. The real nineteenth century was just a shambles. There was War in the world regularly every four years. I carried the facts—the dry facts of history—out to France in 1915. I was always interested in military history. Yes, that's the word, interested. I was just interested because I knew nothing. Battles were just the movements on the chess board of the world to me. I was as innocent, as fatuously, idiotically innocent as most young men of my generation. I carried the interesting facts into my first battle, and there they came to life, they roared and thundered, they dripped with blood, they cursed, mocked, blasphemed, and cried like a child for mercy. They stood up before me like obscene specters, beckoning with bloody hands, laughing like fiends at my little parochial religion, and my silly parochial God. I can remember running over an open space under shell fire trying madly to fit in the dates, and every shrieking shell kept yelling at me with foul oaths: Now do you understand, you miserable little parson with your petty shibboleths, this is W-A-R—War, and History is War—and this is what History means. How about gentle Jesus, God the Father, and the Peace of God—how about it? I saw the face of Christ in His agony, and remembered some Sunday School children singing in shrill childish voices:

> Peace on earth and mercy mild,
> God and sinners reconciled.

Then I found the man I was looking for, and stopped thinking. But as I think again of the nineteenth-century Wars it all comes back to me. It isn't this War, it is History in the light of this War that we Christians have to face. Here is the case in a nutshell. Does God will War?

(1919)

Fed Up

We have been tried as silver is tried, we have passed through fire and water and had a surfeit of self-sacrifice, we have given our best and bravest, and shed our blood in rivers, and we trusted that God would bring us out into a wealthy place, into a new world. But it is no new world that we find ourselves in, but an old world grown older, a world of selfishness grown more selfish, of greed that has grown more greedy, and of folly that knows no limit to its foolishness.

There has come upon us a great disillusionment. We thought that the great Peace Conference was travailing to the birth of Peace, and it has brought forth an abortive pandemonium. Millions who gave up their all in a frenzy of self-sacrifice during the war are asking themselves bitterly what they gave it for. What's the good? And who's to gain? We are fed up. It is dangerous, deadly dangerous, and must be cured—and there is only one cure for it. We must feed our souls on solid food, and not on the slops of sensationalism. We must regain our vision of life's purpose and set up a plain objective.

(1919)

Facing Facts

There are no words foul and filthy enough to describe war. Yet I would remind you that this indescribably filthy thing is the commonest thing in History, and that if we believe in a God of Love at all we must believe in the face of war and all it means. The supreme strength of the Christian faith is that it faces the foulest and filthiest of life's facts in the crude brutality of the Cross, and through them sees the Glory of God in the face of Jesus Christ.

(1918)

Waste

Waste of Muscle, waste of Brain,
Waste of Patience, waste of Pain,
Waste of Manhood, waste of Health,
Waste of Beauty, Waste of Wealth,
Waste of Blood, and waste of Tears,
Waste of Youth's most precious years,
Waste of ways the Saints have trod,
Waste of Glory, waste of God—
      War!

(1918)

A Song of the Desert

On the Hindenburg Line, 1918

I've sung my songs of battlefields,
    Of sacrifice and pain,
When all my soul was fain to sing
    Of sunshine and of rain.

Of dewdrops glist'ning on the rose,
    Cloud castles in blue skies,
Of glory as God's summer grows,
    And splendor as it dies.

Of blossom snowed upon the trees,
    And fresh green woods that ring
With music of the mating birds,
    Love's miracle of spring.

Of summer night in velvet robes,
    Bedecked with silver stars,
The captive beauty of the dawn
    That breaks her prison bars.

The rustling sigh of fallen leaves
    That sing beneath my feet
The swan-song of the autumn days,
    So short, so sad, so sweet.

An exile in a weary land,
    My soul sighs for release,
It wanders in war's wilderness,
    And cries for Peace—for Peace.

(1918)

The Sniper

There's a Jerry over there, Sarge!
Can't you see 'is big square 'ead?
If 'e bobs it up again there,
I'll soon nail 'im—nail 'im dead.
Gimme up that pair o' glasses,
And just fix that blinkin' sight.
Gawd! That nearly almost got 'im,
There 'e is now—see? 'Arf right.
If 'e moves again I'll get 'im,
Take these glasses 'ere and see,
What's that? Got 'im through the 'ead, Sarge?
Where's my blarsted cup o' tea?

(1918)

The Pensioner

'Im and me was kids together,
    Played together, went to school,
Where Miss Jenkins used to rap us
    On our knuckles wiv a rule.
When we left we worked together,
    At the Fac'try, makin' jam,
Gawd 'ave mercy on us women!
    I'm full up today—I am.
Well I minds the August Monday,
    When 'e said 'e loved me true,
Underneath the copper beech tree,
    With the moonbeams shining through.
Then we walked down by the river,
    Silent-like an' 'and in 'and,
Till we came there by the Ketch Inn,
    Where them two big willows stand.
There 'e caught me roughly to 'im,
    And 'is voice was 'oarse and wild,
As 'e whispered through 'is kisses,
    "Will ye mother me my child?"
An' I took and kissed and kissed 'im,
    Sweet as love and long as life,
Vowed while breath was in my body
    I would be 'is faithful wife.
An' I seemed to see 'is baby,
    Smiling as 'e lay at rest,
With 'is tiny 'and a-clutching
    At the softness of my breast.
Gawd above, them days was 'eaven
    I can see the river shine
Like a band of silver ribbon;

    I can feel 'is 'and in mine,
I can feel them red 'ot kisses
      On my lips or on my 'air,
I can feel 'is arm tight round me,
      Gawd! I tell ye it ain't fair.
Look ye what the war's done at 'im,
      Lying there as still as death.
See 'is mouth all screwed and twisted,
      With the pain of drawing breath!
But of course I 'ave a pension,
      Coming reg'lar every week.
So I ain't got much to grouse at—
      I suppose it's like my cheek,
Grousin' when a grateful country
      Buys my food and pays my rent.
I should be most 'umbly grateful
      That my John was one as went,
Went to fight for King and Country,
      Like a 'ero and a man,
I should be most 'umbly grateful,
      And just do as best I can.
But my pension won't buy kisses,
      An' 'e'll never kiss again,
'E ain't got no kissin' in 'im,
      Ain't got nothin' now—but pain.
Not as I would ever change 'im
      For the strongest man alive.
While the breath is in my body
      Still I'll mother 'im—and strive
That I keeps my face still smiling
      Though my 'eart is fit to break;
As I lives a married widow,
      So I'll live on for 'is sake.

But I says—Let them as makes 'em
    Fight their wars and mourn their dead,
Let their women sleep for ever
In a loveless, childless bed.
No—I know—it ain't right talkin',
But there's times as I am wild.
Gawd! You dunno 'ow I wants it—
'Ow I wants—a child—'is child.

(1919)

part two

A Suffering and Triumphant God

We see Christ in the world and in the Church—crucified—crucified in every street of our great cities, crucified in every hovel of our slums, crucified on our markets, crucified on our battlefields, but forever rising . . . If our Gospel were only a Gospel of the Crucified, it would be untrue to facts and a Gospel of despair. But the Gospel of the Cross and the Empty Tomb, of the Crucified Risen Christ, always crucified and always rising again, is the Gospel that faces all facts and gives to life a meaning.

There is in the heart of God, and always has been, a Cross and an Empty Tomb.

(1921)

Christ Crucified Everywhere

On June 7th, 1917, I was running to our lines half mad with fright, though running in the right direction, thank God, through what had been once a wooded copse. It was being heavily shelled. As I ran I stumbled and fell over something. I stopped to see what it was. It was an undersized, underfed German boy, with a wound in his stomach and a hole in his head. I remember muttering, "You poor little devil, what had you got to do with it? Not much great blond Prussian about you."

Then there came light. It may have been pure imagination, but that does not mean that it was not also reality, for what is called imagination is often the road to reality. It seemed to me that the boy disappeared and in his place there lay the Christ upon His Cross, and cried, "Inasmuch as ye have done it unto the least of these my little ones ye have done it unto me" (Matthew 25:40). From that moment on I never saw a battlefield as anything but a Crucifix. From that moment on I have never seen the world as anything but a Crucifix. I see the Cross wet up in every slum, in every filthy over-crowded quarter, in every vulgar flaring street that speaks of luxury and waste of life. I see Him staring up at me from the pages of the newspaper that tells of a tortured, lost, bewildered world . . .

But the Vision of Life in the Cross is not a vision of despair, but of confidence and hope, because behind it there is the empty tomb, and the figure with wounded hands outstretched to bless, ascending into glory.

(1925)

After War, Is Faith Possible?

The Christian religion is, and always has been, the simplest thing in all the world—a passionate devotion to Jesus Christ. A passionate devotion to Jesus Christ as a person, not of the past but of the present, not among the dead but among the living ... All sects and all ages of real Christians, however much their theologies have differed, have really been at one in this, their love of and their devotion to the ever-present Christ ...

The Christian religion is simple—and always has been. Christian theology is complex and difficult and full of mysteries—and always has been. There always have been a large number of souls in the world to whom Christian theology meant nothing, while the Christian religion meant everything. There are still a large number who could no more follow an argument than they could go to bed without saying their prayers, and they are the salt of the earth. You can count among their number some of the choicest souls in the world—brave men and tender women ... In their religion there [are] no problems, only a deep and abiding trust in Christ as God: God for the present and God for the future, in whose hands all difficulties [can] be safely left until He [sees] fit to clear the clouds away. These people are God's own people, whom to know is to love ...

But it is inevitable that the number of people with this peculiar faculty of serene and untroubled power to penetrate the darkness, and find God, should grow less and less, in proportion to the whole, as the process of universal education advances. We have in these last years, for good or ill, embarked upon the colossal task of teaching the world to think, which means that for more and more of the human race, problems and perplexities must creep in to mar the serenity of a childlike faith. And that is why in these days Christian theology is bound to play a larger and larger part in bringing men to God or keeping them from Him.

The Christian religion is the love of Jesus Christ. Christian theology is the interpretation of the universe and of human life in terms of Jesus Christ. That is what Christian theology always has been, the effort of thinking men to express the stars and the stones, the winds and the waves, the laughter and the tears, the pain and the peace of the world in terms of Jesus Christ. That is the real task of the Christian theologian, and it is a tremendous one and enormously complicated. It is a task which men have been always doing and have never done.

We must not on our peril get confused in our minds between theology and religion. There is the faith once and for all delivered to the saints, which never changes; but there is no such thing, and there can be no such thing, as a theology once and for all delivered to the saints, which never changes, unless God were to cease from educating man, and the light which lighteth every man were to cease from coming into the world. Theology can no more stand still than any other branch of thought. It has always been changing, and within the last half-century has changed so rapidly that the minds of many thinking Christians are troubled and confused. But if you will cling fast to this, that the religion is always simple and always the same—which is the love of Jesus—you can face the task of grasping a complex and ever-changing theology without fear. Theology does not interest me, and it does not really interest anybody, unless it be as a hobby, except so far as it helps or hinders religion. Theological questions do not really matter until they become religious questions.

But the number of people who must be more or less theological if they are going to be religious, and to whom some sort of theology is an absolute necessity, is growing rapidly; so rapidly that we must now face the fact that a muddled and confused theology—in which the falsehoods of the past and the half-truths of the present unite to obscure the real truth as it is being revealed to us—a popular theology which is taught in schools, preached from pulpits, talked in the street, and which forms the background of people's minds—is keeping thousands of men from the religion of Jesus Christ . . .

There is no doubt that we clergy are enormously responsible for this. We may have preached the truth but we have not preached the whole truth, and our mental reservations have often made the truth we preached a lie to those who listened. We have been afraid of upsetting people's convictions, and many a golden-hearted parson has shrunk from saying what he really thought of Christ out of respect for dear old Mrs. Brown or Mr. Smith, both of whom clung with equal tenacity to the religion and the theology that they learnt at their mother's knee . . . We have continuously dressed up old lies in modern clothes in order that their ugliness might not shock the children of our generation. The real rulers of our theological seminaries have been Mrs. Brown and Mr. Smith. This would be all very well if we were not really sacrificing hundreds of young souls on the altar of love for these two old ones. Education, poor and limited as it is, has now brought us to the time when we must speak the truth and the whole truth, and risk Mrs. Brown and Mr. Smith. We have got to take up the task of re-interpreting the world, as we now see it, in the full blaze of our modern light, in terms of Jesus Christ.

We cannot, I am afraid, accomplish that task of reconstruction without doing a great deal of destruction first. We must pull down a good many time-honored but tottering ruins before we can build a new temple worthy of the Prince of Peace. The task of destruction is not, and never ought to be, a happy one. It is never pleasant tearing clinging ivy from old walls and breaking down the homes where many noble people have lived and died content, because time has rendered them not fit for habitation. The man who delights in destruction, who loves tearing down for the sake of tearing down, who delights in shocking, hurting, and paining people, is a bad man in whom Christ does not dwell. But the man who will not tear down what truth itself condemns is a coward and a traitor to the God he serves.

For me and for a good many others this work of destruction was finally accomplished during the past four years in a brutal, cruel, and merciless fashion. To a sensitive spirit these years of War have been a perpetual torture chamber in which he has often had to have his half-beliefs, which were like parts of his body, torn away from him without even being allowed at the time to utter a cry of pain.

The War has not led to any great religious revival. I am not surprised at that. I cannot see anything in War to produce a religious revival. I believe it to be an utter and dangerous falsehood to believe that War of itself uplifts, purges, or sanctifies men's souls. That is a lie which only the devil could believe. It is the heart of that mock-heroic sentimentalism upon which militarism is morally, or rather immorally, founded. People stay at home by the fire, or sit in studies and write books, and imagine War to mean dashing over the parapet in defense of liberty and right, and giving one's life in one supreme act of self-sacrifice for the great cause. War can be made into that by very exceptional souls, but in itself it bears no resemblance to it whatever. You don't go out to give your life; you go out to take the other fellow's. You don't go out to save, you go out to kill; and if you don't, you are no good as a soldier. If non-combatants hide behind the sentimental conception of War they hide behind a lie, and a peculiarly cruel lie, and I think thousands of us have been doing just that.

Once and for all let me state here my conviction that War is pure undiluted, filthy sin. I don't believe that it has ever redeemed a single soul—or ever will. Exceptional souls have found their glory in it and have let it shine before men; but the war only brought it to light; it did not make it. The only power that war possesses is the only power that any evil thing possesses, which is the power to destroy itself. If this world-wide War has done us any good it is because in its flames a certain number of old and soul-killing lies have perished self-destroyed. In the blood, the mud, and the stench of the battlefield they worked themselves out to their final absurdity, while the guns roared laughter from behind. Often and often the 9-inch guns have seemed to me to yell out above the rattle of a barrage, "You fools, you fools!" From the bottom of my heart I believe that this work of destruction, however painful it may be, must be accomplished to the bitter end, to lead the children of our generation to the worship of the true God.

What is God like? . . . What do all those wonderful pictures in the Revelation mean—of God sitting on a throne with Christ at His right hand, while millions of angels throng around Him singing gorgeous songs, and bending low in humble worship, singing praises of the triumph and the victory of God—while a German soldier spears a Belgian baby, rapes its mother, and keeps her alive to see the father shot? In God's name, what is the Almighty God like?

That is what the question which has been torturing the minds of millions during this war; making some blaspheme and curse the very name of God; making others turn from the very thought of Him in bitterness and despair; making others still dully and dimly indifferent to religion and all it means; and shutting all alike into a darkness which the love of God has proved powerless to penetrate. To answer them merely as Job's comforters answered the splendid impatience of patient Job with the cry of agnosticism: "It is higher than heaven; what canst thou do? It is deeper than hell; what canst thou know?" (Job 11:7–8) is to produce the same effect upon them as the comforters produced on Job, namely, to make them irritated, sad, and miserable, and to put God farther away and not draw Him nearer.

If a man had come to me on the battlefield and told me that God knew best, and that I must leave it all to Him, he would have made me blaspheme; and the man who comes to me today with the same pious platitude upon his lips makes me want to blaspheme more bitterly still. Because, although the horror of the battlefield has faded from my mind, thought and meditation have produced in my soul a dead and settled loathing of it as an evil, and not merely a very painful thing. Thought and meditation have convinced me that War is not only torture but that it is filthy. To tell me that War is evil, and that the problem of evil is insoluble, is, indeed, finally the truth; but it is not enough. I will not be able to understand altogether; I know I cannot; I know, however much I learn and however much I think, there will be mysteries still. But I must know how God looks at it; I must determine what God's attitude towards it is, or else down comes the darkness and Christ is not merely crucified, He is dead . . .

There is no power nor virtue in this travesty of faith, which makes it mean the taking of all things on trust, the folding of the hands and the bowing of the head, the spiritless submission to the lie that whatever is is right. Faith does not mean that we cease from asking questions; it means that we ask and keep on asking until the answer comes; that we seek and keep on seeking until the truth is found; that we knock and keep on knocking until the door is opened and we enter into the palace of God's truth.

It becomes more and more important as years pass by and men's minds grow that we should prove all things, while holding fast to that which is true. Christ calls us to that courage which bids us give up the snug little homes which sloth and prejudice have built for our minds, our pet infallibilities, in which we could rest and cease to think wrapt in peaceful peace . . . We are afraid—of course we are afraid. "If that is not true," we say, "where am I? How can I be sure of anything? If the Bible is not literally true, word for word, if the picture of God which my forefathers had is a false picture, where am I? What is there settled? Where can I live? There is nothing before me but the open sea where I must journey helpless and exposed to every wind that blows."

And that is true! The world is out on the open sea exposed to every wind. And I am out on the open sea with it, but I do not care because there is One walks beside me and before me and behind me, and God, who caused the light to shine out of darkness, has shined into my heart to give the light of the knowledge of the glory of God in the face of Jesus Christ. We are called upon, the Church is called upon, to go out onto the open sea with Christ, leaving behind the snug homes of patent infallibilities which the guns have battered into dust, and follow Him until we find the truth.

We are not in complete darkness. We are not without a Guide. Theology changes, but religion remains. To fold your hands and say, "God knows best," to take refuge in unreal platitudes, is to cower away from the light that God, through the prayers of the saints, through the courage of the scientists, through the cunning of inventors, and through the tireless patience of the thinkers, has been giving down the ages. The task of the Church and of her children, which is peculiarly her task and peculiarly theirs, is to gather up from every corner of the world all the light that can be found, and set it blazing on this great problem of evil, in order to find the best partial solution for the children of our day, and the one which will provide the surest foundation for the complete solution which the passage of the ages, under God, will bring to light. We must seek for light in every corner of God's universe, never forgetting it is God's universe, and that in it we can find revelation of Himself. We must go down to life's dirtiest and dingiest depths, and up to its fairest and most fearful heights; we must face all the facts—the facts that make us shudder and the facts that make us laugh, the beauty that makes us gasp with wonder and the ugliness that makes us shrink in horror, the good that makes us want to worship and the evil that makes us bow our heads in shame; we must look at them all, face them all, asking always, "What is God like"—the God who is Creator and Ruler of a universe like this? We must not do what we have done, invent a God and then make life to fit Him, blinding our eyes to what does not suit our purpose; creating an absolute by the negative process of subtracting all human limitations from the human being, and choosing what we want to consider limitations, and what we do not. An imaginary God may be very beautiful, but He will not stand the tears and terror, and the fires that are not quenched. We must have Truth.

(1919)

Why Does God Permit War?

The root of the soldier's blasphemy is the same as that of his humor, and that is why they are so often mixed. They are both efforts to solve a felt but unformulated contradiction in life, and they are both essentially Christian, the signs of a lost sheep of the Good Shepherd . . .

Blasphemy and blasphemous humor are both common at the Front because the Front is one vast contradiction.

"I believe in God the Father Almighty, and a trench mortar has just blown my pal, who was a good-living lad, to pieces, and God is Love, and they crucified the sergeant-major, and peace on the earth, good will towards men, and I stuck my bayonet through his belly, and Jesus died to save us from sin, and the Boche has been raping women, and this _____ war never ends" (note the _____, it is important, and would probably be considerably amplified). "Christ, there's the _____ tea up; where's my _____ dixie?"

I have never heard that said because it never was said, but I have heard what was the expression of it hundreds of times, and in a vision I have seen the tears stand bright in Jesus' eyes, and heard Him laugh the grand loving laughter of God.

If the dear old chaps who said it could have seen Him they would have laughed with Him, and would have said, "Sorry, sir, I did not really mean it. As you were, and we will carry on." Why cannot they see Him? Because of the contradiction. The first great difficulty of the private soldier is war.

"Why does not God stop it? Any decent man would stop it tomorrow if he could, and God is Almighty and can do anything, then why does He allow it to go on?"

It is, of course, the old problem of evil in an acute form, and there is no complete and logically perfect solution of it. But can nothing be done to mitigate the mystery of it? Some would reply that in this final mystery reason has no part to play, it is the sphere of faith. Faith in god, and Faith alone, can pierce without dissolving the contradiction and find God good behind. It is, of course, undeniable that Faith has done this again and again, but we must beware of how we play off faith against reason. Faith is super- but not contra-rational. It does not bid us cease from thinking, but rather bids us think the more, strong in faith that there is reason in the ways of God with men, and that God's mysteries are mysteries of the unknown but not of the unknowable. Faith is a food and a stimulant and not a narcotic. It is meant to quicken, not to kill, the power of thought. I do not think it is right to tell men that they must not think about this question, and it certainly is perfectly useless to tell them, because they will not obey.

What do you mean by the word "Almighty" as an attribute of God? It rolls off our tongues in our creeds and prayers and sermons very easily and glibly, but what does it mean?

Everyone ought to read Mr. H. G. Wells's great novel, *Mr. Britling Sees It Through*. It is a gallant and illuminating attempt to state the question, and to answer it. His thought has brought him to a very real and living faith in God revealed in Jesus Christ, and has also brought relief to many troubled minds among the officers of the British Army. I know that from conversations I have had. I have met the book everywhere in the trenches. As yet it has not largely reached the private soldier.

But I am sure that no one, not even Mr. Wells himself, having thought so far could stop there. "After all," says Mr. Wells, "the real God of the Christians is Christ not God Almighty; a poor, mocked, and wounded Christ nailed on a cross of matter . . . Some day He will triumph."[1] However strange that may sound to Christian ears, there is a lot of truth in it. The center of our worship has always been Christ and Him Crucified. We have always worshipped a suffering God . . . But we cannot think of the Cross apart from the Resurrection.

The Gospel of the Cross without the Resurrection would be a Gospel of despair, the revelation of a powerless, pain-racked Deity caught in the grip of creation and held fast. The Gospel of Christ is a Gospel of Hope, a Gospel of all-suffering but all-conquering love faced with an awful and inevitable agony, but patiently and powerfully overcoming it. It is the Gospel of a transcendent God Who makes Himself immanent for Love's sake, and thereby takes upon Himself a burden and an agony beyond our power to understand. The attribute Almighty must be interpreted in the light of the Cross and the Resurrection, and in that light it is seen to mean, not that God has no difficulties and no sorrows, but that God is able to overcome all difficulties and to rise supreme above all sorrows. Omnipotence does not mean that God can do anything which we imagine He ought to be able to do, but that, faced with awful obstacles and

---

1. Wells, *Mr. Britling Sees It Through*, 406.

humanly incomprehensible difficulties, He is nevertheless able to grapple with and overcome them. God is *Pator Pantrokrator*. This revelation of God in Christ is the revelation which the story of the growth of the universe as it is laid before us in science and in history would lead us to expect.

As one reads the amazing story of development which evolutionary science has to tell, one seems to catch a glimpse of that ever-struggling but ever-conquering power Who works unceasingly behind it all. We see Him struggling, but victoriously struggling, to bring order and beauty out of chaos. The Spirit of God is seen at war with necessity. We must call it that for lack of a better name. The Catholic Faith simply calls it Satan, the adversary, and puts its origin in the misuse of free will by spirit created before the world was. This is not a solution but a postponement of the problem. But the adversary is there, in nature as in man.

As one reads the story of science and the struggle of nature towards perfection, one sees staring up through the pages of the textbook the face of Christ patient, pain-pierced, and powerful . . .

It is not for nothing that Spring and Easter coincide. A perfect spring day in a smiling land is the victory of God over necessity in nature, as the Resurrection is the victory of God over necessity in man. It is not mere poetry but truth to say that the summer rose is dyed red with the life-blood of God. All good things are the product, not only of God's love and power, but also of His pain. The raiment of the lily was not bought for nothing any more than is the raiment of the saints. With the dawn of history the struggle of God becomes more powerful. History cries out for that prone figure in the Garden sweating great drops of blood, and demands for its interpretation the Cross of Calvary . . .

To meet the difficulty of war honestly, we have to face the facts not only of this war but of history's thousand wars, and all the cruelty, barbarity, and sin that they have produced. Belgium is but the latest of a thousand lands that have had to weep for their children and refuse to be comforted because they were not. Man's history is one long bloody war, with burning homes, dishonored women, tortured children, and all war's usual atrocities repeated like a filthy tale. That fact must be faced, and Christianity faces it in the tortured figure of God incarnate in Whom all history is summed up. History is an intolerable enigma without the Cross of Christ. But again the Cross without the empty Tomb fails to fit the facts. There is an agony of God in history, but again I would stress the truth that it is a victorious agony. There is progress in history, there is a real development of man, a real development of the individual and of society toward perfection. The Kingdom of God is really coming and has been coming all down the ages. It is on this point that Mr. Wells falls short in his teaching. He does not do justice to the Victory of God. He has temporally swung back to the opposite extreme from the theologians and has allowed the mystery of evil to obscure the mystery of good. Necessity is not really uttermost or ultimate, it is essentially temporary and contingent; it will pass away, and God will be supreme. All this is latent in Mr. Wells's teaching, latent but not yet patent, and it needs to be patent and emphatic. There is no Gospel apart from the Resurrection. "The world is cruel," Mr. Britling's Letty says. "It is just cruel. So it always will be." "It need not be cruel," replies Mr. Britling,[2] and in that great reply is all the latent power of the Christian Faith. It need not be, it must not be, it shall not be. This is that which overcometh the world, even our faith. "I believe in God the Father Almighty," is an act of faith, not a declaration of demonstrated fact. It is the Christian soldier's declaration of entire trust in the striving, struggling, but insuperable Person who works without and within the universe. It is the Christian Army's oath of allegiance, and its battle cry. It is said standing to attention with our faces turned towards God's altar and the dawn of day whence comes the final victory of Light.

Too often in the past this first clause of our Creed has been interpreted and preached in such a way as to force men to lay upon God the responsibility for evil as though it were in some mysterious way His Will. God has been represented as sending and willing plague, pestilence, famine, disease and war. All these have been represented as the visitation of God. This has led to a very popular fatalism which is a pernicious travesty of Christian Truth. Fatalism and agnosticism are man's chief enemies, they cause more sin than drink and selfishness. It is this fatalistic Christianity which has no appeal to men, and it is, often through our bad preaching and teaching, and their consequent ignorance, the only Christianity they know. Christian preaching has very often consisted in pious attempts to make evil good in order to save God's face. We have suffered from what Hilary of Poitiers called *irreligiosa sollicitudo pro Deo*, and have been orthodox liars to the glory of God. Passive resignation to

2. *Mr. Britling Sees It Through*, 405.

evil as though it were God's will has been exalted into a virtue, and consequently the Christianity which should have turned the world upside down has been turned into a method of keeping it as it is and meekly accepting its wrong-side-upness as the discipline of Almighty God. The Revolutionary Christ has been disguised as a moral policeman.

Our preaching of the Cross has been stultified in the same way. The murder of Good Friday has been separated from the other murders that stain man's history and represented as in some mysterious way the Will of God, part of God's plan. The spite and hatred of the priests, the treachery of Judas, the cowardice of Pilate, the brutality of the soldiers, the ingratitude of the crowd, part of God's plan, because God willed that Christ should die—what a God, and what a plan! When Christ cried in the Garden "Thy Will be done," He has been represented as submitting to the Cross as the Will of God, and as being a pattern of patient submission. What a travesty of Truth! God's Will was of course the perfect life, the perfect witness to the Truth; for this end was He born and for this end came He into the world. The cry in the Garden was an act, not so much of submission as of aspiration and tremendous resolve. Christianity is not the gospel of the bowed head but the gospel of the set teeth. "Thy Will be done" in the Garden was the supreme majesty of manhood which sent Christ's enemies reeling backwards to the ground, and is the revelation of that supreme majesty of Godhead which shall at last send all evil reeling backward into its native nothingness. "Thy Will be done" is not pathetic, it is powerful, with the power of the suffering but insuperable God.

Here I think is the teaching which will mitigate if it does not destroy the bitterness of the contradiction of Christ in War. We preach a suffering but insuperable God at war with evil in the world, at war with sin, disease and death, and at war with war.

We preach a God ever crucified by evil but ever rising above it, Christ crucified but risen from the dead. Evil is not and never can be the Will of God, it arises from necessities the nature of which we cannot fully understand.

What the necessities were which God had to overcome in the creation of the material world we cannot understand, because our knowledge of them is limited by our knowledge of the ultimate nature of matter, which is nil.

But our knowledge of the necessities arising in the evolution of man toward perfection is greater because they arise out of the nature of consciousness which is the only thing we know about from the inside, and these two necessities when fully realized meet many of the commonest difficulties in the soldier's mind.

Why Does God Allow Evil?

Even when you have made it clear that God does not will war, still the soldier wants to know why God permits it. And we must answer because He cannot help it. Man must be free. An element of independence and spontaneity is an essential factor of personal consciousness. Man would not be man without freedom. The first necessity God had to meet in the creation of self-conscious personality was freedom. God must leave us free to sin or else destroy us. Man cannot, absolutely cannot, be compelled to do right. There is no such thing as compulsory virtue.

Why Does Not God Punish the Right Man?

A soldier in hospital badly wounded, to whom I had explained the necessity of freedom, replied that he understood that man must be free to sin, and that sorrow must follow sin. "But what I can't see," he said, "is why God does not punish the right man. He does not. He seems to knock a wrong 'un every time. The Kaiser and his lot sin, and my old dad is breaking his heart because my brother has lost his legs. Now what sense or justice is there in that?"

This is a question that worries soldiers as much as any, the apparent injustice of the suffering of the innocent. The reply seems to me to lie in the demonstration of the second necessity that God has to meet in the development of the human race, viz., the necessity of unity. Conscious personality must be in a measure independent, and cannot be completely isolated. A completely isolated human personality is an absolute impossibility. We are human, and we progress as human beings because we are one family, and share our evil and our good. Speech, writing, and the reason which invented and can use them are the hallmarks of humanity, and they are the means of our unity. We share the good that others win, the product of their hands and brains, and so, and only so, do we progress. We reap in joy what others sow in bitter tears, and garner into our treasury of blessings the fruit their labors bear. That is the very law of Love, the Love that makes us one. Rightly used, this power of unity is the greatest blessing we possess, it is the very source of all our highest joy. It is the source from which all knowledge comes. It is the meaning of the mystery of Music and Art. The music that sings in a great musician's brain, the glory of form and color that burns in fire of ecstasy in the soul of the great artist, flow out to bless the brains and hearts of lesser men.

But when by virtue of his freedom man uses his powers wrongly, the evil that he does, the vicious product of his hand and brain, flows out to curse the human family through those very channels which were meant to convey the highest blessings. These two necessary properties of freedom and unity when wrongly used make the suffering of the innocent for the guilty inevitable. That boy soldier's dad and the Kaiser are one in the unity of the human race, and so the evil results of Germany's wrong choice of ideals, her substitution of Mars for Christ, come upon him and upon his children, and they suffer, the innocent for the guilty.

What Is God Doing?

"He is out of it," a man said to me. "Christ suffered once and for all, and then ascended into Heaven to wait until the world comes round, and it seems a long time coming. Christ died once in pain to save us from our sins, but it does not seem to have saved us much, when all this comes as the result of sin after two thousand years."

This is a very real difficulty. There is no one for whom the soldier has such supreme contempt as a bad staff officer who wears red tabs and spurs and never sees the trenches. And to him that is how God appears. Christ was splendid while He was on earth, but He has gone into Heaven. He has retired to the security of Corps Headquarters well behind the line, and from there He directs operations. All the glory with which we invest the glorified Christ, the throne, the host of waiting angels, the triumphal entry into Heaven, all this means just "Red tabs and spurs," and they do not evoke worship or even respect. The pageantry of Courts and thrones which supplied past ages with the symbols wherein to express the glory of God has lost its glamour for the man of today, he is too deeply Christian. Only the Cross is eternal, it is the only real throne. The only crown the modern man respects is the Crown of Thorns.

A muddy, bloody, suffering but unbeaten Christ he can be made to love and follow, but a supreme, transcendent potentate is to him as contemptible as the Kaiser. We need to reinterpret the Resurrection and Ascension if they are to grip the mind of the soldier of today or the citizen of tomorrow. We are witnessing the passing of the monarch absolute from the world in a flood of blood and tears, and all the metaphors supplied from absolute monarchy must pass too. The Ascension needs to be connected with the coming of the Spirit, the coming of God to embark upon another and more terrible course of victorious suffering in the Church and in humanity. God comes again in the Spirit to lead His army, and to suffer with it. God suffers now, and is crucified afresh every day. God suffers in every man that suffers. God, the God we love and worship, is no far-off God of Power, but the comrade God of Love: He is on no far-off heavenly throne, He is up in the trenches, under the guns: for every wound a man receives there is pain in the heart of God, and every cry of agony finds echo in God's soul. God is not a bad Staff Officer, but a gallant and fatherly Colonel who goes over the top with His men. God is leading the world at cost of awful agony to its perfection. The truth of the indwelling of the Spirit of Jesus Christ and the suffering of God in man must be the keystone of our preaching. The Church is God's army, in which He dwells and suffers, and we must preach the Church, and the call to its warfare under the leadership of God.

(1919)

God Is Powerful But Not Almighty

The process by which this world has come to be what it is must have someone behind it. He may be more than a person, and He can't be less. He appears to be a Being Who has within Himself not merely persons but a unity of persons, a sort of Brotherhood. That is what appears to be working its way out through the process, so I suppose it must be in the final cause of it. I am driven to that conclusion. You see, we must look at the movement in the light of its latest results; that is the only way in which we can rightly judge any movement. We must look at nature in the light of human nature, and the best human nature. We cannot look at it apart from ourselves. Trying to understand nature apart from man is like trying to understand a body without a head, which is a hopeless job. We have suffered from that sort of nonsense. When writers talk of nature they very often don't make it clear what they mean, but if it is to have any real meaning, it must mean the whole universe, the whole show complete. You cannot divide it up. It is a universe. Cabbages are no more natural than kings, and Julius Caesar was just as natural as a jelly fish. It is a unity, and a single movement, and we must judge it in the light of its latest results; and when we consider its latest result, viz., "Men," and ask ourselves the meaning of their peculiarly human powers—speech, writing, art, music, printing, mechanical invention, telegraphy, telephony, wireless communication, etc.—they all seem to have one tendency, they seem to make for unity, they seem to make for unity, they are all means to unity, to the Creation of Man—the united human race.

That purpose is not accomplished, it is not nearly accomplished, but it looks as if it was being accomplished. And the queer part of it is that it seems as if it was being accomplished without our individually fully comprehending what the purpose is. It is as though, to spite our stupidity and selfishness, some great Power were working a purpose out, molding our blind and selfish efforts to His Will. Under the guidance of this Power we appear to be blundering on towards brotherhood. The almost dramatic discovery of mechanical power in the last century gives one that impression very strongly. No one, I suppose, has contributed more to the Creation of Man than the builders of railways and inventors of more rapid means of communication, yet one doubts if they knew what they were doing in the least. Their powers of invention were gifts. If any one can be said to be inspired it is an inventor. Inventive power is as much a gift as music or poetry or pink eyes; you don't earn it and you can't force it, it just comes from God knows where—only He must know. The gift comes and makes things for their own sake, or for the sake of money or a woman's love, or just for fun, because it can't help itself. And it is only after ages that the purpose of all the gifts becomes apparent at all—the final purpose.

So one gets the sense of a superior Power or Intelligence gradually working out a colossal idea—the idea of Human Brotherhood and Unity—the Creation of Man. What infinite purpose that is part of we cannot comprehend, but it probably is part of a larger scheme, because this earth is only a speck in an infinite universe. A survey of the process forces in upon the mind that sense of some one turning much more out of our actions than we can understand or foresee. We cooperate half blindfold, and almost without any conscious desire to do so. The Creation of Man seems a thousand times more possible today than it did two centuries ago, and we can hardly say that we have consciously tried to make it so.

As then, this purpose of human brotherhood seems to have been working itself out through the process all the time, and as it seems vastly improbable that it can be doing so by an infinite series of accidents, we come to the conclusion that there must be some one behind it, who must at least be a person, and is probably more, and if we are to give Him a name, it is difficult to see what better name we could give Him than "Father," not merely because He produced us, but also because it is apparently His purpose and plan to make a family of us. He has done a great deal towards it, and it looks as if He was going to do more, and I am drawn very strongly to back Him, to believe in Him, to bet my life upon Him and His plan. So I come to say in a very real sense, "I believe in God the Father, Maker of Heaven and Earth," Author of the Process.

But this Creed of ours goes further and adds the word "Almighty." Now at that word I am inclined to boggle and hesitate. What does it mean? And my hesitation grows greater when I am told that absolute sovereign power is an essential attribute of God, that He can know no let or hindrance to the working of His Will, that He is absolute Master in His own universe, and all things move in obedience to His command. It seems, then, that I am required to believe that every detail of this process is the direct result of His Will, and is good.

Now that is what I cannot do. The process seems to me to be a cruel and a bloody business. I cannot say that war, disease, pestilence, famine, and all the other characteristics of the process are good. If this word "Almighty" means that the Father could have made this world, and obtained the results He desires, in a thousand other ways, but that He deliberately chose this, that makes my gorge rise. Why in thunder choose this one? It is disreputable if He could have done it otherwise, without this cruelty and wrong. It is not commonly respectable. He must be an evil-minded blackguard, with a nasty disposition like a boy that likes pulling the wings off flies. I cannot get up any reverence for such a being. Why, bless my life, He tortures children, voluntarily tortures them to death, and has done so for thousands of years. I can't stand that at all—it's dirty; and when I am told that I must believe it, and that every detail of the process was planned out precisely as He wished, I begin to turn sick. Snakes, sharks, and blood-sucking vermin—what sort of a God is this? He chose this way because He gloried in it! That beats the band. It turns me clean up against the process. I cannot see its beauty for its brutality. I cannot hear the lark sing for the squealing of a rabbit tortured by a stoat, I cannot see the flowers for the face of a consumptive child with rotten teeth, the song of the saints is drowned by the groans of murdered men.

Nothing can justify this method of Creation but absolute Necessity. This way is only tolerable if it is *the only way.* There must be a great necessity binding upon the Creator. He must have taken this way because there was no other way to take. He must hate the process if He is good just as much as I do, and more, and I do hate it with all my heart. And yet I cannot adopt the dignified defiance attitude, and set myself up in judgment of it, refusing to recognize any God but the still small voice within my soul. I can't do that because it is not honest. I couldn't have a soul or a still small voice or a mind or anything else apart from the process; I am the product of it, I am part of it, one with it. I am one with all life, one with earth and sky and sea, one with birds and beasts and fishes. I kill them, eat them, prey on them, but love them still. I cannot separate myself from nature, or nature from myself. I cannot simply defy the process, still less can I wholly assent or submit to it. I must somehow come to terms with it, find a Friend through it, but He must be better than the process is. He must be beyond as well as in it—morally beyond it—or He can be no Friend of mine. He must be as good as I am; my inmost being demands that, and my intelligence demands it because He produced me, and I am better than the process.

If that sounds arrogant I can't help it; I've got to cling fast to the best that is in me, or suffer shipwreck. That is the very disaster that has befallen many souls; they degraded themselves by submitting to a Will of God which in their best moments they knew to be immoral, and by bowing their heads when they should have fought. In a world like this, you cannot respect yourself unless you are a rebel; every decent man must be a rebel.

What I want to be is a rebel in the name of God. But if God is "Almighty God, King of all Kings, and Governor of all things, whose Power no creature is able to resist"—as the Prayer Book puts it—how can I help making Him absolutely responsible for every detail of the process, and assuming that every happening in it is the result of His Will's action on it? The conclusion seems inevitable. Yet what grounds have we for believing that there exists, or can exist, this "Sovereign power of Good that knows no let or hindrance to the working of His Will"? What grounds have we for believing that God is a Being whose Power no creature is able to resist?

As far as I can see, there is no evidence for it whatever, and an enormous weight of evidence against it. I cannot find in heaven or earth a trace of the existence of such a Power. But men say you degrade God if you make His Power less than absolute. If His Power is not absolute, if He is not complete Master in His own universe, then He is not perfect. But who says so? Whose idea of perfection is that? Why must perfection of necessity include the possession of what we call absolute power? What right have we to assert that there is or can be such a thing in existence at all? What does "being Master in His own universe" mean?

It seems to be an essentially human metaphor, drawn from our own experience by a negative process, and arising from our chronic disposition to confuse Power with Force. This feeling that God's perfection demands that He should be possessed of power as complete as that of a potter over a piece of clay seems to be the result of thinking that God's ways are our ways, and of making God in man's image in the wrong sense. We try to protect God's dignity as though, like the dignity of our earthly kings, it depended ultimately on the possession of force wherewith to drive men to His Will, as if God were a despot.

That brings us to the very root of all our trouble. Our ideas of perfection are wrong. They are not the ideas that God has revealed to us, but our own. We do not reverence or worship the Right things or the Right people. We exalt the mighty to their seats, and put down the humble and meek. We still believe in and worship Force, and despise Love. We are willing to respect Love provided it has Force behind it, but without that it seems to us still to be contemptible. Pure Love is still despised and rejected of men. It saves others and cannot save itself, and that to us is pure weakness. We are still ashamed of the Cross, and cannot stand the reckless humility of God. We are still cowards and snobs and sycophants at heart, and our real reverence and respect is still for physical force, wealth, luxury, and outward show.

Even when we profess to despise these things we are not sincere. It is a case of the Fox and the Grapes, we pretend to despise what we cannot get. There is all the bitterness of thwarted desire in the contempt which the have-nots display for the haves. Give them the chance, and they would change places tomorrow and be as blatantly vulgar and as stupidly tyrannical as those who in possession are today. The champions of the bottom dog are only out to make him top dog, not to make him a New Man. Those in possession taunt the dispossessed with envy, and their taunt is true, but they are too stupid and too blind to perceive that two wrongs can never make one right; and so we go round in the putrid circle of our own moral perversity, plunging the world into sorrow, and piercing our souls with pain, because we crucify the Son of God afresh, despising Love and not believing in its power. This problem of power is the very heart of our trouble. We have not grasped God's Truth revealed in Christ, because our idea of power is essentially wrong.

Our idea of power is not God's idea of power revealed in Christ, and it is not God's idea, because our purpose is not God's purpose, our will is not God's Will. Our idea of power depends upon our idea of purpose. It must. Whether a thing is powerful or not depends upon the purpose that you use it for. A bull is a powerful animal for the purpose of ploughing a field, but for the purpose of preserving delicate antiques in a china shop it is not powerful at all. The gentle hands of some frail woman would be power for that purpose. A locomotive engine is powerful for purpose of transport, but not for the purpose of teaching a child its alphabet. Our idea of God's Power depends upon our idea of God's purpose, and we cannot have a clear conception of His Power until we perceive with heart and mind that the purpose of God is Brotherhood, the Creation of "Man," the making of a united family of human beings.

When we have really got that perception clear and clean in our hearts and minds, then we begin to see that for God's purpose, which is the Creation of Man, the human family or unity, there is, and can be, only one Power, and that is Love. For that purpose force is not power, it is weakness. A unity of human beings is an imperfect unity just so far as it is based upon force and fear. That is the lesson that the history of these last strange years should have blasted into our minds. How much we hoped from the unity of the classes and nations in time of war, and how bitterly our hopes have been disappointed! It was a weak and superficial unity, because it was not based upon Love.

Again and again during the year after the war I listened to impassioned appeals to men to unite in the cause of Righteousness, appeals based upon the unity that we had attained and preserved during the war. "Look what you have done," cried the orators, "look what you have done. Look how cliques and classes ceased to be, and a nation came to birth, fired with one spirit, buoyed with one hope, pressing onward like one man, on through the Valley of Death and the sorrows of Hell, on through seas of blood to find triumphant Peace and final Victory. Look what you have done, why can you not do it again? Why need there be dissensions now and bitterness, why need we lose the splendid unity that was born mid the groans of our dead comrades on a thousand stricken fields?"

Well, why need we? Simply because it was not a splendid, but an entirely superficial, unity, because it was not a unity of persons, it was a unity of bodies. A soldier in time of war is not a person but a puppet, who moves when you pull strings. The Army says to a man, "Go—Go—or I'll shoot you," and naturally a man goes under those circumstances. He is deprived of the freedom—the separate and spontaneous life—which is the essence of personality. That is why soldiers are often impatient with politicians. "Why all this talk?" says the soldier. "Why all this talk? Why don't you get the thing done?" Because, O silent, strong, and extremely simple (not to say fat-headed) soldier, my purpose is not your purpose, and my power is not your power. Your purpose is destruction, and mine is creation. Your power is compulsion, and mine is persuasion. Your very existence is the result of my weakness. You only come in where I fail. For creative purposes force is not strength, but the result of weakness, and it never creates anything. That is the very essence of the Christian Truth, and it is because we have failed to grasp it that we crave for a God with what we call "absolute power," Who is Master in His own universe, and are too blind to see that the foolishness of God is wiser than men, and the weakness of God is stronger than men, and why God hath chosen the foolish things of the world to confound the wise, and the weak things of the world to confound the things that are mighty. In the eyes of men there is no fool like God, because in the eyes of God there are no fools like men.

That does not mean that we should abolish all armaments and force tomorrow. It merely means that we should start out on the right basis and recognize that our armaments are symbols, not of our power, but of our weakness, that the great powers are the great weaknesses of our world. It means that we should recognize that we cannot attain to greatness by painting the map of the world red, but only by washing the soul of the world white. Our military power is an exact index of our spiritual and moral impotence.

Until we do recognize that, there can be no peace and no true progress. And so it is that when our minds are cleared of all confusion about the meaning of power, we begin to appreciate the truth of this first clause of our great Creed. There is a Spirit of Unity who works out His purpose throughout the process, and for that process—the Creation of Man, the Human Unity—there is no other Power but His, which is the Power of Love. God is Love, and all power belongs to Love.

There is more real power in that simple truth than there is in the massed armies and navies of all the nations of the world. There is more wealth in it than earth's million banks contain. There is more beauty in it than all the millionaires could buy. There is sufficient dynamite in it to blow our rotten civilization sky-high, and bring down the New Jerusalem out of Heaven, adorned as a bride for her husband. It is the only thing which can make our politics truly progressive and redeem our House of Commons from its exceeding commonness, which can heal the hurts of the suffering peoples and lift the everlasting burden from their souls. O God, for a statesman who would stop quoting the Bible in the spirit of cheap and vulgar parody, or to deck the insincere peroration of a frothy clever speech, and would speak to the peoples with clear insight and vision begotten of this its crowning Truth!

Our supremest need is real faith in the omnipotence of Love. Thousands talk of God Almighty, and have no faith in Love at all; to them the real powers are force, wealth, competition, and self-interest. These are the powers that sway the world. They only believe that God made Heaven and Earth because if He didn't, then they don't know who the devil did. God to them is just the conventional name for The Great Unknown, about whom nothing is or can be certain. Orthodox infidels, they say their Creed and never base an action upon it, because they don't believe in Love. If you told them that God was not Almighty in the strict despotic sense, but that He had to strive and travail to bring His purpose to its birth, they would tell you that they could not accept such a degraded God as that. But this orthodox infidelity has no power to save the world. God is Love, the Spirit of Unity, Brotherhood, Cooperation, Peace, and when we say our Creed we pledge ourselves to live, to think, act, and speak upon our faith in that spirit and in its power. It is impossible to prove that Love is almighty now; it does not reveal itself as supreme, but as struggling, striving, and conquering, calling us to fling ourselves in faith upon it, and prove it almighty in our lives. That is the sense of the Creed. It does not pledge you to the incredible belief that all this weird and awful process is the Will of an Almighty Despot; it pledges you to consecrate your whole life to the service of Love, that you may prove your faith in its final omnipotence in the only way it can be proved, by experience.

When you realize this, the Creed rings out a question and a challenge: Do you believe in the power of Love? It is not a thing you can accept and let it make no difference to your life. It is no mere declaration that you accept the universe as it is, and believe vaguely that all is for the best. You do not hide behind a picturesque and pious agnosticism disguised as Reverence, and talk with bated breath about the awful mystery of omnipotence, and the folly of supposing that poor finite man can do anything but just submit to His inscrutable Providence. You do not take refuge in that pride which apes humility, and insist upon calling God by splendid names that have no meaning. You do not plead that God is Eternal and you are temporal, and cannot do anything but accept the mystery. You declare your faith in the foolishness of the Gospel truth that the Eternal reveals itself through the temporal as Love, and that you propose to consecrate your every thought and word and deed to the service of that Love.

(1921)

God Suffers But Overcomes

What then is God like? I see no evidence anywhere in nature of the Almighty Potentate Who guides and governs all things with His rod, and knows no failure and no thwarting of His Will.

The strange and awful process by which the worlds were made does not look a bit like the work of an absolute and unlimited power of Love Who has but to speak and His Will is done. Nevertheless there is something or someone behind it, and I feel sure that it is someone and not something. I must judge the process in the light of its highest product—that is just common sense. The meaning of every movement must be sought in the direction in which it moves. An upward process must be looked at from its highest point. The highest point of nature's upward process is Man—a person, a being who Wills, and Loves, and Plans. I must judge nature in the light of man. I cannot separate myself and my fellows from the great process. Life is one, from the single cell to the Savior in the flesh. I cannot separate Swine from Shakespeare or Jellyfish from Jesus of Nazareth; they all are products of the process. So behind the process there must be a Spirit which is like the Spirit of man . . .

I must look for the meaning of nature in Man, and then I must look for the meaning of man in the Spirit of Jesus Christ—the perfect man—who is man's God because he is the highest that has ever lived in Flesh. So, finally, I come to look for the meaning of nature in the Spirit of Jesus Christ. I cannot help it. Soul and intellect together drive me to it. Moreover, when I go to nature, seeking not the Almighty Potentate but the suffering, Loving, laboring Christ I am not disappointed. I do find evidence of a spirit like to His—a Spirit of Beauty, Order, and Benevolence striving to express itself in nature. I see this Spirit crucified on Nature's Calvary. I see it thwarted, hindered, baffled in its task, but never stayed or stopped; always it begins again, always it persists. It suffers like Christ, and it rises again like Christ. It is no mere metaphor but the nearest expression of final Truth to which I can attain and express, when I say that I see all nature signed with the sign of the Cross and bright with the glory of Easter Day. I see the whole creation groaning and travailing in pain together until now, and the meaning of the travail—I can find in Christ.

I can only understand nature by looking back at it through Christ. I can only understand God's labor and God's suffering in nature as I look at it through His labor and His suffering in Christ. God suffered in Christ on Calvary because His effort to express Himself through man was hindered and thwarted by man's free will misused (that is by sin), and also by man's ignorance and imperfection. If we go back from man we find that free will has grown, as everything that is human has grown, from roots which are buried in nature. Free will like everything is the result of the great process. Animals have a will of their own, not so fully grown as man's will, but still there. Every horseman knows that, and knows too that in training force is only of use up to a certain point. You must not break the spirit of a horse or a dog any more than you must break the spirit of a man. Go back to plants, and they too have a kind of independence, a will of their own, which cannot be altogether killed without killing the plant. Every gardener knows that. Go back to stones, and the sculptor knows that they have a nature of their own which cannot be destroyed without destroying the stone. The nature of the material is a limitation to which the most skillful worker must submit. Here is the only light we have upon the mystery. When God in His Love willed to begin the great process, He had to submit to limitations due to the necessary nature of matter itself.

These limitations are not eternal or final. God is overcoming them, nature is not finished yet, it is being finished through man. Every effort that man makes to overcome the evils due to matter is made by the power of the striving God that works within him. As he learns to conquer space and time by mechanical invention and scientific discovery, as he lays the railroad, sinks the cable, builds the flying machine, he is perfecting the Body of God, through which His Truth can at last express itself in the perfect Brotherhood of man. That is the meaning of material progress—it is the building of God's Body.

(1919)

The Messianic Passion

"Christos" is the Greek translation of the Hebrew "Messiah," which means the "Anointed One," and was the title of the great Deliverer, Savior, or Redeemer whom the Jews believed would come to save the world from sorrow and sin. But this expectation, this passionate longing for a Savior, was not confined to the Jewish race, it was literally worldwide. To quote Mr. Edward Carpenter's book on *Pagan and Christian Creeds, their Origin and Meaning*: "The number of Pagan Deities (mostly virgin born and done to death in some way or other in their efforts to save mankind) is so great as to be difficult to keep account of. The God Krishna in India, the God Indra in Nepal and Tibet, spilt their blood for the salvation of mankind. Buddha said, according to Max Muller, 'Let all the sins that were in the world fall on me, that the world may be delivered.' The Chinese Tien, the Holy One, 'one with God, and existing with Him from all eternity,' died to save the world. The Egyptian Osiris was called Savior; so was Horus; so was the Persian Mithras; so was the Greek Hercules, who overcame death, though his body was consumed in the burning garment of mortality, out of which he rose to Heaven. So also was the Phrygian Attis called Savior, and the Syrian Tammuz or Adonis likewise, both of whom were nailed or tied to a tree, and afterwards rose again from their biers or coffins. Prometheus, the greatest and earliest benefactor of the human race, was nailed by the hands and feet with arms extended to the rocks of Mount Caucasus. Bacchus or Dionysius, born of the Virgin Semele to be the liberator of mankind (Dionysius Eleutherios as he was called), was torn to pieces, not unlike Osiris. Even in far-off Mexico, Quetzalcoatl, the Savior, was born of a Virgin, was tempted, and fasted forty days, and was done to death."[3]

Now, when you come to think of it, that is a queer business, isn't it? Here you have peoples so utterly severed and disconnected that there is no possibility of communication between them, and yet there grows up among them spontaneously, as it were, a passionate longing for a Savior—a Deliverer—a Christ. "The long tradition of the Savior comes down from the remotest times, and perhaps from every country in the world."

---

3. Carpenter, *Pagan and Christian Creed*, 129–30.

Funnily enough, this has often been used as an argument against the reality of the Christ. The fact that the Messianic passion was not confined, as most of us were taught in the days of our youth, to the Jews, but was almost as universal among men of every race as hunger or thirst, is supposed to make it harder to believe that a Christ or savior has ever come, or ever will. When it is discovered that all the world over men were holding up helpless hands to Heaven in supplication for a Savior, and that the Old Testament only records one part of the age-long preparation for His coming, we are told that this conclusively proves that He never came. Learned men trace the history of this passion back through all the maze of legends, myths, rites and ceremonies that make up the history of man's search for God; they discover that it had immoral or non-moral beginnings, that it was connected with Nature Worship and the Sex Instinct, and then tell us that, having explained its origin, they have not only explained the passion, but have actually explained it away, and proved it to be a delusion.

But that is a queer way of doing things. It is the topsy-turvy method of argument that the idolatry of the scientific method has imposed upon the world of men for years. The analysis of a thing is supposed to be a complete account of it. Find out where a thing came from, and you know what it is. Prove that a man is grown from an egg, and you have explained the man. Of course it is all nonsense. It is not the beginning of a thing that explains its end, it is the end that explains the beginning. You cannot explain a passion or a plant by discovering where it comes from, you can only explain by discovering what it is coming to. If all the world over, a passionate desire for a savior and deliverer sprang up, if black and white, red and yellow men have felt the passion burning in their hearts, so that they have burst into poetry, invented legends, and instituted rites and ceremonies to express it, the only thing that would really explain such a mysterious fact is not the discovery of the long process of its growth from strange beginnings—that only deepens the mystery—but the discovery of some great reality towards which it was leading men.

Of course, if you believe that all the worlds were made by chance, or accident, there is no use asking for an explanation of that, or of anything else; it is all muddle, and there is no good thinking at all. But if you refuse to take up that attitude, the logical result of which is mental and moral suicide, believing that a purpose runs through the ages of creative movement, then this circle of saviors that rings the whole world round would seem to point onwards to someone, or something, some great reality that would explain it. The real object of studying the history of this Messianic passion is not so much to discover where it came from, as to find out from its history what it is tending to.

If you study it in that way, some big broad facts grow clear. The passion, like most other human passions, as it develops seems to undergo a process of refinement. It seems to grow from the passionate longing for a magical and material salvation into the longing for a moral and spiritual one. Men seem at first to long for a Savior who will do something for them, and later for a Savior who will do something in them. First, they desire a Deliverer who will change their circumstances and surroundings, and then a Deliverer who will change them. Of course, it seems absurd to summarize so shortly a process which took ages, but, broadly speaking, that seems true. First, men seem to find the root of all their sorrows in the world without them, and later become conscious that the trouble really rises from the world within. These two strains in the passion do not, of course, succeed one another in an orderly sequence, nothing ever develops that way. Wherever the passion is found these two strains are found in it, but in some races the one is the stronger, and in other races the other. And as men grow in intelligence and insight the moral and spiritual passion grows stronger, and the magical and material more weak. The reason why the history of the preparation for the coming of the Christ among the Jews has gripped the Western world and survived to be read and loved by common men, while the history of that preparation among other peoples has barely survived to be hunted up out of the dust of ages by scholars, is that the great Jewish teachers and prophets had a clearer vision of the truth that what men needed was a moral and spiritual redemption—a Savior who would change the world within.

I do not mean to say that the Jews were the only ones to see that truth, or that there is not a great deal of the lower strain in their passion for a Savior. Neither of these statements would be true. The popular idea of Salvation among the Jews was as material and as magical as most popular conceptions; and the best of their teachers were not free from its influence. On the other hand, some of the legends and sayings current among so-called pagan peoples show great moral beauty and an intense longing for spiritual Salvation. We have no right that I can see to say that all the other sacred books were purely human and the Old Testament alone Divine, that they were merely folklore, while the Old Testament is revelation. That creates a division between the human and the Divine which cannot really exist. But we have a right to say that in the Old Testament story of the preparation we do see the higher truth, the loftier idea of Salvation, struggling more successfully to expression. We have a right to say that in the battle of the sacred books for survival the Bible won a foremost place, mainly on its merits, because of its deeper moral and spiritual appeal, because it touched men's consciences and made them long to be better men in a way that other sacred writings failed to do.

I do not think there is any doubt that we have grossly underrated the moral and spiritual worth of other religions, and have allowed prejudice to blind our eyes to their beauty, and to the foreshadowing of Christ which they contain. It is a tragedy that we should have allowed a spirit of almost savage exclusiveness to have blotted out for us the revelation of God contained in earth's million myths and legends, so that Christians have regarded them almost as though they were the inventions of the evil one. It is a disaster that we should have lumped all other faiths together and called them "pagan"—dismissing them as worthless. It is disastrous because it has distorted our missionary methods and delayed the development of the world religion. It has made us seek to convert the East not merely to Christ, but to our peculiarly Western Christ, and to force upon other peoples not merely our experience of Him, but our ways of expressing the experience. It is disastrous, too, because it has bred in us the spirit of intolerance and contempt for others which is one of the chieftest obstacles to the union of the world.

Perhaps, like other evil things, intolerance was an inevitable accompaniment of development, but it is none the less evil. It has led us to stress and emphasize comparatively unimportant issues in our statement of belief, and to elevate our own peculiarities into the position of principles. It has led us to trust in hatred rather than in love. It has caused us to put prejudice before truth, and to make a virtue of our own stupidity and ignorance. It has often made us orthodox liars for the glory of God. It has thrown us back upon futile and unchristian methods of defending our faith and spreading it abroad, and turned us from the one method which has in it the secret of success, the method of living by it, of basing our every thought, word, and deed upon its truth. It has made us fearful and distrustful of the power of Christ to win, and bred in us a blasphemous anxiety to do God's work for Him, and to build up defenses for His Church, with human hands and human minds, when it needs no defenses but its own eternal truth. It has thus delayed the coming of the day, which must inevitably come, when the faith which has in it most of truth and perfect moral beauty will win the world to the unity of the Spirit in the bonds of lasting peace.

I do not think there can be any doubt that we have paid, and are paying, for this mistake, a heavy price both at home and abroad, and that one of our chief lessons to be learned is that bigotry is no adequate substitute for faith. But when we have admitted all that, the fact still remains that in the Old Testament story of the Messianic passion, and the preparation for the coming of the Christ, the real meaning of the passion comes out more clearly than in any other, and it is true that we can search the Scriptures for witness to the Christ.

But all this is ancient history you say—very ancient, and in fact a bit moldy. What has it got to do with the issues of today? It may have been important for a Jew at the times of Jesus to see that He fulfilled the prophecies upon which his fathers lived, but what has it got to do with me in the year of grace 1920? What do I care whether the Jews were God's sole chosen people, or whether there was a great light breaking through all over the world? I am willing to admit that the latter seems a more rational and likely notion, but how does it affect my belief one way or another?

Well, you see, this Messianic passion and its growth are part of the history of the world; they are a section of the wonderful process by which man's mental and emotional world has been built up, and the study of that process is at least as important for purposes of truth as the study of the process by which the material world was built. And it has to be looked at and judged in the same way. The way to learn from the past is to remember always that the whole universe is a movement, and must be examined with a view to discovering what it is moving to—what its purpose is. We have seen that this Messianic passion is a developing, growing passion, which, as it grows, tends to change its content. It grows from being a desire for a magical and material Savior to being a desire for a moral and spiritual one. It is a passion almost as universal as hunger and thirst; and unless the world is a joke, or a chance, it must have a meaning and purpose.

We can best judge of its purpose in the light of its latest development. In its latest development it is seen as a passion for inward and spiritual Salvation, the longing for a Savior who will not merely change man's lot but will change his heart, redeem his character. It if points onward, as we are driven to believe, to some great reality which will be food for its hunger and drink for its thirst, we should expect that it would be a great moral and spiritual reality. We should expect that the great passion for redemption of the inner man would find satisfaction at last in the appearance upon the earth of a Perfect Character, possessing the power of drawing men upwards into its own likeness. We have seen that the wonder of the Gospel stories is that out of them, with all their inconsistencies, there grows a supremely consistent Character which does possess this power of drawing men upwards into its own likeness. This has been the universal Christian experience. "We all, with unveiled face reflecting as in a mirror the glory of the Lord, are transformed into the same image, from glory unto glory, as from the Lord—the Spirit." This has been the experience not merely of the great saints who have left their record behind them, and made their mark upon the shifting sands of time, but it has been the experience, the fundamental experience, of millions of unknown saints who, by gallant lives of self-sacrifice and love, of purity and passionate charity, have bravely borne the burden of the world, and done their part unseen in our development as a race.

The history of the Christian Church, like the life of its Lord, is a tragedy, and often a sordid and revolting tragedy, but through it all there runs a vein of golden goodness that redeems its squalor and its ugliness. A man who can write, "With the exception of a few episodes like the formation during the Middle Ages of the noble brotherhoods and sisterhoods of friars and nuns, dedicated to the help and healing of suffering humanity, and the appearance of a few real lovers of mankind (and the animals) like St. Francis (and these manifestations can hardly be claimed by the Church which pretty consistently opposed them), it may be said that after the fourth century the real spirit and life of early Christian enthusiasm died away,"[4] as Mr. Edward Carpenter does, is looking at history as a journalist looks at life—from the sensationalist point of view. No

---

4. *Pagan and Christian Creeds*, 208.

saint is worth bothering about who does not make a name for himself, and the Church is to be judged by the faults and failings, the sordid sins and squabbles that mar the history of its highest officials.

But the history of the Papacy is no more the history of the Church than the history of the British Cabinet is the history of the British People. That judgment is a vulgar judgment, vulgar with the pernicious vulgarity of intellectual pride which lives in the world of books, and lives in that world without the imagination that comes of touch with real human sorrow, and with real human sin. The fire of Christian enthusiasm has at times burned low, but it has never died; it remains the soul of Western civilization and the hope of the world. And it is because this Character of Jesus meets the Messianic passion of mankind at its purest and best, and can prove itself bread for its hunger and wine for its thirst, that we claim for Jesus the title of the Christ.

The Messianic passion is not dead. It is very much alive. There is in the world of today a very intense conviction, which after the last five years [of war] ought to be more intense, that there is still something wrong—radically wrong. And there is, too, a longing which is intense and ought to be intenser for someone or something to put it right. The Messianic passion is still there, and the two strains in it are still evident. There are those who long for a magical and material redemption, for a savior or a system which will change man's lot, and make the world an entirely pleasant and comfortable place to live in, and there are a smaller number who have seen deeper and know that man's great need is moral and spiritual redemption, a Savior who will not merely change man's lot but transform man's soul, and who perceive that only so can man's lot be changed—by the changing of his heart.

To bet your life upon Jesus as Christ means that you throw in your lot with this smaller number. To believe in Jesus as the Christ means that you stand irrevocably opposed to the million and one Godless and materialistic schemes of redemption in which the world abounds. It confronts you with the same choice exactly as that which faced Jesus of Nazareth. He came to a race in which the Messianic passion was intense, and found the people longing for a Savior, but mostly longing for the lower kind of Savior—a military Messiah Who would lead a great revolt and set God's people free; a National Deliverer Who would conquer the Roman conquerors and drive them from the land, and then take His power and reign in justice, restoring the Kingdom of Peace and Prosperity to suffering Israel. Expectation was keen, thousands were ready to rise, only waiting for a leader and a signal.

The Kingdom of God which John the Baptist proclaimed meant to many of his hearers an earthly kingdom of peace and plenty and national freedom. They sought a Savior Who would change the world without. There were a smaller number—very small—who looked for a higher kind of Savior, a Deliverer Who would come to save not merely Israel from its sorrow, but the whole world from its sin. Very few indeed, if any, had this idea of the Messiah, pure and uncontaminated by any lower elements; probably even the best had an idea of an earthly kingdom, in which righteousness should rule, and which would be founded by a great supernatural Leader Who would compel His enemies to submit. None saw the Truth as Jesus saw it. None fully grasped the fact that those who take the sword must perish by it, and that the everlasting Kingdom must be built on Faith and not Force. Jesus had to choose between the higher interpretation of His Mission and the lower, between the material Salvation which the people craved and the spiritual Salvation which they really needed. He chose the higher path, and in that choice lies at once the triumph and the tragedy of His Life. Once that choice was made, Calvary, or something like it, was inevitable, and on that choice, and on the way in which He carried it into action, depends His claim to be The Christ, The Savior of the world.

That choice still pierces to the heart of our most modern problems. Still bright within the soul of man the Messianic passion burns, and still the two strains in it persist. The world is full of movements, plans, and schemes to better the world without bettering the souls of men, to obtain material without moral and spiritual Salvation. There is still the bitterness caused by tyranny and oppression, the tyranny of force, vested interests, financial scheming and wire-pulling—the whole of the sordid forces of reaction which remain in the hands of those who find this world satisfactory and sufficient for their small souls as it is, and would not have it changed.

This secret slimy selfishness that saps the life blood of the nations and feeds on the sorrows of the poor and friendless is still there, piercing us through with many sorrows, plunging the world into wars, worming its way into our politics, breeding rot and corruption in high places. It is still there, doing the dirty work it has done for centuries. And it still causes the passion for deliverance to burn in men's souls. The ruling classes still stand over against the ruled, the governors against the governed. And, as in Christ's day, so in ours, many believe that Salvation can be won by violence and threats of violence, by meeting force with force, and tyranny with counter-tyranny. The vision of the great proletarian republic, when the workers shall rule the world, is held before us as the ideal end. Salvation must come through class war and the victory of the downtrodden and oppressed. The modern zealots—socialists, syndicalists, class-conscious proletarians—still proclaim war on the hated bourgeoisie, bidding us believe that you have only to destroy the competitive system of industry, and the rule of the classes over the masses, and earth will be a paradise. Everywhere we are forming ourselves into great fighting unions to secure our own interests, and we are told that when the Union of the Unions comes, and the people rise as one man, then the day of salvation will dawn for man. That on the one side, and all the cynical forces of reaction on the other, and the common man of all classes blind and bewildered between the two, that is the world of today.

And the only light in it is still Jesus, the Christ. The Character stands firm and judges these movements right or wrong, or disentangles the mixture of right and wrong which makes them so bewildering to the honest man of the day who has to earn his bread and keep his children. Jesus stands and tells us that force is folly and hatred waste of time, that "a man's life consisteth not in the multitude of things that he possesseth," that there is more in life than pleasure, that giving is better than gain, that the secret of life is service and self-sacrifice.

He is, of course, despised and rejected by both sides. The reactionaries patronize Him and render Him lip service, but in their hearts believe that He is quite unpractical and does not count. The revolutionaries hate Him, and declare that His Gospel of Love is opium to the people, who need to be fed fat with hatred, that they may be strong to revolt. Business is business, and Christ has nothing to do with it, says the commercialist. "Conscious labor or planned organization of social labor is the name of the expected Messiah of the New Age. Our hope of Salvation is not a religious ideal, but rests on the massive foundation stone of materialism," says Mr. Belfort Bax, the Socialist.[5] Christ tells the businessman that he is

5. Belfort Bax (1854–1926), influential socialist advocate and editor of *Justice,* the

an immoral scoundrel, and the socialist that he is a silly fool, and points another way. What is wanted is the transformation of the human heart into His likeness. All schemes are futile which are not aimed at that.

(1921)

---

newspaper of England's Social Democratic Federation.

In God's Heart

We cannot see the Cross and the Resurrection as two distinct and finished acts; we see them as one—one great act in time revealing a process of Eternity, revealing the Love of the suffering but triumphant God. We see redemption, not as a finished and completed thing, but as a purpose that is being worked out, and is to be completed in the fullness of God's time. So we see it in ourselves, and so we see it in the world. We cannot say of ourselves that we are dead to sin and alive only to goodness; we cannot say that it is no longer we that live, but Christ that liveth in us, that we are new creatures; we cannot say that the Cross in our own hearts is empty, that we are risen with Him; but what we can and do say is that we are dying to sin, that Christ is crucified every day, but that He rises again, that in our lives He is suffering, but we are filled with the conviction that He is to be triumphant, that He has gotten a hold on us, and will not let us go, that although He is but feeble, is as it were just a baby in a manger, hidden away in the poorest room in the crowded inn of our lives, He makes us feel that He is to be one day the Lord of Glory, the King of Kings.

That is how we see Christ crucified and risen again in ourselves, and that is how we see Him in the world and in the Church—crucified—crucified in every street of our great cities, crucified in every hovel of our slums, crucified on our markets, crucified on our battlefields, but forever rising again. Again and again men cry that He is dead and buried, antiquated, impossible, mythical; again and again He comes back, takes hold on human hearts, and sends them out to preach His truth, aflame with the old new Love. Once more we see how the great idea of the moving universe—the idea of progress and development—comes in to throw new light and make a wonderful harmony of the apparent contradictions of Christian experience. Looked at in the light of that idea, the old, old story takes once more the powers of youth and goes out to win the young. If our Gospel were only a Gospel of the Crucified, it would be untrue to facts and a Gospel of despair. But the Gospel of the Cross and the Empty Tomb, of the Crucified, Risen Christ, always crucified and always rising again, is the Gospel that faces all facts and gives to life a meaning.

There is in the heart of God, and always has been, a Cross and an Empty Tomb.

(1921)

Facing Up to Suffering

One of the strongest and most deeply-seated instincts that sway normal men is repulsion from pain and suffering. It is a natural repulsion with a very obvious purpose, and intensely strong, and strongest in the healthiest people. If a man likes inflicting pain, or desires to endure it, and there are heaps of men and women who do, healthy-minded people agree that he is either mad or bad, or both. Yet one of the strongest impressions that Christ made upon the men of His own time, and one of the strongest impressions He makes upon the men of today, is the impression of His sufferings. He was, and is, seen to be "a man of sorrows and acquainted with grief." And His Gospel has often been stated, and is still often stated, in such a way as to glorify suffering as a good thing, sent by God, and give the impression that Christ taught, and would have us believe, that pain and suffering were good things, and that a man who suffered was to be admired and reverenced for it whether He suffered for any good purpose or not. Christians themselves have often been morbid people, and believed that suffering of any sort was the Will of God, and always tended to purge the soul and make for purity of heart. We all know the kind of Christian who manufactures his own crosses by the dozen, and then pathetically claims your admiration for the way he bears them; the morbid hysterical woman who walks the way of sorrows paved by her own distorted and self-centered imagination with the air of a saintly martyr done to death for truth. We all know these people, and they are the despair of our lives, for there is no more soul-destroying evil than self-pity that mistakes itself for sacrifice.

If we are to have healthy minds and live healthy lives, we must assume quite definitely and clearly that pain and suffering are evil things, and that to endure them without necessity is folly, and the most futile of all follies, and to inflict them without necessity is sin, and the most sinful of all sins. There is no sin so vile and so degrading as deliberate cruelty, and the essence of cruelty is the infliction of unnecessary pain. We cannot be too definite about the sinfulness of cruelty of any sort whatever. But we must also recognize that, evil as pain and suffering are, they are by no means the worst of evils, and that to endure them *for a good and sufficient reason* is the highest wisdom, and to inflict them with *a good and sufficient purpose* is the most perfect kindness. Only the purpose must be good and sufficient. We must have a perfectly good object, and we must make absolutely certain, as far as we humanly can, that we cannot possibly attain that object without inflicting suffering and pain.

That sounds like rather ponderous and platitudinous (those words have an imposing appearance, haven't they?—just like fat men with loud voices) common sense; but the most ghastly sorrows have been endured by men and women, and especially children, because the truth was not recognized and good religious people looked upon pain and suffering as good things which it was always beneficial to inflict and endure, and which always tended to purge and purify the heart. They have been convinced that men could only be saved from sin by suffering, and that God sent suffering into the world for that good purpose. This idea has led Christians to tolerate and regard as inevitable a great deal of totally unnecessary and avoidable suffering. It has led them to condone and even regard as beneficial ghastly social conditions, involving the daily torture of men and women. It has enabled them to contemplate a dirty, unorganized, wasteful, and stupid world as God's appointed place of preparation for the next. The Church has given its blessing to a stupid and cruel chaos on the ground that it was God's appointed preparation for a wondrous order after death. Only the other day a good Christian was telling me of some outdoor services in a poor quarter, and described with great satisfaction the crowd of dirty, unkempt, and degraded-looking people that thronged around the preacher. He was delighted with the service. Here was the real thing, the preaching of the Gospel to God's poor. So picturesque and romantic. It did not strike him that the existence of such people and their miserable pig sty houses was a reproach to the Gospel and a wound in the heart of Christ.

Of course, when he was challenged with it, he saw it, *but he had to be challenged.* He had to be shaken out of his piety into practical humanity. It was necessary to make him, a good Christian man, see that this stupid and avoidable suffering was a sin. He was still under the spell of that perversion of Christ's Gospel which leads to the sinful and morbid glorification and sentimentalizing of stupid cruelty. The same attitude has been commonly taken by Christians toward disease. It was God's chastening, to be meekly accepted and submitted to. It was the cup of suffering given by the Father, and must be drunk to the dregs. It was a special privilege to be allowed to share Christ's sufferings, and the sufferer must look upon it as such. These things are sent by a watchful Providence to test and try us.

So in a vicious circle the morbid lie worked round, fastening the chains of sorrow tighter round man's hands and feet. Cruelty walked proudly round the streets arrayed in the shining robes of Christ.

The error is fatal because it disguises cruelty and gives it a religious sanction, and that is the very thing sin always seeks—a good disguise. Again and again men have tortured their fellows in the name of God, pretending that it was for their own good, and deceiving themselves, when really it was the morbid and savage love of inflicting pain that was urging them on. "See thou to what damned deeds religion draweth men" is as true of the Christian religion as any other. Men have found doctrines to disguise and cover the bestial cruelty and vindictiveness of their own natures. There is no doubt that much of the powerful appeal which the teaching of the Divine frightfulness and eternal punishment had for their elect was due to the freedom it gave them to reel in thought over the vengeance which they could not inflict themselves, but which God would inflict for them upon their enemies. It was due to the making of God in man's image, and the picturing of God's justice as being like our degraded and makeshift justice.

Few words have been so misused as "Justice." Justice has been supposed to demand that a sinner should suffer whether any good purpose was served by the suffering or not. He "deserves" to suffer, and this is enough. Nine men out of ten do not know what the word "deserve" means. It is a word that covers a multitude of sins—like charity. It covers up any quantity of vindictiveness, and cruelty, and callousness. The truth is, that no one deserves a pang of pain unless it is necessary for his own good, or the good of other men, unless it serves a purpose which cannot be otherwise accomplished. This idea of "Justice" as something distinct from Love has been a curse to the world. Even now our prisons are full of men and women who "deserved" to suffer, and who will be all the worse for it, and all the greater danger to society because of it, and several steps nearer Hell than they were before they suffered. Suffering was inflicted on them in the name of "Justice" because we were too lazy, too ignorant, and too stupid to get to the root of their sin and save them from it. The history of this world's course of "Justice" would turn a strong man sick. All through time man, with his genius for self-deception and hypocrisy, has dressed up his sin in the robes of this attribute of God, and then fallen down and worshipped it. The really just man is the man who inflicts and permits only absolutely necessary pain, and *who suffers himself in doing so*. The more perfectly just a man is, the more he will strive to avoid inflicting pain, and the more keenly he will suffer himself when he has to inflict it—of necessity. God's Justice must mean an infinity of effort to avoid inflicting or permitting pain and suffering, and an infinity of sorrow to Himself when He has to permit or inflict it—of necessity. God's Justice is God's Love.

If Justice means the rationing out of pain and pleasure to people as they "deserve" it, this world is not just at all. Pain is not distributed according to desert in this world. Looking for that sort of justice in life is like looking for a needle in a haystack when it is not there. The best people suffer most again and again. Life is not fair, and cannot be made fair, except on the surface, and that with great difficulty. It is true that we can remedy, and must remedy, the glaring surface "injustices" of life, the disgusting extremes of riches and poverty, the ridiculous differences of opportunity for education and development, but these are only surface injustices, and when we have remedied them all, life will not be fair. And in our effort to remedy them we shall discover, and do, that our greatest enemy is this idea of desert. People who have been given by God greater brain power and higher ability look upon themselves as deserving all they can get, and as being in some mysterious way better than the common ruck of men. They have a right to affluence while others starve. The deserve to live in fine houses with large gardens and a tradesman's entrance while others pit it two families in one room. They deserve these blessings. Under that blessed notion they disguise their selfishness. And it is all a pack of stupid nonsense. They don't deserve anything, and are not a ha'porth better than any decent man who earns 3 pounds per week, and often not as good. They were given these gifts of brain and ability to serve and help with, they were given them as *trusts* for a noble purpose, and unless they fulfill the trust, they are just common thieves. There is no desert about it.

And when you have killed that lie and remedied the surface injustices, you will not have made the world fair. Still the natural gifts which make for pain or pleasure are unequally distributed without any attention to desert. Brains, beauty, charm, genius are not distributed according to desert, and they are treasures beyond the power of money to buy. Of course, in the orthodox religious scheme of things beauty and charm do not count, they are only skin deep, but as a matter of fact they are the most coveted gifts in the world, and productive of intense pleasure, and are tremendous powers for good or evil. There is no greater devil than a beautiful and charming devil, and no saint so powerful as a charming saint. They are distributed unequally, and with no attention to desert. Stupidity, awkwardness, shyness are not distributed equally, or as they are deserved, and they are the cause of agonies. Misfortunes, accidents, disease, and death are not sent to those that deserve them. What is the use of pretending that they are? You may be a saint, but that will not prevent you from falling down the cellar steps and breaking your leg. Life does not always punish the guilty and reward the innocent. The Jews tried hard to believe that it did, but it only broke their hearts, and it will break the heart of anyone who tries to believe it, unless he is the kind of person who can see a hundred children burned to death and thank God they were not his, or hear that a battalion of fine men has been cut to pieces and thank God he was not there. That kind of gratitude to the Almighty is fairly common, and I often wonder what He thinks of it. An exceptionally fortunate person might persuade himself of the idea that the world was just, provided he never felt the truth

> That loss is common does not make
>
> My loss the less but rather more.
>
> Never morning wore
>
> To evening but some heart did break.[6]

It is not true that if you are good you will escape pain, or that if you are sinful you will incur it. The better you are the more pain you may be called upon to endure, and the worse you are the more pleasure you may manage to obtain. I know of no task more hopeless than the endeavor to maintain that God's government of this world is just in the sense of awarding reward and punishment according to desert. When you get down beneath the surface into the underworld of private hopes and fears and horrors, where the real tragedies of life are played out, and have laid bare before you the tortures which good men and women suffer, and when you know with what brutality the law of heredity works out, this copybook lie about the way to happiness being goodness, and the

---

6. Alfred Lord Tennyson, "In Memoriam," VI.

way to sorrow sin, turns you sick. It is just soothing syrup and untruth. God is not just in that sense of the word. This world is not a complete, finished, and justly ordered place where all things happen as they should, where all the good little boys get halfpennies and all the bad little boys get smacks. If belief in God depended upon maintaining the truth of that lie, then belief in God were impossible.

But belief in God does not depend upon it. The Christian religion starts off by aiming a blow at that lie. That is its chiefest glory. It begins with the best Man that ever lived hanging in agony on a Cross, and so faces up to facts right away. There is its splendor. It is rooted in the most stark naked act of injustice that the mind could well conceive. There stands Perfect Man, with the spittle of a drunken soldier streaming down His face, a crown of thorns set sideways on His head, with blood from the great wounds in His head, with blood from the great wounds in His back sousing red through the dirty purple cloth that mockery has thrown across His nakedness—there stands Christ. Behold the Man! All history is summed up in that scene. There is no truer picture of what history reveals than a Crucifix. As it stood in a broken Flanders village, looked up to by broken bleeding men, as it stands in some rotten slum today while the squalid crowd pass seething by, it is the Truth—the Martyrdom of God in Man. Life is as brutal as it is brutal, as repulsive as it is repulsive, as unjust as it is unjust, and, thank God, as perfectly beautiful as He is perfectly beautiful. That is the secret. The Cross is not God's Will, but God's Woe. The Christ is God's Will—He is perfect Beauty. But His beauty is not for all to see. To many there is no beauty that they should desire Him. They cannot see Christ for the Cross. It stands in the way. It blots Him out. They have been taught, perhaps, that the Cross was God's plan, that God willed it; it was part of His scheme, and they are repelled. What a God! What a plan!

They would be prepared to admire Christ for His sufferings if they could see any good and sufficient reason for them. "This have I done for thee; what wilt thou do for Me?" pleads the preacher. "What hast Thou done for me?" answers the man in the street. "What purpose did this suffering serve?" "It saved the world from sin," says the preacher. "But it didn't," says the man in the street, "you know it didn't. You are talking cant—pious cant. It didn't save the world from sin. Sin and sorrow still continue, misery and wretchedness are with us yet, and fall like the rain upon the just and the unjust too. Men still torture men and women, children still go hungry, there is still rape and murder, lust and war. Our streets are full of it, our papers ring with it, the world remains unsaved, and the heaviest burdens still fall upon the best of men. Calvary made no difference. It is a summary of life's problem, but not a solution."

"But Salvation is possible now," says the preacher; "it was impossible before. Man can now be saved from sin. God's justice has been satisfied. You see, God's justice required that man must suffer for his sin, his rebellion against God, before he could be forgiven. All the world would, by the law of justice, have been doomed to eternal torment in an everlasting Hell if Jesus had not suffered and saved us from that awful fate. God could not forgive, even if man repented, unless the law of justice were satisfied and the punishment which sin deserved was borne by man in Christ. You do not understand the awful Holiness of God."

But the man in the street gets frantic here. "No, I don't," he says, "and I don't want to. I don't want to understand a justice that demands eternal agony for threescore years and ten of ignorance, sorrow, and sin. Who is this just God? I do not believe there is such a Being. If there is, He must be the Devil. If I could meet Him, I would tell Him what I thought of His justice even if I went to Hell for it afterwards. Justice which demands eternal punishment for anything is not justice, but vengeance, cruelty, and hate. I tell you straight, this just God of yours is nothing but the reflection of your own dirty mind, which is still back in the days when they hanged a woman for stealing ribbon. You may twist yourself into philosophic knots as much as you like, and pile up explanations that don't explain to your heart's content, but you cannot get over the fact that a 'justice' which demanded everlasting punishment for anything would be just another name for inhuman brutality. That is all this divine 'justice' is, it is a survival, a superstition in the worst sense.

"What I want to know is, Why did Jesus suffer? What good did His sufferings do? What difference do they make today? What good purpose was served by them which could not have been served without? If you cannot give me intelligible answers of some sort, I am prepared to pity Jesus, as I am prepared to pity any other noble visionary who has been put to death, because he was before his time, but I do not see why I should worship Him because of His sufferings, which are just one more gruesome act in this world's sordid tragedy of errors. I admire the men who suffered for me in the war, because I see what good their sufferings did, I see what they have saved me from, and I don't see how I could have been saved without them. But I cannot see what good the sufferings of Jesus did, or what they have saved me from, or why, if there be an Almighty God of Love, I could not have been saved without them. I cannot see why men should not have been forgiven, if they repented, without this brutal murder as a sacrifice. Jesus forgave men freely when He was on earth, and never Himself mentioned any other condition of forgiveness but repentance. He told us to forgive seventy times seven if a man repents, and went further, and told us to forgive our enemies, bless those who cursed us, and do good to those who ill-treated us, and that we were to do this because we have to be perfect as our Father in Heaven is perfect. Yet you say that a callous legal murder had to be committed before it was possible for God to forgive a repentant man. To be quite frank, this doctrine strikes me as being not merely incredible, but immoral as well."

These questions, half formulated, and altogether unexpressed, crowd into the mind of the man and woman in the street when he or she is persuaded to come and be saved, and the preacher pleads pathetically for gratitude to Christ for His bitter sufferings. Visions of similar brutalities which he has seen and is anxious to forget flit before the soldier's mind—men with their bowels in their hands, men with bodies ripped and torn, murdered children, ravished women; and the great God who needed a propitiation to save the world from sin, and then did not save it, sits up and looks down on it all. The preacher cannot explain. The theologian explains himself into a knot which no one could untie. Dr. Dale explained the Atonement to me as a youth, and was harder to grasp than the Cross itself. Dr. Moberly was worse.[7] I have never read a book on the Atonement that did not puzzle me more than the puzzle. As for getting a plain message for plain men out of them, it would take God Himself to do it, no man could. The miracle was that God sometimes did. He can get through any cloud of lies to find a soul in desperate need.

Plain men do not understand justice that demands eternal punishment, and cannot picture a Father who requires propitiation before He forgives a repentant child. The fact is that our preachers spend, or did

---

7. Robert William Dale (1829–1895), English nonconformist theologian whose major work was *The Atonement* (1875). George Moberly (1803–1885), Bishop of Salisbury. The work Studdert Kennedy is probably referring to is Moberly's 1868 Bampton lectures published as *The Administration of the Holy Spirit in the Body of Christ*.

spend (they have largely given it up as a bad job now and taken to brief, bright, and brotherly talks to the people on popular subjects, their time explaining, not the Gospel, but the symbols and metaphors which its first evangelists used in the struggle to give its message to the men of their day, men whose minds moved in a different world from ours, men whose religion was steeped in bloody sacrifice, whose states were ruled by despots, and whose work was done by slaves, men whose idea of justice was full of cruelty and destitute of love. We sacrifice reason and imperil morality in order to keep these pseudo-sacred symbols and metaphors intact. It all leaves the decent man in the street cold. He finds it dull, dreary, and repulsive. Better go out into God's green fields and listen to the choir of birds, better to see God's Love in a cloudless sky, than sit in a stuffy church and hear a perspiring parson wrestling to explain how "Justice" and the awful Holiness of God demanded a peculiarly brutal murder as propitiation in order to avoid damning a world of men to Hell.

They have my sympathy. But there is a sublimely simple truth that saves. Get all that out of your head. Burn all the books of explanation. Fisherize the whole boiling and sack the lot. ("This is dreadful," exclaims the nice good man who thinks such things too sacred to talk naturally about. "What becomes of Catholic theology?" I don't know—and—Oh, I don't want to be contemptuous or anything, but I don't care. As a matter of fact, I have never been able to discover what Catholic theology is. It changes with every generation of Catholics. It cometh up, and is cut down like a flower, and never continueth in one stay. It is the mortal body of an immortal truth.) We have suffered many things for these dead symbols, it is time that someone read their funeral service, and they were decently interred in a museum. Let us get out. Swing back to the universe as it is. Here we stand beneath the stars, with the challenge of the world before us. What does it mean?

Remember what we know. Remember first that the universe is a movement—an unfinished movement. It is on a pilgrimage—a journey. Where to? That is the question. And it is in order to answer that question, and only to answer that question, "Where to?", that we have turned back and asked ourselves the question, "Where from?" we have sought to pierce the darkness of the past in the hope of discerning the direction in which the world is moving, and so guessing the final goal to which it strives. We have seen the age-long preparation of the world for life, and then the strange beginnings of life itself. We have traced its struggle upwards stage by stage, we have seen vegetable, animal, human life emerge, and we have marked how each higher type of life has had to struggle for its existence, only surviving if it proved strong enough to overcome the lower life. That has been true in the story of man as in the story of animals and things. We have watched the growth of man, and have gained the impression that behind and within it there seems to be a Power which makes for unity of man with man, which strives to make the Human Unity or Brotherhood, to create Man. We have marked the growth of unity against the obstacles of human stupidity, imperfection, and sin, and in that growth there came a crisis, a breakthrough, parallel partly with those great crises when life itself began, or when mind emerged out of matter, there came the crisis of Christmas Day—the Incarnation. In the fullness of time God broke through once more, and a higher life than the merely human, a new order of goodness, appeared upon earth, and appeared as a solitary Personality amid millions of a lower order of life.

What would you expect, what would the whole story of the process lead you to expect? Are not Gethsemane and Calvary, or something like them, natural, inevitable? Was it not written in the rocks and stones, written in the strange book of Life's history, that the Son of Man must suffer many things, and be rejected of the elders and chief priests and scribes—the whole of the lower and older order of life; and was it not written, too, that He must be raised up—that the higher order must survive? Can you not almost see that naked Figure, with His wonder and His wounds, growing out of the pages of your scientific textbook? Has not the whole process been the crucifixion of the higher by the lower life, is it not all summed up in the Cross? The process is bloody, so is the Cross; the process is repulsive, so is the Cross; the process is unjust, so is the Cross; the process is glorious, so is the Christ. Behold the Man—Perfect Man—the Character. Never does His glory shine so brightly as it shines now. No man has ever seen the sun who has not seen it break its way through inky clouds and bathe the world in sudden silver beauty from on high, so no man ever sees the Face of God until it breaks upon his vision through the clouds of Calvary. Never was God so human, never was man so Divine. That is the truth: the martyrdom of God in Man, not the punishment of Man by God.

This is the truth that lies behind all these old world symbols and metaphors, behind the Propitiation and the Sacrifice. The Incarnation is the Atonement—and the Atonement the Incarnation. Good Friday is Christmas Day, and Christmas Day Good Friday, and Easter Day, and Ascension Day, and Whitsunday, because they are all Christ. It is Christ that saves, not the Cross; it is Christ that redeems, not His sufferings. The Cross does not save, any more than the process creates. The Cross never saved any man, and never could. You are not to be saved by anything that happened in the past, you can only be saved by God acting now in the present. You cannot be saved by any Church, Sacrament, Priest, or Creed of God—you can only be saved by God Himself. Calvary is not past, it is present. The Cross is still set up, the crowd still stands and mocks, the soldiers still play dice, the faithful still draw near to worship God in Man. That Christ Who hung there hangs there still, and calls to you and me, challenging us to take up the struggle of the higher life, bear its burden, endure its shame, and win its inward Peace.

The Cross was the most natural thing in the world—the most natural and inevitable, as natural and as inevitable as all the rest of the hideous process by which life has been, and is being, evolved, and of which it is the first scene in the final act. There is no Almighty potentate who made the world perfect, and then permitted it to come to a disaster, put it under a curse for thousands of years, and then intervened and sent His Son to undo the curse by offering a propitiatory sacrifice. It is all a tissue of ancient metaphors in which men strive to express in terms of their day the overwhelming experience of finding God in Christ. He had to be expressed in terms of their religion and their philosophy, but we are not bound by them, or saved by believing in them. We are only bound by the Spirit of Christ, saved by our faith in Him, not in what He was, nor in what He did, but in what He is, and has been from the beginning, from the time that this mysterious business first began and the world of worlds was born. The Gospel does not ask men to believe in suffering as being good, or as being the Will of God. The Cross was no more the Will of God than any other murder or atrocity that stains the story of man's life on earth. The Cross is common, it is Christ that is unique. It was no more the Will of God that Christ should suffer than it is the Will of God that a good and patient wife should have her brains battered out by a drunken husband with the leg of a table, or that a young mother should be ripped open and left disemboweled on her own doorstep by a drunken soldier. It was the Will of God that the travail of the process should bring in the fullness of time the perfect Life to birth, and that it should be lived out in its perfection to the end. It was God's Will, because God was and is that Life, and He was travailing in the process, and is travailing still.

The necessity of Calvary was the necessity that has been binding on God since the beginning of time, it was the necessity inherent in the task of creation. We can never fully understand it, anymore than we can fully understand anything else. It is not sufficient to account for the facts to say that God chose to give man a free will, and that man chose evil rather than good. There is a truth in that, but it is not, cannot be, the whole truth. All the misery and evil in the world, all the cruelty and crime, is not due now, and never has been due, to man's deliberate choice of evil. It was not merely sin—in the full sense of willful sin—that has caused God's age-long Calvary, or that hung Christ on the Cross. All through the ages men have crucified God, not knowing what they did, crucified Him through their ignorance, stupidity, and imperfection as well as through deliberate choice of wrong against right. There has always been a voice crying in the heart of God, and appealing to His Fatherhood, "Forgive them, for they know not what they do." It is not possible to account for all the hideous misery that has marked the growth of Man as being the consequence of sin—unless you interpret sin in a wider sense than the word can really bear. It must be taken to include ignorance, dullness of imagination, feebleness of mind, and a host of other factors for which man cannot be held wholly responsible either as an individual or as a race. Religion in the past has suffered because it concentrated all its attention on sin as deliberate rebellion against God, and passed over the part that ignorance and feebleness have played in making His age-long Calvary. This has been due to the fact that we have separated the Creation of the world from its Redemption, basing our thought upon the doctrine of the Fall and man's free will. But there is a sense in which Creation and Redemption go on side by side, and have always gone on side by side, because the Creator and Redeemer are One God. Redemption is not an afterthought of the Creator—it is an eternal aspect of His work. The Lamb was slain from the foundation of the world. There has always been a Calvary in God's heart.

The first and last enemy of God the Creator, is Death—nothingness, non-existence. That is what evil is in its essence—nothingness. Evil is self-destructive and tends to death; it is based on a lie and ends nowhere. God's first creative act brought Him up against the enemy, and He has been up against it ever since, and must be up against it until creation is complete, and the world is made at last.

Calvary is the revelation in human terms of what Creation—Creation in that larger, truer sense which includes Redemption—means to God. It is the struggle of Life with Death. Christ is life and the Cross is Death. Man is saved by Life and not by Death, by Christ and not by the Cross. When we say that man has free will, we mean that he has become conscious of the struggle of Life with Death in the world and in himself, and can resolve or refuse to cooperate with Life. Sin, deliberate sin, is conscious refusal to accept the struggle for existence which Life must make—conscious refusal to bear the Cross. The only cure for sin is Life—more Life. The selfish man is a dying man. His world is small and must grow smaller. The loving man is a living man. His world is large, and must grow larger. What the world needs, what it always has needed, is more Life. That is what Christ can and does give, not by what He did, nor by what He was, but by what He does, and by what He is now—the same yesterday, today, and forever. God does not punish the sinner; sin is its own punishment; it means inevitable decay, and decay is painful, and it ends in death—extinction. The pain may not be terrible, may not be anything like as keen as the pain of growth, but it is useless and ends nowhere . . .

It is not by the sufferings of Christ that you are saved, but by His Life-force; it is not the Cross that you are called upon to worship, but the Christ, Who is the Life of the World.

(1921)

The Sorrow of God

Yes, I used to believe i' Jesus Christ,
    And I used to go to Church,
But sin' I left 'ome and came to France,
    I've been clean knocked off my perch.
For it seemed orlright at 'ome, it did,
    To believe in a God above
And in Jesus Christ 'Is only Son,
    What died on the Cross through Love.
When I went for a walk o' a Sunday morn
    On a nice fine day in the spring,
I could see he proof o' the living God
    In every living thing.
For 'ow could the grass and the trees grow up,
    All along o' their bloomin' selves?
Ye might as well believe i' the fairy tales,
    And think they was made by elves.
So I thought as that long-'aired atheist
    Were nubbat a silly sod,
For 'ow did 'e 'count for my Brussels sprouts
    If 'e didn't believe i' God?
But it ain't the same out 'ere, ye know.
    It's as different as chalk fro' cheese,
For 'arf on it's blood and t'other 'arf's mud,
    And I'm damned if I really sees
'Ow the God, who 'as made such a cruel world,
    Can 'ave Love in 'Is 'eart for men,
And be deaf to the cries of the men as dies
    And never comes 'ome again.
Just look at that little boy corporal there,
    Such a fine upstanding lad,
Wi' a will uv 'is own, and a way uv 'is own,

And a smile uv 'is own, 'e 'ad.
An hour ago 'e were bustin' wi' life,
    Wi' 'is actin' and foolin' and fun;
'E were simply the life on us all, 'e were,
    Now look what the blighters 'a done.
Now look at 'im lyin' there all uv a 'eap,
    Wi' the blood soaken over 'is 'ead,
Like a beautiful picture spoiled by a fool,
    A bundle o' nothin'—dead.
And it ain't only 'im—there's a mother at 'ome
    And 'e were the pride of 'er life.
For it's women as pays in a thousand ways
    For the madness o' this 'ere strife.
And the lovin' God 'E looks down on it all,
    On the blood and the mud and the smell.
O God, if it's true, 'ow I pities you,
    For ye must be livin' i' 'ell.
You must be livin' i' 'ell all day,
    And livin' i' 'ell all night.
I'd rather be dead, wiv' a 'ole though my 'ead,
    I would, by a damn long sight,
Than be livin' wi' you on your 'eavenly throne,
    Lookin' down on yon bloody 'eap
That were once a boy full o' life and joy,
    And 'earin' 'is mother weep.
The sorrows o' God must be 'ard to bear
    If 'E really 'as Love in 'is 'eart,
And the 'ardest part i' the world to play
    Must surely be God's part.
And I wonder if that's what it really means,
    That Figure what 'angs on the Cross.
I remember I seed on t'other day
    As I stood wi' the captain's 'oss.

I remember, I think, thinks I to mysel',
> It's a long time since 'E died,
Yet the world don't seem much better today
> Than when 'E were crucified.
It's allus the same, as it seems to me,
> The weakest must go to the wall,
And whether 'e's right, or whether 'e's wrong,
> It don't seem to matter at all.
The better ye are and the 'arder it is,
> The 'arder ye 'ave to fight,
It's a cruel 'ard world for any bloke
> What does the thing as is right.
And that's 'ow 'E came to be crucified,
> For that's what 'E tried to do.
'E was allus a –tryin' to do 'Is best
> For the likes o' me and you.
Well, what if 'E came to the earth today,
> Came walkin' about this trench,
'Ow 'Is 'eart would bleed for the sights 'E seed,
> I' the mud and the blood and the stench.
And I guess it would finish 'Im up for good
> When 'E came to this old sap end,
And 'E seed that bundle o' nothin' there,
> For 'E wept at the grave uv 'Is friend.
And they say 'E were just the image o' God.
> I wonder if God sheds tears,
I wonder if God can be sorrowin' still,
> And 'as been all these years.
I wonder if that's what it really means,
> Not only that 'E once died,
Not only that 'E came once to the earth
> And wept and were crucified?
Not just that 'E suffered once for all

  To save us from our sins,
And then went up to 'Is throne on 'igh
  To wait till 'Is 'eaven begins.
But what if 'E came to the earth to show,
  By the paths o' pain that 'E trod,
The blistering flame of eternal shame
  That burns in the heart o' God?
O God, if that's 'ow it really is,
  Why, bless ye, I understands,
And I feels for you wi' your thorn-crowned 'ead
  And your ever pierced 'ands.
But why don't ye bust the show to bits,
  And force us to do your will?
Why ever should God be suffering so
  And man be sinning still?
Why don't ye make your voice ring out,
  And drown these cursed guns?
Why don't ye stand with an outstretched 'and,
  Out there 'twixt us and the 'Uns?
Why don't ye force us to end the war
  And fix up a lasting peace?
Why don't ye will that the world be still
  And wars for ever cease?
That's what I'd do, if I was you,
  And I had a lot o' sons
What squabbled and fought and spoilt their 'ome,
  Same as us boys and the 'Uns.
And yet, I remember, a lad o' mine,
  'E's fightin' now on the sea,
And 'e were a thorn in 'is mother's side,
  And the plague o' my life to me.
Lord, 'ow I used to swish that lad
  Till 'e fairly yelped wi' pain,

But fast as I thrashed one devil out
    Another popped in again.
And at last, when 'e grew up a strappin' lad,
    'E ups and 'e says to me,
"My will's my own and my life's my own,
    And I'm goin', Dad, to sea."
And 'e went, for I 'and't broke 'is will,
    Though God knows 'ow I tried,
And 'e never set eyes on my face again
    Till the day as 'is mother died.
Well, maybe that's 'ow it is wi' God,
    'Is sons 'ave got to be free;
Their wills are their own, and their lives are their own,
    And that's 'ow it 'as to be.
So the Father God goes sorrowing still
    For 'Is world what 'as gone to sea,
But 'E runs up a light on Calvary's 'eight
    That beckons to you and me.
The beacon light of the sorrow of God
    'As been shinin' down the years,
A-flashin' its light through the darkest night
    O' our 'uman blood and tears.
There's a sight o' things what I thought was strange,
    As I'm just beginnin' to see:
"Inasmuch as ye did it to one of these
    Ye 'ave done it unto Me."
So it isn't just only the crown o' thorns
    What 'as pierced and torn God's 'ead;
'E knows the feel uv a bullet, too,
    And 'E's 'ad 'Is touch o' the lead.
And 'E's standin' wi' me in this 'ere sap,
    And the corporal stands wiv' 'Im,
And the eyes of the laddie is shinin' bright,

> But the eyes of the Christ burn dim.
> O, laddie, I thought as ye'd done for me
> > And broke my 'eart wi' your pain.
> I thought as ye'd taught me that God were dead,
> > But ye've brought 'Im to life again.
> And ye've taught me more of what God is
> > Than I ever thought to know,
> For I never thought 'E could come so close
> > Or that I could love 'Im so.
> For the voice of the Lord, as I 'ears it now,
> > Is the voice of my pals what bled,
> And the call of my country's God to me
> > Is the call of my country's dead.

(1918)

Indifference

When Jesus came to Golgotha they hanged Him on a tree,
They drave great nails through hands and feet, and made a Calvary;
They crowned Him with a crown of thorns, red were His wounds and deep,
For those were crude and cruel days, and human flesh was cheap.

When Jesus came to Birmingham they simply passed Him by,
They never hurt a hair of Him, they only let Him die;
For men had grown more tender, and they would not give Him pain,
They only just passed down the street, and left Him in the rain.

Still Jesus cried, "Forgive them, for they know not what they do,"
And still it rained the wintry rain that drenched Him through and through;
The crowds went home and left the streets without a soul to see,
And Jesus crouched against a wall and cried for Calvary.

(1919)

part three

The Plain Bread of Religion

What is truth? O God, what is truth? Many a man has asked that question in these later years, not in cynic disbelief but in desperate and unutterable need. Many a man has asked it, not as the rhetorical flourish to easy agnosticism, but secretly, painfully, passionately, as he sat in silence with dead Billy's photograph on the mantelpiece, a demand-note for the rates on the table by his side, and a review on his knee containing a closely-reasoned article upon the shaken Creeds. And many a man has dumbly asked it, as he stood at some street corner, listening drearily to the verbal vinegar of a communist orator, with a demand for eviction in his pocket and a vacuum in his dinnerless inside . . .

What the plain man in the street wants to get at, is the plain bread of religion, the unchanging and unchangeable Christ, that, with a soul made strong by that refreshment, he may fling himself upon his work in a complex world: knowing what it means, knowing whence he comes and whither he goes, and what his world is for.

(1923)

Four Great Certainties

The modern revolt against dogma is partly the result of shallow thinking, and partly the consequence of false dogmatism. There is dogmatism false and true, and false dogmatism is a vile thing. It belongs to the carnal mind which is at enmity with God. It has behind it nothing but a mixture of pride, fear, intellectual sloth, and the will to dominate others; and it expresses itself in an attitude of harsh and unreasoning intolerance. It is a disgusting and repulsive thing, because it is rooted in sin—in common ordinary wickedness. It disguises itself as a strong-minded love of principle, and, in that guise, imposes upon many noble men, destroying their influence and power for good, and leading them to behave more like drill-sergeants than pastors, and to treat their flocks as if they were platoons. It is, and always has been, the curse of Churches. There is also a dogmatism common in the young, which is the outcome of a shallow, ill-founded enthusiasm, tinged with the self-importance of youth. This is very little more than a childish complaint like measles; but it is intensely irritating, because it is rooted in human folly, and only God and His Saints have really learned to suffer fools gladly.

But there is a dogmatism which expresses the most precious thing in the world, which is spiritual certainty; and that dogmatism is absolutely necessary to religion. It is beautiful, because it is rooted in honest love of God and man; it is fired by vivid and vital spiritual experience; it feeds upon constant prayer and communion with God, and it inevitably expresses itself in humble earnest work, and unconscious self-sacrifice, for the higher welfare of mankind. Its hallmark is Humility. It is first of all pure, that is, rational, in the highest sense of the word, caring only for God and His Truth. It is then peaceable, knowing that Truth must speak for itself, and needs no support but its own manifestation. It is ever ready to hear and consider another man's point of view, and, taking it into the inner sanctuary of the soul, to lay it at the feet of Christ for His judgment upon it. It is patiently prepared to make allowances for human frailty, and entirely without tinge of contempt. Yet it is certain, unshakable, serene and humbly confident. This is the true dogmatism, the spiritual certainty, which is of the essence of religion.

Religion exists not to answer all questions, or to clear up all mysteries; if that were its purpose, it could never be accomplished, for life grows, not less, but more mysterious as the intellect enters more fully into its truth. The stars were wonderful enough in all conscience, when we thought of them as lamps of light set in a solid sky to guide the sailors on their journey over the trackless sea; but they are a million times more wonderful, now that we know them to be blazing worlds, that move through the vast infinities of space in accordance with exact mathematical laws. Our own bodies were wonderful enough when we thought of them as created in a moment by the fiat of the Almighty from the dust of the earth; but how much more wonderful they have become, since the sciences of physiology and embryology have taught us to trace their growth through countless stages, from the humblest kind of beginning to their present strangely complex end. Knowledge does not take from, it adds to, the wonder of the world. It is an infallible rule that, the more a man knows, the less he knows he knows. He knows that he knows nothing compared with what there is to know—that he is but a child playing on the shore of an infinite sea of truth, and picking up tiny pearls of wisdom that, by the grace of God, are cast up at his feet. Religion leaves a million questions unanswered and apparently unanswerable. Its purpose and object is not to make a man certain and cocksure about everything, but to make him certain about those things of which he must be certain if he is to live a human life at all. Religion does not relieve us from the duty of thought; it makes it possible for a man to begin thinking. It does not put an end to research and enquiry, it gives a basis from which real research is made possible and fruitful of results; a basis without which thinking only means wandering round in circles, and getting nowhere in the end, and research means battering at a brass door that bruises our knuckles, and does not yield by the millionth part of an inch.

We must be certain about some things, before we can enquire about anything; and the first of these necessary certainties is the certainty of self. You say about something "I am as sure of this as I am of my own existence," but are you so sure of that? Descartes said that all doubt must end at the fact of his own existence, but in very truth that is where all the deepest doubt begins. Are you sure that you do exist in any real sense? Is there any settled, steady, reliable person that you can with confidence call "I"? Are you anything more than a stream of sensations? Some time ago a man sat in my office—a clever and cultured man who had reached a position of prominence in an honorable profession—and what he kept repeating over and over again to me was, "How could I have done it? How could I have done it?" Now, which was the man, the man who had done that deed, the man who sat there hating it—or the man who, as events proved, could do it again not long after? The truth about him was that, educated and cultured as he was, he was not in any real sense a person at all, he was still two or three "persons" which had not yet attained to any sort of unity. And is not his a common case? Search into yourself and see.

Often, as I sit and listen to the inner tragedies of life which are disclosed to me, I think of the comic story of Billy the Lizard. An explorer came back from abroad to his country house, with a chameleon which took the color of whatever material you placed it upon. He displayed it with pride to the members of his household, and then went away, leaving it in charge of the butler who had affectionately named it "Billy the Lizard." After a time he returned, and his first question was, "Well, John, and how is the Lizard?" The butler looked serious and downcast, and said: "Well, you see, Sir, it was this way. We had a few of the villagers up to look at him, and we put him on some red flannel and he turned red all right; and then we put him on some green baize, and he turned as green as Ireland; and then some silly ass put him on a patchwork quilt—and poor old Billy bust." There are many of us who are nothing but "poor old Billies" bursting and bust. The world we live in is a patchwork quilt, a bewilderingly complex patchwork quilt, patched with all the colors of the rainbow, and we madly try to adapt ourselves to its complexities. We are as children tossed to and fro by every wind of doctrine, and by the cunning craftiness of men, whereby they lie in wait to deceive, not so much men, indeed, as incarnate moods, more unreliable than English weather. We change our characters according to the company we keep. We pride ourselves upon our sanity, merely because we never fail to be bitten by the fashionable craze. We don't know where we are or whither we are going. We don't know what we want, and won't be happy till we get it. And while we remain in this state, living, and thought about life, are, in any real sense of those terms, perfectly impossible. We lightly assume that we are rational beings; but it is an assumption that, for many of us, has no justification whatsoever. We are not born rational; far from it, we are born reasoning, which is a very different thing. The value of reason depends entirely upon its basis, and it may be, and often is, based upon nothing but passion, prejudice, and a whole series of unexamined delusions; and in that case reason moves like a drunken man who goes round and round a lamp post, mistaking its crowning flame for the lights of home. It is commonly stated that men act upon reason and women act upon impulse; whereas the truth is that men act upon impulse and find a reason for it afterwards, and women act upon impulse and don't bother about the reason at all.

We must always remember that there is no such thing as pure reason. To begin with, you cannot separate intellect either from emotion or from instinct; and to go on with—which is more important—you cannot divorce the conscious from the unconscious mind; and, as we dig deeper into the mystery of the mind, it becomes more and more evident that it is like an iceberg, two-thirds of it are underneath, underneath the conscious level, and upon the health of that buried part depends the balance and vigor of the whole. By far the most important part of an argument consists of the evidence upon which it is based; and the kind of evidence which we select to argue from, out of the mass that is being continually submitted to us, the kind of fact that we tend to remark and remember, and the kind of fact that we tend to forget, is unconsciously determined for us by the kind of person that we really are. The assumptions from which we argue are built up out of the things to which we attend; and the things to which we attend, always a limited selection out of the innumerable things which claim our attention, are mainly determined by our character, by what we actually are. And so, the first absolutely necessary certainty is the certainty of self; and there is no way by which you can come to the certainty of self, to the certainty of what you are, by which you can come to anything like internal unity, by the exercise of reason alone. No amount of knowledge, no great weight of learning, can deliver you ultimately from the necessity of making an act of Faith. You must set up a hypothesis and then test it—that is the only way in which you can get at anything. It has been said there is no science until there is a hypothesis on its trial, and that is true of science and of life too. The method by which Newton came to the law of gravity is the method by which we must all come to the law of Life. We must make our great guess, set up our grand hypothesis, and then test and verify it by living as though it were true. There is no other way. With our great guess for a guiding star, we must go exploring in our world of space and time, groping in the dark, and finding of the pathways blocked on every side; until at last, as we follow faithfully, a mystic certainty arises like the sun, drives all the mists away, and shows in front of us the radiant, living mountains of God's Truth. And of the great certainties which must be sought and found this way, the certainty of self comes first, for without it there can be no certainty of anything whatsoever.

Herein lies the rock upon which all our dreams of a better social order, all our dreams of peace upon earth and goodwill toward men, come to shipwreck. You cannot make peace among people who are at war within themselves. There can be no peace except to men of goodwill, and the difficulty is to be sure of a will at all, never mind a good one. We assume that we have a will, as we assume that we have a self, and we say "I have a will of my own," but have you? Never, until you have a God of your own. The battle between the will and a desire is, at its root, a battle between two desires or more, and the dominant desire wins. But while we have no one dominant desire, or while we have widely different and conflicting desires which dominate us by turns, there is no peace, no possibility of peace without or within. There is no peace for those who have not got in some measure to the certainty of self; and in order to secure that, we must have our dogma, our great hypothesis by which we live, and which we verify by living.

And here it is that Christianity comes in with the great Prayer "Our Father." *Lex orandi lex vivendi*—the law of Prayer is the law of life. There is the great hypothesis. "Now are we the sons of God, and it does not yet appear what we shall be, but we know" (therein is the mystic certainty) "that when He shall appear we shall be like Him, for we shall see Him as He is" (1 John 3:2). That is the great hypothesis—that is the truth about me—and to that truth I must cling. I am the Son of God revealed in Jesus Christ. Whatever I think, or feel, or do, which is not consistent with that fact, is not true; it is not I; it can lead me nowhere and gain me nothing. However many are the gifts I may be offered they are all shams, lies, and delusions apart from Christ's likeness, and will turn to dust in my hands. That is the truth, the final, absolute, and ultimate truth about me. It is a dogma, and an intolerant dogma in a sense, as all dogmas are. It does not permit of compromise. If I am the son of God revealed in Jesus Christ, I am not just a little better than the beast, I am a little lower than the angels; and made so only that I may be crowned with glory and honor. Every kind of thought or action based upon the belief that I am anything less than this, an immortal soul made in the image of God—any idea that my life is limited like the life of the animals, or controlled as theirs is controlled—is a tissue of falsehood and all action based upon that falsehood can only issue in disaster.

If I am the son of God, nothing but God will satisfy my soul; no amount of comfort, no amount of ease, no amount of pleasure, will give me peace or rest. If I had the full cup of all the world's joys held up to me, and could drain it to the dregs, I should still remain thirsty if I had not God. If the feast of all the good things of life, pleasures and powers that have been and that are, could be laid out before me and I could eat it all at one meal, I should still be hungry if I had not God. Nor would it satisfy my soul, if I could be assured of an infinite extension of this present life at its best, apart from God. If the feast of this life's goods could last for ever, yet would I start up from the table satiated but still unsatisfied, because I had not God. There is not enough in ten material worlds to satisfy a fully developed human soul—I must have communion with God. Whatever tends to break that communion is an enemy of mine, however much it may pretend to be a friend. However stubbornly I may stick to the delusion that I can live without Him, however closely I may cling to the idol that I put up in His place, sooner or later, in this world or in the next, the idols and delusions will have to go. There are not in reality two worlds or two lives, there is but one; and that is life eternal, which is to know Thee, the only true God, and Jesus Christ whom Thou hast sent. That is the first great dogma; and the certainty of its truth which comes by living on it, never by reasoning about it, is the first dogmatic certainty which I must have if I am to live, in the true sense of that word. This is the first slice of Plain Bread which Jesus gives to me—I am the son of God, and am destined to wake up in His Likeness and to be satisfied with that.

The first slice is that by which we come to certainty of self; and the second is like unto it, and by it we come to certainty of other-self. Complete uncertainty about other-self makes life in the world impossible, and thought about it impossible. From the very beginning I find myself surrounded by the mystery of other-selves; they press upon me on every side, from the time when I first look up into my Mother's face, to the time when I lie down at last alone to die—and yet not alone, for I only relinquish my hold on the hand of the one I leave behind, to grasp the hand of the Other I go to meet. If I am to live, I must be in a measure certain about other-selves.

Next to the uncertainty of self, the most common cause of tragedy in life is the uncertainty about other-self, the uncertainty of what lies behind the eyes into which I am always looking, of what is going on behind the masks of the myriad human faces that surround me everywhere. Often, from the very beginning, tragedy dogs our steps. A child instinctively stretches out its hand in trust and love to the first other-self it meets, which is its Mother; and then later grows to find that trust and love betrayed, grows to find that its first guess was apparently wrong, and that behind the mask of a smiling face there was, not a friend, but an enemy. And in that trust betrayed, there is symbolized and summed-up the bitterness of human life apart from God.

Life is not life at all until a man or woman has attained to two certainties—certainty of self and certainty of at least one other-self in the world. It is not only not good, it is not possible, for man to live alone. There is no mystery like the mystery of a crowd; and, the more one knows, the more mysterious it becomes. Again and again I have stood before a crowd of what the enemies of the Church would call with a sneer "dull respectable people," and have been tempted to think of them as "dull" and "respectable," but not for long. Knowledge soon comes, and proves that they are neither as dull nor as respectable as they seem; a frank and public confession of their secret hopes, longings, and memories, would supply copy for the Sunday press for a twelve-month, and provide passages which might well appear in the biographies of the world's heroes and saints. Through all that was written, there would run, and run richly, the veins of tragedy and comedy, of splendor and of squalor, of glory and of shame, which go to make up human life; and one of the commonest cries that would rise from the heart of the crowd would be "It was not mine enemy that did me this dishonor, for then peradventure I would have hid myself from him; but it was even thou, my companion and mine own familiar friend; we took sweet counsel together and walked in the House of God as friends, and yet it was thy hand which struck me in the dark, and the wound remains still bleeding and unbound" (cf. Psalm 55:12–14).

That is the cry of any husband to any wife, of any friend to any friend—the uncertainty of other-self. The need is desperate and imperative, and once again the Prayer comes to us in our hour of need, with its great hypothesis, "Our Father." First of all, there is One other-self of which we can be sure, one other-self upon whom we can rely and from whose Love we never can escape—there is God. I am alone and yet not alone, because the Father is with me. It can become for us a spiritual certainty, the Love of God. "I *know* that neither length, nor breadth, nor depth, nor height, nor any other creature can separate me from the Love of God which is in Christ Jesus" (Romans 8:39). God's answer to the cry of humanity for a comrade and a friend is the gift of Himself.

But there is more than that. He not only gives Himself, He gives us brothers. He bids me set up as my second great hypothesis, that all these other-selves, that press around me everywhere, are my brethren. Whatever in their conduct or character seems to contradict that, is not the real truth about them. Whatever they do or say, they are still the sons of God and brethren of mine; and if I think or act towards them on any other understanding than that, the action will be, in itself, a falsehood, and will lead me nowhere, and gain me nothing. I shall certainly come up against facts—apparently the hardest of hard facts—which go to contradict this hypothesis. I shall be disappointed, disillusioned, again and again, and yet the closer I cling to that faith, and the more I defy fear and self-pity in its name—the more utterly I refuse to compromise with any other hypothesis—the stronger will become the certainty of its final truth. Apart from the hypothesis, there is no chance of certainty about other-self whatsoever. No amount of worldly wisdom, no amount of experience, no great weight of learning, no observation in the world, however close, will ever yield us the certainty of other-self upon which we can act with vigor, and suffer with joy and gladness, and so come to a real knowledge of the world as it actually is at heart. It is impossible to verify the hypothesis without suffering for it, that is why most of us never do verify it. We are afraid to suffer, we do not dare to Love, and so we never come into touch with reality at all, but pass our time in a world of conventional make-believe. No man can believe in the Brotherhood of man and be comfortable, it is a creed that takes away all our cushions and leaves us with a cross. But it is the only way to life. We know that we have passed form death unto life, because we love the Brethren. We do not live, unless we live in and through the beloved community. That then is the second slice of Plain Bread, the Brotherhood of Man, the second great necessary certainty.

The third great certainty is the certainty of Nature. From the very beginning I find myself conscious of another reality set over against myself, the reality of what I see and hear and touch, and from the beginning there is an uncertainty about it. It is true that I have my senses to go by, but experience goes to prove that I cannot trust them. The man to whom seeing is believing lives in an unreal world. To him the earth is flat, the sun goes daily round it, and sinks into the sea, the stars are tiny point of light set in a dome of sky, and matter is a solid and unchanging thing—and that is a world of dreams. Moreover, my senses do not and cannot tell me anything about what it means to me, this other reality; they can observe but they cannot interpret it; they cannot tell me whether it is friend or foe, and if I trust them to decide they will deceive me. And yet I must be certain of what this other reality means to me and to mankind: I must decide whether I am to treat it as a friend or a foe—an immense amount depends upon that.

Here once again reason unaided will not help me, I must make a great venture, an act of faith, I must set up a hypothesis and live by it; I must assume either that it is a friend or a foe, and test it as such. At first man assumed that it was a foe, nor can we wonder at this when we think of the first man in the real Garden of Eden, which, as science shows us, was no ready-made paradise. There he lived in the trackless jungle or tropical forest, swept by the rushing mighty winds, drenched by torrential rains, parched by the rays of the burning sun. When one thinks of him standing and looking up at the everlasting hills that rose in snow-clad mystery against the sky, tossed about in his little boat on the waves of a story sea, cowering in his darkening cave, while the lightning tore the clouds asunder, and the whole world shook at the voice of the gods; with evidence all around him of powers so much greater than himself, small wonder that his first instinct was that of terror, and that he tended to people the unseen world with a thousand gods, who, if they were not his enemies, were but capricious and fickle friends. But the hypothesis of fear is unfruitful, out of terror nothing comes. It is sometimes said that, in contrast to this original attitude of fear, man has arisen in his might and conquered Nature. We talk glibly about subduing the powers of the material world, but we have not subdued, and cannot subdue, them, we have merely made friends with them. We have, as it were, stretched out our hands to the stars above us and the stones beneath our feet and cried

"Our Father." We have assumed that at the heart of Nature there is reason like our own; we have looked for mathematical order in the movement of the stars and have found it; we have searched for method in the growth of life and have discovered it; we have hushed the wrangling of our fears, our passion, and our pride, and have trustfully bent our ears to the lips of the earth and sky, and listened intently to the song they sing, and, on the whole, it is true that the more clearly audible that song becomes, the more certain we grow that it is the song of a friend, a reasonable and reliable friend. As scientific learning advances it goes to establish, more and more firmly beyond the possibility of doubt, the great hypothesis or guess upon which it is based, that at its heart the external world is reasonable, reliable, and friendly. As we make friends with it, our powers over it grow, and it showers gifts upon us with a prodigal generosity of which, we feel, we are only just at the beginning.

The newly discovered order of Nature is infinitely precious to the religious man, revealing, as it does, the faithfulness of God with Whom there is no variableness nor shadow cast by His turning. Nevertheless, it is impossible to hold this faith unless we hold it in the teeth of doubt, and there are many still who say, "Who will show us any good?" If we have discovered order and reliability in Nature, we have also discovered and continue to discover in it, fresh visions of chaos, cruelty, and apparently purposeless waste. We have had laid bare before us the vision of "Nature red in tooth and claw" and the "struggle for existence," and we must face facts. But if we do, let us be sure that they are facts we face. Nature "red in tooth and claw" is, not so much fact, as interpretation of fact. A friendly critic of this book, read in proof, reminds me of the "incredible cruelties which modern research reveals," and takes as a single instance the mussel beds of the Wash. "I don't know what the mussels live on," he says, "some small sea organism or other anyhow which cannot enjoy being eaten. The star fish comes along, carefully provided with the means of *cruelly* forcing open and devouring the mussel. The sea gull comes along, provided with the means of *cruelly* tearing up and devouring the star fish. What happens to the sea gull is another story . . . . But does this argue love to the destroyed one? It is all very well to dissemble your love—but why? From this standpoint, *which might be indefinitely multiplied* every living thing is in a sense a parasite upon some other living thing."

This very typical criticism consists, not merely in a description of fact, but in an interpretation of it, the interpretation being not so much stated as suggested—especially by the insertion of the word "cruelly." The facts are indisputable. The whole order of Nature is that living things live on other living things, every living thing is in a sense a parasite upon some other living thing, there is no getting round that fact, and if it must be interpreted as cruelty, then the whole Christian creed falls to the ground in ruins. But must it be so interpreted? Cruelty is the infliction on a living creature of *unnecessary* pain by a being who delights in pain. Do we find cruelty in the fact? To begin with, to talk about a mussel or a star fish, or for that matter of that a sea gull, suffering pain, in anything like our sense of the word, is not to state facts but to make great and unfounded assumptions. *They simply have not got the wherewithal to suffer it.* I think every competent scientist would be with me in warning people against this kind of sentimentalism, which makes mussels and star fish like men and women. As a doctor friend of mine remarked the other day, pain is an extremely relative business even among men, and what is agony to a sensitive and delicately nurtured woman is mere inconvenience to a navvy and, in the same way, what to a navvy would be agony, may be presumed to be uncomfortable tickling to a mussel or a star fish.

The people who are most intensely troubled about the cruelty of Nature are, for the most part, extremely sensitive people, who read their own sensitiveness into every living thing. But when God brings His creatures to that pitch of sensitiveness to pain, He provides them with the means to turning pain into peace and joy by making it a sacrifice to Love. Men and women find the most exquisite pleasure in enduring pain for the sake of a glorious purpose or a beloved friend. The Sacrifice, which in the animals is unconscious, becomes conscious in man, and, with the power of conscious sacrifice, comes the power to interpret pain, and by the alchemy of Love transform it into glory. The animals cannot offer conscious sacrifice, but neither can they suffer as men can, or, at any rate, it seems unlikely that they can, for the truth is, that we know nothing whatsoever about the feelings of a mussel at the moment when it is eaten by a star fish, or those of a rabbit worried by a stoat, nor can we enter into the mind of a mouse when it is being played with by a cat, but it seems probable that they are anaesthetized to a great extent. A man with a war wound which would have caused him under normal circumstances tremendous agony, has been known to shout with joy because he had got a "blighty," interpreting pain as pleasure. There are natural anaesthetics, like excitement or fear, and though we do not know, we have good grounds for guessing, that Nature has many ways of alleviating agony. Nature is not as red either in tooth or claw as she is painted. "The struggle for existence" is also not so much a fact as an interpretation of fact—an interpretation which is very doubtfully true. It reads into the process of evolution the agony of human warfare, with its accompaniments of callousness, cruelty and degradation. But although the sparrow falls it is not certain that it falls without the knowledge of the Father, and that its falling is not falling on to sleep and peace. The dead bird is a pitiful sight, and it is right that it should stir us to pity, but may it not be that we pity it because He first pitied us and the bird alike?

The whole question sums itself up in this: Can we, who know so much more than the early Christians did about the process of Nature, still maintain the Christian interpretation of the process as meaning the Fatherhood of God? Can we still cry "Our Father" and maintain that Christ is the *logos* or meaning of the natural world, and that through Him all things were made and without Him was nothing made that was made? I believe we can. But mind you, if we cry "Our Father," it is to the Father of Our Lord Jesus Christ we cry, the Father Who was revealed in Him, and in that revelation the mystery of the Cross is central. Christ reveals the meaning of the world as Sacrifice. Never did He more clearly reveal the Father than when He hung there broken, battered and bleeding, between the earth and sky. The Father Whom we worship is revealed in Christ crucified as well as in Christ risen, and Christ ascending, and in that revelation there is no sign of what I call, for lack of a better term, "easy omnipotence." Neither creation nor redemption is revealed as being accomplished by a turn of the eye or a wave of the hand, and, as we shall see later, the shadow of the Cross falls over Nature, and bids us see in it, not man tortured by God, but God suffering with, in, and for man, that He may bring him to glory.

The Christian interpretation of evolution is that it is *an ascension through sacrifice to perfection, and in that sacrifice, all creatures join, from the protoplasmic jelly fish to the Man, Christ Jesus.* The true parasite is the living thing which eats but is not eaten, which gets but does not give, and is in Nature, comparatively rare, and tends to become rarer. Sensitive men and women shrink from saying or thinking that animals have less than a human capacity for feeling pain because they fear it will lead to cruelty, it bids us fight it with the sword of gratitude. Inasmuch as we must accept the sacrifice of the animals in order to live, it bids us receive that sacrifice as a sacrament, with reverence, and with a thankful heart, and bids us love the animals, and indeed if we do not we cannot love the Christ. Cruelty to animals means that in a Sacramental universe we eat and drink the universal sacrifice without discerning the Lord's Body, and therefore eat and drink damnation to ourselves. Christianity and cruelty to animals cannot really co-exist any more than love and hatred, fire and water.

The shadow of the Cross is there, and though we must beware lest we exaggerate its darkness by mistaking fiction for fact, yet there remain dark facts to be faced, which make it necessary that, if we hold the faith of Our Father, we hold it in spite of doubts. Nevertheless the faith can and must be held. The supposition that at the heart of all things there is a friend, and a reliable friend, has proved to be so fruitful of real results, that we must not be shaken from it by apparently cruel contradictions, but must seek to enter more fully into truth, and find out how far, as a matter of fact, cruelty and waste are part of Nature's very self and how far they are a part of Nature as we, in our ignorance of the great end God seeks to achieve, and in our state of rebellion against His laws, imagine her to be.

Every child has two fathers, the father as he is in himself, and the father as the child in his ignorance conceives him to be, and, if the child have a good father, his growth depends upon his trust in him that he is a friend, even when he appears to be a foe, for without that trust he cannot attain to the fullness of loving communion. So it is with us and God. "Our Father" is the beginning and the end of science, as it is the beginning and the end of life, for the beginning of science is the supposition that the world is in reality a rational world, and the end of science is to understand, and so hold communion with that rational reality. The beginning of life is the supposition that God is Love, and the end of life is to comprehend, with all the Saints, what is the length, and breadth, and depth, and height, of that Love which passes knowledge. So science and religion meet and in the end are one . . . The whole creation groaneth and travaileth together in pain, and, apart from Him, it is a groaning and travailing in the dark, but God Who commanded the light to shine out of the darkness has shined into our hearts to give the light of the knowledge of the Glory of God in the face of Jesus Christ, and in that light I can look into Nature's darkest horror chambers, and see there, at the very worst, a Cross, the universal Sacrifice, and behind the Cross an empty tomb, and a figure with hands outstretched to bless ascending into glory. I see Christ's cross in Nature's sorrow, and His glory in her joy, and can in Him lift up my heart in gratitude upon a summer day. This is the third slice of Plain Bread, the third great certainty, which provides the necessary mystic basis of human knowledge and human life . . .

The fourth and last certainty is the certainty of Death. Of all things in the world it is in a sense the one thing of which we can be sure. We may try to forget it, but it will not forget us. Nor can we ever really forget it, until we have faced it and come to a decision about it. In the midst of life we are in death, unless we know that in the midst of death we are in life.

In the midst of life we are in death, its shadow falls over everything . . . There is a stage in a small child's life, when one of its greatest joys is to be taken up by its father and swung in the air, and I can see now my own small son standing, with shining eyes, "Do it again Daddy, do it again." And in him I see a picture of the whole world of men and women standing before the great All Father Who makes the sunset and the rose, and crying as they fade and fail, "Do it again Daddy, do it again"—always trying to recapture the ecstasy, and never quite succeeding. There is only one way by which we can ever capture, and hold fast forever the joys that come and go, that is by capturing and holding fast the Father Himself from Whom they come. Always we must stand in a world of dying things and dying people crying out through our tears, "Do it again Daddy, do it again," until the moment comes when the Father reaches down, snatches us to His heart, and holds us there forever.

The more we grow in the love of Beauty, Truth and Goodness, the more completely human we become, the more intense must grow our hunger for immortality and our abhorrence of death. The idea that belief in immortality is an ancient doctrine fast losing ground is an exact reversing of the facts, it is a comparatively modern doctrine which the growth of human personality, and its firmer hold on a wider world make inevitable. It is the man in his infancy who cries: "How good is man's life, the mere living, how fit to employ all the heart, and the soul, and the senses forever in joy."[1] It is the man in the fullness of his manhood who cries: "Whom have I in heaven but Thee, and what is there upon the earth that I desire in comparison with Thee?" (Psalm 73:25) And that experience of being caught up in the arms of the Father is one of the fundamental religious experiences. Saints of all sorts, from St. Paul to the bright-eyed wholesome Salvation Lassie, have felt, and expressed in widely different ways, the same joy. Faith in immortality is, and must be, the logical conclusion—using logic in its fullest human sense—of the instinct of self-preservation. As man grows, so grows his divine discontent, that discontent which severs him completely from the rest of the animal creation, and bids him reach out to fuller and fuller life. And there is in him an instinct to preserve that life. He can find endless reasons to justify the instinctive craving, but it is the instinct that sets him reasoning, and, unless the world is a fraud, that instinct points to something real by which it can be satisfied . . .

The shadowy hosts whom Virgil pictured in the underworld like autumn leaves in the Vale of Vallambrosa, crowding by the river bank, and stretching out their hands backward to the life that they had left, not forward to the life which was to come. But, as man grows, the hands turn round and are stretched out forwards to the future, not back to the past. We become conscious that the most perfect things in life like Love, Beauty, and Truth, fall short of perfection. And yet, God has given so much, can we believe that He will not give more?

From the purely intellectual point of view there are many sound philosophical arguments for immortality, and even from the scientific standpoint, it is difficult to dismiss as negligible the evidence which in these latter years has accumulated for the survival of the human personality after death. The value of the evidence is indeed difficult to estimate; we have to allow for fraud, self-deception and ignorance, yet it is impossible to ignore the possibility to which so much of it points. But certainty about death only comes with certainty about God and His Love. We can never reach the point of victory and triumph over death until we reach the heart of the Father in Jesus Christ, and it is that triumphant certainty that we need, and need, not for the future only, but for the present. We cannot live this life aright unless we see it in its true perspective, see it as the foreground of eternity. Apart from that we tend to see all things in a

---

1. Robert Browning, "Saul," 9.

wrong proportion; big things become little, and little things big, and we labor for that which is not Beauty, and strive for that which is not Bread. There is no peace for man as long as he lives in the Valley of the Shadow of Death. It is only the tender mercy of Our God whereby the Dayspring from on high can visit us to give light to them that sit in darkness and in the shadow of death, only through His tender mercy that our human feet can be guided into the paths of peace. Apart from this triumphant certainty life becomes vulgar and sordid. When the shadow of death falls over all the beauty of the world, the hunger for life in man is so strong that it tends to brutalize him, and drives him to grasp at everything he can get, without caring how he gets it. "His selfishness is satiated not, it wears him like a flame; his hunger for all pleasure howso'er minute grows pain,"[2] and life tends to become a struggle of swine about a swill trough—a struggle in which there is no tenderness and no mercy. Unless, then, life mocks man and has no meaning, the instinct of self-preservation must have its perfect work and must lead to Truth, not falsehood. The Christian hypothesis is that life is as good as God revealed in Christ, and that behind the Cross there is ever and always the resurrection. And it is only by taking that hypothesis, and living life as though it were true, flinging ourselves upon it recklessly in the faith that God keeps the good wine until the last, that we can come to that triumphant certainty which destroys death, and makes us sure that in the midst of death we are in the Life Everlasting. This is the fourth slice of Plain Bread, Victory over death.

(1923)

---

2. Robert Browning, "Pauline: A Fragment of a Confession."

Master Passion and Neighbor Love

The man in the street says frankly: "I don't profess to be religious. I don't know much about it. It's a queer business. My religion is to do to others as I would be done by. It doesn't matter what a man believes so long as he does what's right. I'm not an atheist, mind you. I believe in the Supreme Being, but I can't see what difference religion makes. There's a lot of hypocrisy about it. I've known chaps go to Church on Sunday and do you down for tuppence on Monday morning." Now what all that amounts to is this, "Do your duty to your neighbor and your duty to God will take care of itself. The popular version of the two great commandments would turn Christ's version upside down and say: "The first and great commandment is, 'Thou shalt love thy neighbor as thyself,' and the second is like unto it: 'If you are inclined that way, and want to be religious, thou shalt love the Lord thy God more or less—and it's safer less than more, because too much religion drives men potty, and makes them cranks.'"

To a large extent this popular "Christianity" is a revolt from the deeper and more blatant blasphemy which bade men love God—go to Church—support religion—sing hymns and say prayers, and their duty to their neighbors would look after itself. It is a revolt from the religion which damned souls to build churches, sweated work people to endow charities, and manufactured prostitutes by low wages to build rescue homes for fallen women and buy a peerage. It is the rejection by the people of the religion of the classes who patronized God as the best of all policemen, the power that kept poor people in their places by threats of hell and promises of heaven. People felt that it was better to have no God at all than to worship a policeman, and I entirely agree. But it is only by contrast with this caricature of Christianity that popular religion can be called Christian.

It is only because we have had so much of the Gospel of Jeremy Bentham, "Each man for himself and God for us all, as the elephant said when it danced among the chickens," that we can still regard the Gospel of godless goodwill as the Gospel of Jesus Christ. Any religion which does not put God first—far and away first—has no real claim to be Christian. You cannot change the order of the two Commandments and retain the Truth. It is shallow nonsense to say that it does not matter what a man believes so long as he does what's right. A man cannot act right unless he believes right, because men always act according to their belief. A man may not act according to the belief he professes, but he will always act according to the belief he really holds—he cannot help it. All men have a God or Gods, even if they are only idols. A man's God is what he believes in and lives for.

The oldest religion, and the most popular religion still, is the worship of many gods. Man is a natural polytheist. The heathen idols do not die, although their images be broken and all the temples be cast down. Venus, Mars, and Bacchus still live to challenge Christ. We are fools if we suppose the heathen ever bows him down to wood and stone. Men have always worshipped the powers and passions which they felt to be greater than themselves. Venus stood for that life force which vanquishes our reason and drives us on to propagate new life—the force that brings Nirvana in a beloved woman's arms. Mars stood for the tremendous passion that sweeps like a storm through a people, and calls them out to War. Greater than love of wife or child, greater than conscience, apparently greater than God, this power of passion still remains to turn men into beasts. Bacchus stood for the power of intoxication and ecstasy that drink possesses. He bade men drink and drown their troubles, their weakness, and their fear in the magic cup that held laughter, strength, and courage to their lips. Who that knows our modern world can say the ancient gods are dead? It still is a battle between the one God and the many, between the high and holy passion for purity, justice, and truth, and the gusts of lower passions that sweep away our manhood and make us lower than the beasts. It is battle between the passion which includes and inspires reason and these many passions that destroy it. A man must always act upon his neighbor according to his master passion—his real belief.

He must always love his neighbor as he loves his God. That your love of your neighbor depends for its force on the love of your God is not a Christian dogma but a law of social life, as the law of gravity is of natural life, just as universal and just as inevitable. You must love yourself as you love your God, and your neighbor as yourself—that is the law of life. Jesus of Nazareth did not make it. It was made when man was made. You see it in action everywhere. A man who worships drink gives his neighbor beer; the man who worships lust gives his neighbor food for lust to feed on; the man who worships money gives his neighbor not money, but the love of it.

You must spread your master passion, and your master passion is your god. If you have no passions of any sort, then you have no life to live and none to give away. You are not a man but just a bit of driftwood on the sea of life, tossed this way and that, without a guide because you are in truth without a god. You can give your neighbor nothing but your own futility. If you are a full-blooded animal man with many passions you will spread them all inevitably, but most of all you will spread your master passion, the one you really live for—the one that is your god.

Into this maelstrom of conflicting passions Christ comes, not bringing a new law, but a new passion—a new God. Over against the multitude of gods that men have always worshipped, the multitude of many passions and desires by which they have been swayed this way and that, He dares to set a new passion, which He declares must master all the rest and make them willing slaves if the world is to be saved, and that passion is the passion for Himself. He claims to be, not the servant or the prophet or the preacher of God, but to be God—the very image and the perfect revelation to men in human terms of man's true God, who claims the passionate devotion of the human race by right of the eternal Truth.

That is the Christian religion—the master passion for Jesus Christ. Without that master passion for the perfect man who showed us God, our love of our neighbor is a thing of little worth. Goodwill that is not fired by it is not strong enough to meet and conquer the beast that lives in the heart of the world. Goodwill cannot raise us, inspire us, drive us on to sacrifice and suffering for right, and that is what we need to build the better world. Codes of laws and moral teaching will not do it. Put cold codes of morals between me and a master passion, and I will smash the miserable code to pieces and get me to my God. Put a law between me and my love, and love will laugh your law to scorn, and cast me into the arms of my God. Laws and moral teachings are not strong enough for men. St. Paul knew that. Laws and codes, however perfect in themselves, are no good for men—they have no power of life; trying to hold men with laws is like driving mad horses with silk threads. If there had been a law given which could have produced life, then, of course, righteousness would have come by the law. Moral codes and beautiful philosophies are futile, you can only fight the old gods in the power of the new God. You can only fight the idols in the power of the Christ. Are moral teachings going to battle with the lust for women and the love of gold? Are they going to conquer hatred, envy, jealousy? How white-livered and cold a man must be to suppose they could . . .

When Venus calls us as the shadows fall to easy heaven and certain peace, when the hoarse and blood-choked voice of Mars rings out across the world and calls the nations out to war, when Bacchus stands and offers us the red wine of forgetfulness—what can save us? What can save the ordinary man from damning his soul and destroying his world? The piping of professors? The books of the philosophers? The knowledge of the scientists? Vague goodwill and good nature? You cold-blooded saints of the study, have you ever walked in the streets? Have you ever lived? Only a passion can conquer a passion—we must have God.

(1919)

The Three Temptations

The effect of baptism on Jesus was to make him feel that the time for action had arrived. The certainty that he was called to do a unique work and was endowed with unique powers burned now like a fire within him. He hurried away from the Jordan to the lonely and desolate region that lies beyond it. In the graphic language of the records, "he was led by the Spirit into the wilderness to be tempted by the devil" (Matt 4:1). You deprive the Gospel account of its reality and power if you take it literally and imagine the temptation in the wilderness as a dialogue between a plain and obvious devil, with horns and hoofs and all the appurtenances thereof, and Christ.

Jesus was alone, as utterly alone as a man can be. Had you passed that way you would have seen nothing but a solitary pale-faced majestic Jew sitting on a rock, or pacing up and down some rugged path lost in thought. But no one is ever really alone. Loneliness is a feeling, not a fact. The blind man may say there is no sun, but the light still blazes around him. The deaf man may say there is no sound, but the chorus of the summer woods swells on and is not stilled. The lonely man may say "I am alone," but God and his fellow men are all about him, his loneliness is in himself. He is lonely because he is not fully alive and awake and cannot realize the truth. But Jesus was fully alive and awake, and therefore he was never alone. God and the world were always with him. He carried them both together in his heart and in his head. We all can carry God and the world in our hearts and heads to a certain extent, and the greater our power of doing that, the more universal our sympathy and thought is, the greater we are as men and women.

It is because Jesus of Nazareth impresses us as having powers of universal thought and feeling which were unique and unparalleled that we say his humanity was divine. There in the wilderness he was nearer to God and more closely united with his fellow men than he was in the streets of Nazareth. He went away from them that he might draw them closer in. But he who carries God and the world in his heart and head must suffer. There must inevitably arise within him a conflict, and the greater his power of thought and feeling, the greater that conflict is. This inner conflict is inevitable because the world is partly ugly and evil, while God is wholly good and beautiful.

The man who knows and loves both God and the world must, therefore, suffer, and endure an inward conflict. It was that inward conflict which was tearing the soul of Jesus as he sat alone. Just because he loved God and the world, he was up against the ugliness and evil in the world. He was quite certain that in reality the world was the Kingdom of God, and that if men could see it as it really is, if they could be awakened out of the sleep of the animal life, and look around them with open eyes and open ears, then the ugliness and evil would pass away as a hideous dream disappears at the touch of Love's awakening. But how were their eyes to be opened and their ears to be unstopped?

The First Temptation

With the problem of evil as we put it to ourselves, Jesus never seems to have concerned himself at all. He never asked himself, "Why is there any evil in the world?" or "Where does evil come from?" He has nothing to tell us about the origin of evil. He never tried to explain it even to himself. He was entirely absorbed in destroying it. He called it "Satan," or "the adversary," and his only concern with it was to tear and root it out of the world.

It is impossible to say whether he believed in a personal devil or not. He talked about him as a person, but that is a natural form of speech. He once called poor old Peter "Satan." But he certainly did not mean that literally. He gives the reason quite clearly to Peter. He called him Satan because he was thinking mean cowardly thoughts, and trying to hold Jesus back from his fight with evil, and the suffering it entailed (Matt 16:23). He wanted to make an earthly king of Jesus and put him on a throne and, as we shall see, Jesus had decided for very good and sufficient reasons that that was not the way to destroy evil.

The thing we want to grip firmly in our minds is that this temptation in the wilderness was the conflict that he endured in thinking out his plan of campaign, and deciding how men were to be awakened, and made to see that the world is really the Kingdom of God, and wholly good and beautiful, and that the evil was in themselves and could be destroyed.

How were men to be awakened to the Truth and enabled to live it out in their lives? That was his problem. The first answer that suggested itself was "Feed them." Would it not be best to begin by destroying poverty and want, and giving the people bread?

This problem of the people's bread was always on his mind, and in his heart. He had lived among the poor. And there in the dim grey light of the morning when the rocks and boulders round him, by a natural association of ideas grew to look like loaves of bread, he was surrounded, I believe, by an innumerable phantom host of the world's hungry people. He saw them stretching out into the distance like an endless sea. Mothers clasping puny children to their dry and shriveled breasts; fathers tearing open their ragged shirts to show the bones beneath their skin, and holding our lean and skinny arms in supplication; while all around him, like the moan of the sea, there went up the cry of a world of want, "Bread! Bread! For God's sake give us Bread. If thou be the son of God, command these stones that they may become bread." And he, seeing the multitude, had compassion upon them, for divers of them came from afar, so very far, through so many bitter disappointments, with broken boot soles flapping round their feet, along miles and miles of dirty pavement, miles and miles of filthy streets. "Bread! Bread! For God's sake give us bread!" It was the supreme problem of his life, and how was he to solve it?

He felt within him the pulse of extraordinary powers. He knew that in some strangely unique and wonderful way he was the Man, the chosen Man.

If it ought to be done, he had no doubt it could be done. If it was God's will then there must be God's way. Surely this was the most pressing and crying problem. Here was the greatest need, to feed the people. Was it any use giving them God unless he gave them bread? How could they worship unless they were fed? Was it not mockery to tell them of a Father's love unless he satisfied their human need? And yet—he knew man and needed not that anyone should tell him what was in Man.

Intellectual power consists in the capacity to learn by experience, and his intellect was as clear as light itself. He had tried it—this giving men bread. It did not work. What did they do? Snatched it, gobbled it up, lay down in the sun to sleep, and presently came crying for more. Memories of beggars at Nazareth came crowding in upon him. He saw a beggar eating outside the carpenter's shop, ravenously tearing the loaf with his hands, looking over his shoulder now and then with that furtive look of fear that an animal has when it eats. Jesus was an utter realist. He never allowed his passion, not even his passion of pity, to cloud his intellect. He saw right to the heart of the problem of bread, and arrived at clear and definite principles upon which the solution of it must depend.

The first of these principles was the principle of Work. Bread is a curse when it is not earned. Unearned bread, in the end, corrupts both body and soul. It does not wake men from the sleep, or rescue them from the sensual slough of the animal life. It pushes them deeper into it.

Man cannot live on unearned bread. He must work. He must work with and for God and his fellow men, and by working with and for them, learn to love them. It is by work that man must learn to live by every word that proceeds from the mouth of God. That is to say by the eternal principles of justice, honesty, mercy, and mutual love. He must consciously co-operate with God and with his fellow men in the building of the Kingdom, and in the great school of voluntary co-operative service, must learn to value the Kingdom more highly than himself. To give men bread without calling upon them to earn it, is to rot them both body and soul.

It was his insight into this great truth which lay behind his horror of riches. It was not that he regarded riches as bad in themselves. He was not a lean, hungry ascetic who despised the good things of the world, and bade men seek for heaven by turning their faces from the earth. That was one of the things his critics and enemies complained about. They called him a glutton and a drunkard because he ate and drank like other men, and loved a feast with his friends.

What he dreaded about riches was that they took men out of the working fellowship of God and man. They tempted men to believe that they were really independent of God and of their fellow men. They tempted men to live private lives on private means, and that life is damnation because it is a lie. The man who believes that he can really live a private life on his own private property is damned because he is cut off from the family of God which lives by the work of the world. You see this point brought out with perfect clarity when a man who was staying in the crowd, listening to his teaching, cried out, "Master, speak to my brother that he divide the inheritance with me" (Luke 12:13). He saw right through that cry. Here was a man who cared more for the inheritance than he did for the brotherhood. He wanted to use Jesus, nay, he would have used God himself, as a means of getting that bit of property. Both the brothers were probably like that, and there was the root of their trouble. They had lost their brotherhood in their desire for inheritance. You can never satisfy men like that. You cannot give any decision which they will both accept as just, because they really do not want justice, they want the lot.

Jesus went to the root of the trouble when he said, "Take heed and beware of covetousness, for a man's life consisteth not in the multitude of things he possesseth." Get back to the brotherhood again and you will soon find a way to divide the inheritance. Then he told them the story of the rich fool.

He had a run of luck and raked in plenty, and said to himself, "Now I have any amount of private means and I can live a private life. I need never do another hand's turn for anyone as long as I live. I will have a good time." Then God whispered in his ear, "Thou fool. This night shall thy soul be required of thee."

I do not believe that that was a summons to death. I think it was the realization of the truth that sooner or later comes to all who live on unearned bread, and cut themselves off from the working fellowship of the world; the truth that easy money is muck that has no value and no meaning.

It was because the rich man is inevitably tempted to cut himself off from the fellowship of service that Jesus saw that his money was a danger to his manhood. The same danger, as Jesus clearly saw, exists for the beggar, the scrounger who, being able-bodied, is content with given bread. If Lazarus could work and would not, he must go to hell like Dives, because no man can live by bread alone, not even though he be content with crusts from a rich man's table.

The clarity of Jesus' vision was unclouded, and he saw that the rich man who lives without effort in a world of work was a miserable, poverty-stricken soul, exactly like the lousy, shiftless, drunken beggar who, with loose mouth and wandering eye, preys on the pity of decent men. There was not in his eyes anything to choose between them. They both were naked outcasts from God's world of working men.

It is this first principle of work which if honestly applied would begin the Christian revolution.

The second great principle of Jesus which is contained in this saying, "Man shall not live by bread alone, but by every word that proceedeth out of the mouth of God," is the principle of responsibility, the responsibility of men to God.

Every power that a man possesses is a trust to him from God for the use of which he is responsible. Responsibility was the needle's eye through which the rich and heavily burdened camel might hope to pass by the grace of God.

If, in his riches, the rich man recognized an awful and dangerous responsibility; if he did not allow his riches to cut him off from the working fellowship of God and man, but set himself with all his heart and mind to use them according to God's will and for the glory of his Kingdom, he might save his soul alive, and hear God's great "Well done!"

This principle of responsibility is stated clearly by Jesus in the parable of the talents (Matt 25:14). It is from this story that the word talent has come to be used in its present sense of inherited capacity or natural endowment. Jesus being a realist recognized the fact that men are born unequal. We are by nature differently and very unequally endowed. There are, in every generation, born men of one, two, three, and four talents. We are born unequal, and cannot by any system of education or reform be made equal.

The only way to reduce men all to one level is to reduce them to a dead level. We shall never be equal until we are dead. We cannot make the man of one talent equal to the man of four, though we might, by tyranny and persecution, make the man of four talents almost equal to the man of one. We can level men down, but we can never level them up.

These natural and inevitable inequalities are the cause of much misery and sin, because we use, or fail to use, our talents with a sense of responsibility to God.

The man of many talents says, 'These are mine to use for myself, and I have a right to use them as I will." The man of one talent says, "What is the good of bothering? Life is unjust and unfair. He has four and I have only one." Tyranny, envy and hatred are the inevitable result. There arises what we in modern times call class war. Our misuse of our national inequalities becomes stereotyped and fixed into our customs, laws and institutions, and social strife and discontent threatens to tear the working fellowship into pieces. We pass laws to restrain the man of four talents, and to protect the man of one.

But the strong man uses his talents to override or get round the laws, and we go round in a circle, and always will, unless we recognize the principle of responsibility. We only break the vicious circle as we get more and more men who look upon every power they possess as a trust from God to be used according to his Will, and for the glory of his Kingdom.

When the principle of responsibility is recognized, then the talented man, the naturally rich man, becomes a public servant. The greatest becomes the servant of all. Instead of allowing his riches to cut him off from the working fellowship of God and man, the rich man sees that it brings him closer to it. He has much, and therefore owes much to God and man, and he spends his life discharging the debt.

This is the basis of the Christian social order. As Jesus put it to his disciples when they were quarrelling about who should be greatest, "The kings of the heathen lord it over the people, and call themselves their benefactors. That must not be the way with you. He who is greatest amongst you must count himself as least, and our chief must be the servant of all" (Luke 22:25).

The third great principle contained in the saying, "Man shall not live by bread alone," is the principle of purpose. The only way to secure for all a higher standard of life is to set before all a higher purpose for living. The only way to secure for all a higher standard of living is to set before all a higher purpose for living.

So long as men continue to live the animal life, eating, drinking, lusting, breeding and looking for nothing more, they must live under the law which governs animal life, the law of mutual conflict and death. There is no poverty amongst animals because death, with majestic mercy, lays its great hand unerringly upon the weak and weary and sinks them back on sleep.

Without the Father's knowledge truly no sparrow falls to the ground, and yet the sparrows fall. God does feed the birds of the air, and clothe the lilies of the field, that survive in their natural struggle for existence, but he cannot much more clothe man, unless they seek first the Kingdom of God.

So long as our life purpose remains on the level of the beasts, the law of the beasts must be our law; the world must be a jungle and hunger be its lord.

Therefore let your first thought be not what ye shall eat, or what ye shall drink, or wherewithal shall ye be clothed, for this is the low life purpose of animals and animal-minded man; but seek ye first the Kingdom of God, the reign on earth of justice, mercy, honesty and mutual love, and all these things shall be added unto you.

This principle of purpose is one that we are slow to grasp, and our common sense view of life, the view, that is, which we accept without examination and act upon without question, is that everyone looks after himself, and minds his own business. It will by force of competition work out for the good of all in the end. Jesus says that it cannot, and will not do anything of the kind. On the contrary, so long as men are content with this low life purpose, and live like the beasts, by bread alone, so long will there be poverty, misery and war upon the earth.

The fallacy which underlies the Gospel of enlightened self-interest as the savior of mankind is the over-optimistic belief that the light is as natural to man and as easily come by as the self-interest. But man's natural self-interest is blind, as blind and blinder than the other passions.

Men do by nature mind their own business, but they do not by nature know what their own business is. They busy themselves often in work which means their own undoing. They spend themselves for that which is not bread, and labor for that which satisfieth not.

The amount of human energy which runs to waste in mutual strife, and in the production of poisonous trash is appalling. If this waste energy were caught up, concentrated upon, and consecrated to a high life purpose, it would be more than sufficient to feed the hungry, clothe the naked, and give the thirsty drink, there would be enough to build the New Jerusalem and pave its streets with gold.

Slowly, very slowly, we are beginning to realize that Jesus was right. We begin to see that so long as with blind eyes and a low life purpose, man strives with man, class with class, and nation with nation, most of the colossal energy that the human race controls runs to waste, producing only blood and tears, and a dim vision of what could be done if that energy were directed to a noble end begins to dawn upon us.

The first principles of the Kingdom of God are the only foundations upon which it is possible to build a truly civilized society. They are not impossible ideals, but the only practical rules by which to live.

Man cannot live by given bread. Man needs God's school of honest work, that he may use in that his powers, recognizing them as a trust from God given to him for the high and holy purpose of building the Kingdom here on earth. We cannot live our lives on prose, we need the poet's flame of Truth, and a vision of God's purpose.

The Second Temptation

Jesus came to found a Kingdom. He came to found a Kingdom here upon this earth, where fields are green and skies are blue and blood runs red like wine. He was a practical Man and he set about his task in a practical way. Before he went out on the great adventure he sat down to plan his course of action out. What was he to do? That was the question. In order to found the Kingdom he had to win men to himself. How was he to win them?

We have seen that the first way which suggested itself to his mind was to feed them. It was the way of bribery. He rejected it and we have seen why. Bribery and corruption go together and he knew it. To give men what they ought to earn is to sap the fiber from their souls. Man shall not live by bread alone, but by every word that proceedeth out of the mouth of God. Bribery would not do. How then was he to win men?

There is another way in which men have, all through the ages, been moved to follow leaders and to found Kingdoms on the earth. It is the way of superstition. Superstitious fear, the dread of the unknown, has been one of the great forces molding the destiny of man. It is a curse from which, in its cruder forms at any rate, we are now very largely free; but for more years than we have any record of, it played an enormous part in the lives of men. It was this method that Jesus was tempted to employ. There was a legend amongst the Jews that when the Savior comes, he would come floating down from the clouds of heaven to take command of all the earth. Jesus knew himself to be possessed of extraordinary powers. He had no doubt that he could find a way to do whatever was God's will. If a miracle was needed to start the Kingdom going, then a miracle could be worked. Suppose he took it that way.

He had a vision of the Temple at Jerusalem glittering like some snow mountain in the sun, and himself standing on the topmost pinnacle above the thronged and crowded courts. He sees himself outlined against the sky. Then suddenly he throws himself over. The ancient promise is fulfilled. God's angels catch and bear him up and he floats down in majesty before the astounded and awe-stricken multitude. Would they not follow him then? But he knows man and needs not that anyone should tell him what is in man.

Magic was not unknown in the east then. It is not unknown in the east today. The fakir or miracle monger was a common figure in the crowded streets at feasts and market days. He remembers the look in the faces of a Galilean crowd when some son of the Pharisees had cast out a devil or performed some "miracle" of healing. The momentary hush followed by an outbreak of jabbering and gesticulation as they jostled and pushed one another round the miracle man, yelling for more. They would follow him in crowds, but they would only follow him for what they could see and what they could get. If he performed this great miracle and came down from the Temple's dizzy heights, they would doubtless follow him in multitudes, but they would follow him only for the same low reasons. They would crowd round to see the show and get what they could get. It would not make them any better as men and women. It would not change their hearts and minds or make them the kind of people of whom his Kingdom could be built. It would set men looking to God to do things *for* them, instead of looking to him to do things *in* them and *through* them. It would debase or degrade rather than inspire and uplift them. It would teach them to expect God to work continual miracles for them and get them out of all their difficulties without any effort on their part. They would always be attempting or trying to make God put everything right for them instead of working together to put things right for themselves. "Thou shalt not tempt the Lord, thy God." That is the curse of false religion, the evil of superstition.

True religion brings out all the good there is in man and sets it to work making the world a better and a lovelier place, building the Kingdom of God. False religion teaches men to leave everything to God and expects him to build the Kingdom without our aid and over our heads. There is a lot of false religion in the world still. Men still tempt God. They come to him for what they can get. They pray to him for what they want, and if they do not get it, then they give up praying altogether, and say it is no good.

Now Jesus was very emphatic in his teaching about prayer. He told us we were to pray and to keep on praying. He evidently never thought that men could live rightly unless they prayed. He told a very human story with a touch of fun in it about prayer. There was a man who had locked up for the night and gone to bed with his wife and children when a friend came knocking at the door and wanting to borrow a loaf of bread. The man very naturally told him to get out of that and not come bothering him at that time of night, but the friend kept on knocking at the door and saying how badly he wanted this loaf. It was not for himself, he said, but for someone who had turned up to visit him. At last the man got so sick of the knocking that he got up and handed out the loaf. It is a homely, human story, and the point of it is that the builders of the Kingdom must persistently pray to God.

But if you take his pattern prayer, and read his teaching in the light of it, you begin to see that the purpose of prayer with Jesus was not to get God to do things for you, but to enable God to do things in you and through you. The purpose of prayer with Jesus was to make you a better, finer man or woman through whom God could work his will and build his Kingdom on earth. Our Father who art in heaven, hallowed by thy name. thy Kingdom come on earth as it is in heaven. Thy will be done on earth as it is in heaven. In order that we may do thy will give us—us, mind you, not me—our daily bread. Forgive us our sins against thee as we forgive them that sin against us. Lead us not into temptation—but if in the course of duty, temptation comes, deliver us from evil. We turn to thee for help and inspiration because there is the Kingdom, from thee alone can come the power enabling us to build it, and in thee is all its glory that is to be revealed through us in this world, and the worlds beyond for all eternity.

When you pray like Jesus it is clear that you are not asking God to do things for you, you are asking God to give you the desire and the power to do things for Him. That is a different story, isn't it? Jesus taught that there was no good thing which God does not desire to give us. The difficulty lies in preparing ourselves to receive, to appreciate, and to use rightly the gifts that He is striving to impart. The tragedy arises from the fact that God cannot give us more than we prepare ourselves to receive. There are in each and all of us unknown and immense capacities for good. We are, indeed, if we would only realize it, the sons of God. All the treasures of an infinite universe of goodness, truth and beauty are ours if we will set ourselves with single minds to seek the highest. But we must ask and keep on asking; we must knock and keep on knocking. Only to those who persevere can the glory of the Kingdom be revealed. The difficulty according to Jesus does not lie in persuading God to give, but in preparing ourselves to receive. The Kingdom of God, the fairer, finer, cleaner world is ours as we ourselves develop our longing and desire for it.

This was the very core of Jesus' teaching. God is good and desires our good. He could not and would not ever do us any harm. God loves us whether we love Him or not. He loves His enemies. That is why we must love our enemies. Jesus said, "The old teachers used to tell you to love your friends and hate your enemies, but I tell you to love your enemies, bless the man that curses you, do a good turn to the chap that hates you, put up a prayer for those that have a spite against you and seek to hurt you. That is the only way you can be like God, your Father. He does not ask whether a chap is a saint or a scoundrel before He sends him sunshine. He serves them all alike because He loves them all alike."

Anyone can like those that like him. That is easy. It is liking the other fellow when he does not like you that is the rub. Trying to turn your enemies into friends, that is the job. That is what we must do because it is God's job; it is what God is always doing. That is what shocked and surprised people about the teaching of Jesus. He was so broad-minded, friendly, and human, and he made God so broad-minded, friendly and human. People could not believe it then. They cannot altogether believe it now. A God of power they could understand. A God who could work miracles and prove His power, punishing His enemies, and rewarding His friends they might worship and follow because they would be afraid of Him. They would follow Him for what they could get, and in order to insure themselves against His anger. A God like that is awkward to deal with when he starts throwing His weight about, and they would feel that it was prudent to keep on the right side of Him. There has always been a lot of that sort of religion knocking about the world; there is still. God pays His debts without money, people think. Look out or He'll get you. If He does not get you here He'll get you hereafter. It is safer to keep in with God. As an old fellow in a play I once saw says to his son, "Mark my words, my lad, God is a fair stickler for His position. 'E will 'ave proper ruces'. And if tha says boo to 'Im 'E'll say a fat sight more than boo to thee,

part three: The Plain Bread of Religion · 147

an 'e never forgets nowt, 'E don't, never forgets nowt. Tread on 'Is toes, my lad, and 'E'll tread on thine until tha squeals 'ell out of 'even, and then there's a great gulf fixed, as the old Book says. If 'E gets thee there 'E's got thee fair and there'll be no shiftin' quarters."

That is something like the way in which many people have always thought about God. But it is not Jesus' way. He wanted to lead men not to the fear but to the love of God. It would not have served his purpose to terrify or overcome people by display of miraculous power. That would not have changed their hearts or made them love one another. He wanted to make men hate evil, not fear the punishment of evil. He wanted to make them love Good, not the reward of being good.

There was only one way for him. He had to show men what real goodness is like, and earn their love. That was the way he chose. He acted as he believed God would, if he were a man.

The Third Temptation

That is what led him to reject the third and last way of winning men which presented itself to him, as he sat and pondered over his plan of campaign in the wilderness. The third and last way was the way of the sword.

If he could not bribe men by giving them bread, or awe them by working miracles, could he not force them by wielding the sword?

It was the way by which up to his time all kings had chosen to found and consolidate their kingdoms. It was, moreover, the way his own people would expect him to take. They were expecting a military messiah, and there could be no doubt that they would follow him if he set up his standard and called for volunteers.

This way made a very strong appeal to his natural ambition. Jesus was human, and we cannot suppose that he was without ambition. He was a great man, remember. He was a greater and more magnetic personality than Napoleon. He felt the power within him. Great men do. He longed for a chance to work his will upon the world. He had a vision of the kingdoms of the earth and all the glory of them. He could add to that glory. He could make it real. Why should he not take that way? He himself, by his own power, has made us feel that it was impossible for him to take it, but there was nothing to make it clear that the way of the sword was not God's way. The men of his time would have said unanimously and without hesitation that it was God's way, and that he would have been right to take it.

Jesus was a patriot. He loved his own land and his own people with a deep and passionate love, as all fine men must do. His love for the holy land and the holy city burns its way still through the ages. "O Jerusalem, Jerusalem, that stonest the prophets and killest them that are sent unto thee, how often would I have gathered up thy children together as a hen doth gather her brood under her wings, and thou would'st not. O if thou had'st, even thou, in this thy day, the things that belong unto thy peace. But now are they hid from thine eyes" (cf. Matthew 23:37).

The passion of that cry has its way with us yet, and it is hard to read it unmoved. He loved his people, and they were oppressed and downtrodden. The insolent, swaggering, all-conquering Romans trampled them under foot. They groaned under a crushing load of unjust taxation, and the children cried for bread. Was it not high time that someone struck a blow for freedom in his country's cause? Would not any strong man's heart burn within him, and his hand instinctively feel to find his sword?

We know that the temptation came to Jesus, and by the way he tells the story we can guess that it was a fierce and fiery temptation.

His heart did burn within him. His hand did feel instinctively to find his sword. He was a warrior by nature, and came of a warrior race. He had soldier's blood in his veins. It did not count for nothing that he was David's son. But he rejected the way of the sword more fiercely than either of the other two. There is a kind of cold fury in the words, 'get thee behind me, Satan." They have passed into a proverb of repulsion and disgust.

We can measure the power of the appeal which the temptation made to him by the ferocity with which he rejected it. But why did he decide against the sword? Was it because he felt himself unable to wield it, and saw only failure staring him in the face if he tried? Was he afraid? That would contradict the whole of his life. He appears to have feared nothing and no one on earth. Fearlessness is one of his outstanding characteristics.

If he had believed it was God's will, I do not think he would have hesitated. What would have been the result? Who can tell? Here was one greater than Napoleon. Who can tell?

European history might have read differently. The armies of the Carpenter might have hurled a Roman Caesar from his throne. Whatever

part three: The Plain Bread of Religion · 149

way he chose, we may be sure he would have made history, this solitary Jew in the wilderness, who saw in a moment of time all the kingdoms of the earth, and the glory of them.

But he deliberately rejected the way of the sword . . . He was a realist, and went to the root.

These Romans were not the real oppressors of his people. They were themselves oppressed. They were but slaves who bullied slaves. Caesar was neither here nor there. If they cast off the Roman yoke they would bind another on their own necks more galling still. They would make a Jewish Caesar. Make him one, perhaps. Dress him up in purple and fine linen, and put him in a palace to sit upon a throne, chief slave in a world of slaves.

No! Let them pay their pence to Caesar. He must win their souls to freedom and to God. And the sword was no use for that purpose.

There could be no freedom by the sword, since the sword was the sign of slavery. They that take the sword must perish by the sword, for they are the slaves of fear. He saw that two thousand years ago. We have not seen it yet. There is a dim light dawning, but it is still dark. We cannot see it because we are still afraid. The old savage terror still lurks in the secret places of our souls, and keeps us in bondage. Therefore we wave the Union Jack, sing Rule Britannia, breed vile disease and build Dreadnoughts, because our souls are full of dread.

It was the clear and unclouded perception that force and fear are but two sides of the one thing that made Jesus lay aside the sword as useless. It simply would not and could not serve his purpose. He had to go down to the roots and deliver the human soul from the tyranny of fear. There was only one way of doing that, and that was to teach them the secret of love. Love alone can cast out fear. So by word and deed he set himself to teach men the way of love. He bade men fling themselves on life with courage and with confidence, trusting God and trusting one another, consecrating all their energy to the coming of the Kingdom, and he assured them that if they did that all their real wants would be provided for. Much of his teaching still sounds absurdly unpractical and over-optimistic to us because we still are afraid of one another and of life. It sounds absurd to say to men, "Don't worry about what you are to eat and what you are to drink, and what clothes you are to wear. Live like the flowers and the birds." But if you go on to the end it is not so absurd as it sounds.

He does not tell us to sit still and do nothing but try to be like a lily or make a noise like a bird wanting worms. He says that we are to be up and doing. "Seek first the Kingdom of God and His just and honest order of society and you'll get food, drink, and clothes in plenty," he says.

And there is nothing absurd about it. It may not be common sense. But the more common such sense becomes the better it will be for the human race. There is not a doubt that if all the energy of body and mind which is now wasted and frittered away on futile efforts to protect ourselves against our neighbors and secure our selfish interests, to uphold our prestige and credit, and what we are pleased to call our "honor"; if all that energy were redirected to the single and clear-sighted purpose of constructing a just and honest order of society we could satisfy the reasonable wants of every man, woman, and child in the world, and have a bit over to play with.

For bed-rock sanity I'll back this economic teaching of Jesus Christ against what millions would call common sense. They would and do turn Jesus' teaching topsy-turvy. They say, "Seek ye first what ye shall eat and what ye shall drink and wherewithal ye shall be clothed. In other words, make it your first objective to improve your standard of life—and the Kingdom of God will be added unto you." That is what men call common sense, but it is fat-headed, shallow-pated nonsense. It does not and never will work. Materialism is not practical. It inevitably leads to waste and war. The energy that should go into creation is turned to purposes of destruction, and the hungry are not fed. It is the order of the far-off land, and not of the Father's home.

(1932; posthumous)

Sin Is No Private Matter

Throughout the whole course of evolution, it is evident that life in all its forms, from the lowest to the highest, comes, and can only come, to the individual through a community. That appears to be an everlasting law, a final necessity; the parts only grow through their unity with the whole. And it is so with the Eternal Life, and with the redemption and completion that come with it; there is no redemption or completion for the individual apart from the community, there is no Love of God apart from the love of Man—the two great commandments are an eternal unity. From the very beginning, there grew out of Christ a new social order, a new community; and only in and through that community and its life could redemption come. Every command and every saying of His, from the Sermon on the Mount to His last recorded words on earth, presupposes that the Eternal Life is a social life, and is ministered through and in a new social order.

Herein lies the distinct difference between the gospel of Our Lord Jesus Christ, and all those religions which offer man heaven through ascetic and solitary contemplation of the Being of God. It is of the very being of Christianity that it is a social life. Perfection and redemption alike come through the body. If you take out of the New Testament the idea of the Kingdom of God, and the Beloved Community, which is the seed from which it grows in time, there is nothing intelligible left. It is in the beloved community that the gift of Eternal Life, and therefore the power of man's redemption and completion, is to be found: "Whose soever sins ye remit, they are remitted unto them; and whose soever sins ye retain, they are retained" (John 20:23), was said to the body of the apostles; and said, I believe, not because they were apostles in any sense that ranks them above all other Christians, but because they formed the first Christian Body.

The Sermon on the Mount lays down the law of the Kingdom; throughout, from beginning to end, it presupposes a new order of community life: "For I say unto you, take no thought what ye shall eat, or what ye shall drink, or wherewithal ye shall be clothed (for after all these things do the Gentiles seek), for your Heavenly Father knoweth you have need of all these things" (Matthew 6:31–31). It is the law for the true Israel of God. The Kings of the Gentiles lord it over them, and their oppressors are styled benefactors, but it must not be so with you. No, let the great men among you be the humblest ministers, and your leaders the servants of all. It is a new order of life; and through that order comes the forgiveness of sins.

And so when the Church goes out on her crusade against sin and sickness, she goes out with the call to men to be baptized for the remission of sins. She calls them to be grafted on to the beloved community, and, partaking of the new life which pulses through it, to be healed of their sickness and their sin. Infant Baptism as it is practiced in the Church today is a caricature of what it was meant to be, and lacks reality, because the sense of the Church as the Beloved Community, in which the new Life is to be found, has become so weak. It was meant to be a Sacrament and has become a ceremony because the Community Life of Christian Churches is so poverty-stricken. Often the Sacrament is administered without any congregation to welcome the child, in a half lighted Church on a weekday evening, with no one present but the relatives. It is regarded as a private concern of the parents, not a public concern of the Church. Hence it has become a charm, a magic survival, and people bring their children to the priest to be christened as they bring them to the doctor to be vaccinated. Soon they will begin to wonder whether it is of any use at all, whether it is anything but a convention. The duty of Godfathers is to give the child a silver mug, and not to care for its soul, because the reality has gone out of it, and the reality is membership of a living, loving body of Christians, through which the Spirit gives new life, and in that new life remission of sins.

Our modern idea that sin is a private business, and that salvation is a matter between the individual and God only, does not appear in the New Testament at all, and is entirely foreign to the whole spirit of Christianity. Indeed, the whole notion of an individual who exists and grows by communion with God apart from communion with man is, from a Christian point of view, nonsense. And herein, I believe, lies the weakness of our redemptive work; for it is weak. We are not destroying evil as we should do, we are not healing sickness and saving men from sin as our Saviour meant us to. Everyone who is engaged in Christian work knows that that is true . . . Wherein does the weakness lie?

I believe that in all our Churches, and in every branch of Christendom, it is due to one root cause, the lack of real community life in the Body, and this pernicious idea that sin is a private matter between the individual soul and God, and has nothing to do with anybody else. No one must come between me and my God, a common saying of pious people, is a definitely anti-Christian saying, which regards brother man as a barrier to, and not a means of grace; and that is in itself sin.

I do not think that even the Churches which profess and call themselves Catholic, really escape this weakness. Catholicism has taken unto itself strange meanings in these latter days, and the practice of what is called "private confession" is no guarantee of real community life, it is very often purely private, a reconciliation of the individual soul to its God, rather than a restoration to a living body which lives with the Life of God.

The ancient practice of public confession sprang from, and was filled with, the reality of community life. When some man was drawn from the streets of Rome, or the docks of Corinth, into the little Christian Brotherhood, and was baptized for the remission of sins, becoming thereby a partaker of its vivid and conscious social life, so that he learned to say "I know that I have passed from death unto life because I love the Brethren," he experienced the forgiveness of sins. And if he fell away, and was sucked back into the evil streets again, when his soul grew sick and he began to long for the clean air of the Christian Brotherhood, he would creep back some Saturday night when the Brethren were met in preparation for the Eucharist and, standing up before them all, would confess his fault and ask to come back into the family. And then the elder Brother, the *presbyteros* or priest, *speaking for the family of God*, would absolve him from his sin, and take him back again to share in the common life. But it was the community that absolved, it was in the family that the power of healing and regeneration lay. Although this truth underlies so-called "private confession," it is a truth that is obscure—obscure for two reasons, as it seems to me—first of all, because we think of a Priest far too much as one who represents God, rather than as one who represents the Brotherhood in which God dwells, and through which His Life is imparted to men; and, secondly, because the community, the Church which he represents, is, as a matter of fact, poverty-stricken in its Christian social life.

(1923)

Community, Suggestion, and Salvation

There is not, there never can be, anything approaching to the magical or mechanical about the Sacraments; they cannot and do not work as charms, nor does it seem to be possible to guarantee their actual efficacy because they are administered by Churches which are theologically orthodox and ecclesiastically correct. It is not possible to guarantee that a man can administer effectual absolution, because he is a successor of the apostles in direct historic line; the apostolic succession is powerless to make a dead Church live. The Prophet must still lift up his cry of warning to the Priest, "Begin not to say within yourselves, we have Peter and Paul for our Fathers, for I say unto you, that God is able of these stones to raise up children unto Peter" (cf. Matthew 3:9).

What, you say, does the presence of God and His power depend upon the character of the Priest? Then we are in a poor case indeed! God forbid. The presence and the Love of God depend upon nothing and no one; but His power to heal does depend, and has always depended upon the faith of His Church and the vitality within it. It is as true today as it was in the days of His flesh, that in thousands of places to which He comes, and in which He longs to heal and to save, He cannot do many mighty works there because of their unbelief. It does not need any community, it does not need any sacrament, it did not even need the death of Christ, to secure God's Love for you, to secure that He will come seeking you; He does that everywhere at all times, for everybody; but it does need a community, and it does need sacraments, as the centre of community life, in order that that Love may be enabled to break through the barriers that sin erects, that He may pour into your soul His own Eternal Life, and heal your sin. This is the awful responsibility that is laid upon us all, that in this matter, as in all others, we are our brothers' keepers; and from that responsibility we cannot escape by any sin-proof system or material organization. We cannot keep the Church alive, and preserve her powers of healing, by mere doctrinal discipline, however strict, or ecclesiastical order, however perfect and correct.

The rebellion against organized religion—so far as it is justifiable and not the result of mere ignorance and shallow thinking—is a rebellion against a body which is felt to have no soul. Insofar as this rebellion is a claim that each man's religion is his own private affair, and has nothing to do with his brother, and needs no community through which to express itself and in which to grow, it is the negation of religion and the denial of Christ. But insofar as it seeks for a living body, demanding the fruits of the Spirit as proof of its life, and refusing to be content with doctrinal, ecclesiastical, or historical guarantees, it is the rebellion of the Christ Himself against the tomb in which His enemies—many of whom are Christians—would confine Him.

I shall be told, perhaps, that I am denying the validity of my own Orders, professing disbelief in my own Church, and depriving men of the certain settled conviction that the Church is the Ark of Salvation. I am doing none of these things. I believe that Christ is in the Anglican Church, that the community is alive with His life, that there is, in her, regeneration for the remission of sins; but I believe—because I am compelled by bitter compulsion to believe—that there are parts of her where that life beats very feebly, where the Christ is crucified afresh, and where He cannot do any mighty works because of unbelief. And I believe—because I am compelled to believe—that it is literally impossible to confine the healing and redeeming power of God within any branch whatsoever of the Christian Church, or by any boundaries of ecclesiastical organization.

I know of Nonconformist Ministers who can, and do, absolve people from their sins by the power of the community they represent. I see no escape from it, and to deny it would be a sin against the Holy Ghost. I know altars within the Anglican Communion, from which a constant stream of healing and redemption flows; I know of others, where literally nothing is being done at all. You say, I cannot know that, the altars may be empty, but the angels may be there. I have no doubt whatsoever that they are; but Jesus did not come to save angels, but sinners. And the same thing applies to every other body in Christendom calling itself a Church. *Its power to help and to heal varies, according to the vitality of Christian Brotherhood that is to be found in it.* If you tell me this makes the whole thing uncertain, that there is no positive guarantee, no infallible hallmark whereby you can know the ship of salvation as made by God, I reply that it is and always has been uncertain; that there is not, and there never has been, any absolute guarantee; that there is not, and cannot be, any infallible hallmark except the Love of the Brethren. And where that is not present, there is no Church in any real sense, and there is no saving power, and never has been.

The attempt to organize or construct a vast and complex institution, by mere adherence to which a man can be certain of salvation, is the most utterly futile of all the attempts to build Utopia; and, like a very large number of other Utopias, would mean for man, not salvation, but hell, if it could become reality.

This attempt to find or found the infallible institution, has meant the death of real religion. It has led to a mechanical idea of the Sacrament of Absolution, which has largely destroyed its efficacy. The Church—secure in its ecclesiastical orthodoxy, or anxiously and ingeniously defending it—has neglected, or been distracted from, its proper business of destroying evil, and effectively absolving or freeing people from the power of sin. And sinners in their desperation have turned to gross superstition, or to psychiatrists for help and healing which they do not get in their Church. This may be partly because psychiatry is "scientific," and the authority of "science" is a power to conjure with in these days. Formerly people took the priest on trust, and followed blindly where he led; nowadays the scientist has taken his place, and it is assumed that what is claimed to be scientific must be true. The authority of the doctor is more absolute than that of the priest, and the psychiatrist comes in under his wing, so to speak. It is no good complaining about this change. The scientist has largely won his authority because he has produced results, and we have largely lost ours because we have not. But neither of us is really doing the job.

The conclusions of psychiatry are tentative and its methods of healing largely experimental; and the cure seems sometimes worse than the disease. Nevertheless it is there, and has come to stay. If some of the conclusions are tentative, there appears to be a solid residuum of ascertained truth; and the method in many cases produces wonderful results. And these results, so far as they go, are exactly the results which religion ought to produce. Men and women are set free from the bondage of bad habits, from fears and depressions, which have driven them into much that we call, and rightly call, sin. Bitterness, jealousy, envy, hatred, malice, and all uncharitableness, as well as positive vice, may all spring from, and be due to, some suppression or complex, and may disappear when the complex is dissolved. If absolution means anything, it includes in its meaning freedom from the power of these sins. Doubtless absolution, first of all, means restoration of the soul to communion with God; but if that restoration is effective, it ought to carry with it liberation from the power of evil. If men and women find that they can obtain that liberation from the psychiatrist, which they fail to obtain in the Church, then they will turn more and more to him for help in their trouble.

Well, you say, so long as they obtain it, what does it matter where? The psychiatrist is God's minister as the doctor is, and, in his sphere, is doing priestly work. It is only another proof that you cannot confine God's Mercy within the channels which you choose to suppose are the orthodox ones. The power which the psychiatrist wields, is every bit as much God's power as the power of the priest. Far be it from me to call good evil, or to deny that, so far as the analyst heals men of sin and sickness, he is doing God's work, and doing it by God's power; but there are other considerations. Redemption means not only that men "do not perish," but that they have "everlasting life"; not only that they are saved from degeneracy, but are given a higher order of life; they are not merely rescued, but completed. Now, supposing we admit that the psychiatrist does heal men and women of mental sickness, which is he cause of so much that we call sin, and that his work is so far good—has he the power of completing that work, and lifting the life on to a higher level altogether? Healing on the lower level may often be a dangerous thing for the man or woman, looked at as an immortal soul. Without for one moment casting any aspersion on the good work of the medical profession, it is doubtful whether they do not cause as well as cure disease—whether the constant suggestion of sickness with which we are today surrounded, and our readiness to have recourse to medicine for its cure, does not induce us, at times, to postpone or refuse that radical alteration in our whole way of living and thinking, which would lead us to real health. The divorce between the functions of the doctor and priest is in many ways dangerous to both. These considerations apply as forcibly to the psychiatrist and the nerve specialist as they do to the medical practitioner.

From a Christian point of view, what the analyst is really doing is to dissect the carnal mind, and by observing its behavior over a wide field, and tabulating his results, to discover, or attempt to discover, the laws by which it works, and so cure its diseases. The process leads one into strange places, and it is sometimes difficult to prevent a feeling of nausea as you proceed. Of course, the obvious reply to that is, that the healer must be prepared to deal with sickening things; the surgeon must open the abscess and let out the filth it contains. An operation, to a layman, is a sickening business. If there is all this hidden ugliness in the depth of the human mind, it is better to face the facts, and get down to it. Because a thing is unpleasant, it is not therefore untrue. We must not be turned away from the pursuit of important truths, because they lead us into evil-smelling places. One must admit the right of the pure scientist to investigate anything; and if this investigation is necessary for the cure of the many moral and nervous disorders which afflict us, we must be grateful to the men who undertake it. But if the claims of Christianity are true, it ought not to be necessary. We ought to be able to cure these disorders in the name and by the power of Christ. We ought to be able to deliver man from bondage to the carnal mind, which we hold to be at enmity with God. Christianity declares that the carnal mind can be destroyed by the pouring in of the new life.

With respect to psychological method, Christianity definitely joins itself to the "Suggestionists," as opposed to the "Analysts"—it declares that what the analyst adduces as facts, are not facts at all, but distortions of fact; and that they can be destroyed, without analyzing and observing them, by the inspiration of the Holy Spirit. The Christian method of cure is, as to its method—Suggestion. The New Nancy School, of which Coue was Moses and Baudouin was Aaron, has rediscovered and re-emphazised the basic element in Faith—that, ultimately, it is what you worship, rather than what you will, that makes you what you are.[3] It is what dominates your imagination, fills your thoughts—what haunts you, so to speak—that determines your character and actions. Baudouin's law of reversed effort merely puts into scientific language the experience of St. Paul, "The good that I will to do—I do not. The evil that I will not to do—I do; O wretched man that I am! Who will deliver me from the body of this death? Thanks be to God Who giveth us the victory through Jesus Christ Our Lord" (Romans 7:19, 24–25). The law of reversed effort is the psychological fact underlying the doctrine of salvation by Faith and not by works. The other name of that doctrine might be Salvation by worship and not by will. An effort of pure will means a divided mind—part of us suggests that we can—part of us that we can't—and the suggestion of

---

3. Emile Coue (1857–1926) and Charles Baudouin (1893–1963), pioneers in auto-suggestion as a form of therapy. Based in Nancy, France, the mantra of the New Nancy School was "Day by day, in all respects, I get better and better."

impotence wins. But when a man has found his God, he cries, "I can do all things through Christ Who strengtheneth me." This is the Christian method of salvation. To say that Christianity is only suggestion is to confuse method with power. Suggestion is a method, not in itself a power; it can be used for evil as well as for good, and indeed is at present much more commonly used for evil than for good. We are subject every day to a continual battery of suggestion. If God works by suggestion, so do the world, the flesh and the devil, and it is a doubtful point as to how far the analyst, when he cures, does not work by suggestion too—how far it is the continual suggestion of the cure, that in the end has power to heal, rather than the analysis. The problem of the healing of sickness and sin boils down at last to the question of how to overcome evil suggestion by good.

The claim of the Church is, that within the Christian Brotherhood there is the Eternal Life, the Way of Worship, which can, through Faith in and worship of God as revealed in Jesus Christ, completely counter the power of evil suggestion, destroy its results, and set the sinner on his feet again. Nor, thank God, is this claim without evidence to back if. If the Christian Church is weak in positively redemptive work, if she fails to save the sick and sinful as she should, yet it remains true that she is the greatest preventive power that the world contains against the ravages of sin. Millions of men and women are healed of and preserved from sin and disease of the mind in the early stages, by her ordinary worship, by the ministration of the Word and Sacraments. That is a fact, I think, beyond dispute. What we must realize is, that the tremendous power of mass suggestion, which we call the world, can only be confronted, and its victims cured, if they are received into a body which is filled with a vivid, vigorous, and conscious community life of the Spirit. Individuals are powerless to cope with a power so subtle and all-pervasive as this mass suggestion. If we are to save and rescue sinners, there must grow up in our Church a Spirit of Love and Brotherhood, a Christian community-life, transcending class and national distinctions, as pungent, as powerful, as impossible to escape as the Spirit of the world. No Apostolic Succession, no Ecclesiastical correctness, no rigidity of orthodox doctrine, can by themselves and in themselves give us this; it comes, and can only come, from a clearer vision of the Christ, a more complete surrender to His call and to the bearing of His Cross.

God can and does forgive us our trespasses; but only as we forgive them that trespass against us—that is, only as we become members of a Church really militant here on earth—which is pledged and resolved to bear in its own body the sin of the whole world.

(1923)

A Sin-Bearing Community

"The Lord hath laid on Him the iniquity of us all." What does that mean? Who is this Lord, who lays on the innocent the sin of the guilty? Who burdens the Christ with the sin of the world? What is God like?

The Bible contains many ideas of God. The man who sits down to read it, taking every part of it as equally valid and equally inspired, and endeavors to form from it any sort of idea of what God is like, will rise from his task with a mind in strange confusion; and the more he attempts to reduce it to order, the more will that confusion grow; until it amounts—as, in fact, it has amounted in men's minds—to an utter chaos, which can only echo the hopeless and agnostic cry: "It is higher than heaven, what canst thou do? It is deeper than hell, what canst thou know?" (Job 11:8)

The attempts to reduce to some sort of order the conflicting ideas of God contained in the Bible, on the basis of the equal inspiration of every part, is the cause of those many theories of the Atonement, which bewilder the man who attempts to probe more deeply into the heart of Calvary. Thank God, none of those theories has ever been made an Article of Faith, and it has never been supposed that salvation was connected with adherence to any particular theory. In this, as in every other question that besets the Christian Faith, the first necessity is somehow to get clear in our minds what God is like. No doctrine can be true which gives us an unworthy idea of God.

To every dogma we must apply the acid test of the Incarnation. "Beloved, believe not every spirit, but try the spirits whether they are of God; because many false prophets are gone out into the world. Hereby know ye the Spirit of God. Every spirit that confesseth that Jesus Christ is come in the flesh is of God; and every spirit that confesseth not that Jesus Christ is come in the flesh is not of God" (1 John 4:1–3). *No doctrine is true which makes Jesus less than God, or makes God less than Jesus.* That is the first test of Christian Truth.

A great many of the peculiar dogmas which separate and divide us would be dissolved, under that test, into the nonsense of which they are composed. They make God less good than Jesus.

Supposing it is true that God comes to the Roman Catholic or the Anglican who kneels at the altar, and does not come to the earnest Presbyterian who seeks Him in the Kirk; what is God like? Is He like

Jesus? If God forgives the sinner who makes his confession to a Roman Catholic or Anglican Priest, and does not forgive the man who makes it to a Wesleyan Minister who prays with him afterwards, what is God like? Is He like Jesus? If God demands that Jesus should be tortured on the Cross before He can forgive sinners; if the Cross is necessary to turn away His wrath against man; what is God like? Would Jesus make such a demand?

A thousand mysteries begin to clear away, if we cling persistently to that great Name of God which is given by St. John: "God is Love"—the Love that was revealed in Jesus. That is not one of His attributes; that is His very Self. Cling to that Name, and use it, in all these great passages:

"All we like sheep have gone astray; we have turned every one to his own way; and Love hath laid on Him the iniquity of us all" (Isaiah 53:6).

"Love, for our sakes, in His own Body bare our sins upon the tree" (1 Peter 2:24).

"Him that never knew sin, Love made to be sin for us" (2 Corinthians 3:21).

Doesn't a light begin to break through?

I remember being called upon to visit a man who was in prison for forgery and embezzlement. He was the crookedest, hardest-hearted specimen of humanity that it has ever been my luck to strike, and I could not move him an inch nearer repentance. The only sign of softening that he showed at all, was when he asked me to go and see his mother. I went. She came down, looking worn and sleepless, and that I expected. But there was something about her which I, being young, could not understand. She was bitterly ashamed, and in my pity for her I wondered, what has she to be ashamed of? And then there came the light, and I murmured to myself: Surely she hath borne his griefs and carried his sorrows; the chastisement of his peace is upon her, and with her stripes he shall be healed, if there be any power that can heal him. He has gone astray and turned to his own way, and Love hath laid on her the iniquity of her son. The mother-heart which knew but little sin, Love hath made to feel exceeding sinful for his sake. I understood and, in a measure, the eternal mystery cleared. That love which a woman can pour out upon her son, and which makes her so entirely one with him, that his sin is her sin, his disgrace is her disgrace, his shame is her shame, is the nearest that we can get upon earth to the love of God; to what God is.

part three: The Plain Bread of Religion · 163

It was that love, extended to infinity, which beat within the human heart of Christ, God Incarnate, and made Him feel to every man, every woman, and every child in all the world, as that mother felt for her son; so that our sins became His sins; our disgrace His disgrace; our shame His shame; and in His own Body He bore our sins upon the tree.

This is what forgiveness costs. Forgiveness is love in action, and love means sin-bearing. Forgiveness can only be accomplished by sin-bearing, and sin-bearing means a cross. It means that to God, and it must mean that to man; for "if any man will be My disciple, let him take up his cross and follow after Me," and the meaning of the Cross is Love bearing the sin of the beloved, because of His unity with him. We call any trouble, even if we bring it upon ourselves, a cross, and many of our bitterest crosses are homemade; but the real cross is Love's suffering for the sake of the beloved. We can only be forgiven, as we bear that cross; we can only be forgiven as we forgive. We can only know the Sin-bearer, as we bear the sins of others. We are redeemed in order to be redeemers, and are not saved until God makes us saviors. The Christian must go with his Lord into the Garden of Gethsemane, and must pass from there to Calvary, filling up in his body what is lacking of the sufferings of Christ, for His Body's sake, which is the Church.

If the Church is a Church indeed, it is a body of sin-bearing people; people who love with the love of God that is shed abroad in their hearts, and who, because they love, are compelled to bear the burden of the world's sins. They are a body of people who can forgive because they are forgiven, who have been loved into being lovers. Unless the Church of Christ is by love so united with the whole of mankind, that the sin of the world is the sin of the Church, the disgrace of the world, the disgrace of the Church, the shame of the world, the shame of the Church—then it is not a Church at all. However highly organized, however doctrinally orthodox, however correct ecclesiastically, it is not a Church, but a counterfeit, if it does not bear the sin of the world.

If the Church exists to bear the sin of the world, then the Church which does not bear sins has no power to absolve them. The true Church is made up of those who do not run away from the Garden of Gethsemane. There are many gates out of that Garden; but for the Christian, who is a Christian in truth, they are all locked.

There is the gate by which the Pharisee went out; the Gate of Contempt. He judged others that he might escape from judging himself; he sought by self-righteous condemnation to escape being condemned; he was a religious individualist, and separated himself, as his name implies, from the brotherhood of mankind. Partly the Pharisee is blind, and partly he is afraid. He is afraid to love, because he would have to suffer in some form or other. It is always fear that drives men out of the Garden; as, on that dreadful night, it was out of fear that they all forsook Him and fled.

There are many kinds of Pharisees.

There is the Pharisee of the Study; who sits with his lamp burning late into the night, and explains in perfectly polished phrases exactly where the world is wrong, and why it is that only a very few—including himself, of course—can possibly be saved; showing with great self-satisfaction how certain it is that there will never be any inconvenient crowding outside the narrow gate.

There is the Catholic Pharisee, who regards everybody who does not go to confession as in some strange way beyond the pale of humanity. If people find his services repulsive, and his way of conducting them utterly unedifying, he beams with pride, and regards it as a sign of grace in himself. He meets his fellow Catholics, and they all flatter and fondle each other, and talk their particular kind of cant. They really are a little herd of animals, snuggling up to one another, as the herd beast always does, for warmth. Their type of mind has no connection with Christianity.

There is the Extreme Protestant Pharisee, to whom everybody who signs himself with the Sign of the Cross is worse than a heathen, and cannot be a brother.

All these go out of the Garden by the Gate of Contempt, because they are afraid to join that Figure Who lies with His face to the earth, in agony and bloody sweat, refusing to claim any superiority, and only crying in His heart: "How often would I have gathered My children together as a hen doth gather her brood under her wings, and ye would not" (Luke 13:34).

They are afraid to join the Christ, Who bears the sins of the world. But let us be quite certain of this. Those who leave the Garden by the Gate of Contempt may be Baptized, Confirmed, Communicant, Ordained,

Consecrated; they may have gone through every form of ritual and partaken of every Sacrament there is; and yet they are not Christian.

There is the Gate of Pietism; and many go out thereat, with eyes fast closed in prayer, absorbed in an ecstasy of devotion, singing revivalist hymns, repeating enormous prayers, surrounded by mists of incense, and drunk with the smell of altar lilies, with sweet little altar boys swinging censers, with red caps, carpet slippers, and white gloves; doing humble reverence every now and then to the Body of the Lord, still they go out of the Garden, and leave Him there to bear the sins of the world. These are of that countless host who go to Church for comfort, for a sensation, as a refuge from the world; who must have the best of choirs, the most eloquent of preachers, the most perfectly rendered Eucharist before they will go at all; whose religion is purely a personal business, and concerns themselves and God. There is always a crowd round this gate, and in it there are more women than men.

Then there is the Gate of the Cynics. It is a favorite one for men. They hurry out, muttering words of worldly wisdom. It has always been the same. Human nature cannot be changed and the man who worries over it is a fool. Men are just beasts, with a very thin skin of civilization; pierce an inch below the surface, and you will find a brute. Doubtless religion is good for the masses, but educated men can't be expected to believe in it; it is all sentiment and wash. You can't get down to any facts there. We are always changing the names of things, but the things remain the same; and in the end each man must look out for himself, and the weak must go to the wall. That is the first law of life and the last one, however much it may be disguised: so the Cynics say.

It is a strange crowd, this crowd that throngs about the Gates of the Garden. There are in it men and women of every sort, but there is one secret thing that binds them all together, a thing that they will not confess even to themselves. They are all of them afraid; afraid to love. They cannot stand looking at that Figure; they cannot face His pain. Down in their uttermost depths they are all common cowards who are afraid to love. Thousands of them attend Churches, but none of them understand the meaning of the Church. They are not forgiven, because they dare not forgive. The real Church is made up of those who have not forsaken Him and fled, but have stayed in the Garden of Gethsemane and have gone with Him to the Cross, because Love hath laid on them the sin of the world, and its sin has become their sin, its sorrow their sorrow, and they are content to bear it; aye, more than content, because they bear it with Him. They are glad. They are glad with the gladness of God.

There is always that joy. Sorrow and joy are not opposites; the one is the soul of the other, and those who are the living Church know that the *Via pacis* is the *Via ruces,* and rejoice to walk in it. But for them the Church is not, and never can be, an end in itself; it is a means to an end; a means to the salvation of the world and the building of the Kingdom of God. It is not the Ark of Salvation for themselves, it is the Agent of Salvation for mankind. It is not a refuge of peace, but an army preparing for war. They seek in it, not security, but sacrifice. This is the infallible mark of the Church, the hallmark of the Cross. And if the sin of our modern slums, and the degradation that they cause; if the sin of our overcrowded, rotten houses, and the ugliness and vice they bring; if the sin of unemployment, with the damnation of body and soul that it means to men and women, boys and girls; if the sin of the heartless, thoughtless luxury at one end, standing out against the squalid and degrading poverty at the other; if the sin of commercial trickery and dishonesty, and wholesale defrauding of the poor; if the sin of prostitution, and the murder of women and children by venereal disease; if the sin of war, the very sin of sins, which is but the bursting into a festering sore of all the filth that the others have bred in years of miscalled peace; if all that is not laid upon the Church as a burden, and Christ's members do not feel it as their own, then the Church is not a Church at all; and no amount of organization, propaganda, and evangelization can make it live. It has missed its vocation. It is not really redeemed, because it is not redeeming. It is not forgiven, because it dares not forgive.

Full forgiveness of sins means deliverance from their guilt, their power, and their consequences; and if that is possible at all, *it is only possible in and through a community* alive in every part with the love of God, that love which is always taking the sin of others on itself. Only in such a community can guilt be transformed into gratitude, the real gratitude which shows itself in the passion of service.

When the miracle of the forgiveness of sins has actually taken place, and the man or woman has seen God in His glory, as the forgiven sinner always does, and has risen out of the depths of shame and darkness of guilt into which that vision always plunges him—the next stage is to love much, because much has been forgiven. Guilt must pour itself out in gratitude; and unless that gratitude is to waste away in emotion and evaporate into sentiment, it must take form in practical service, in positive attack upon the forces of evil; and so the forgiven sinner is always a soldier in Christ's Church militant here on earth.

Only in and through a sin-bearing community, alive with the love of God, can the power of sin over the sinner be really and permanently broken. The individual standing alone is not strong enough to resist the force of mass-suggestion which the world brings to bear upon him. The carnal mind can only be met with the mind of Christ, the life of the world with the life of Christ; and that life is a community life, ministered through and in the Christian brotherhood; and it is only as you become a member of a vigorous Christian community, that the power of sin can be finally broken. That is what we all find by experience. It is ever restoration to the Christian family that brings the power of the transformed life.

(1923)

Faith

How do I know that God is good? I don't.
I gamble like a man. I bet my life
Upon one side in life's great war. I must,
I can't stand out. I must take sides. The man
Who is a neutral in this fight is not
A man. He's bulk and body without breath,
Cold leg of lamb without mint sauce. A fool.
He makes me sick. Good Lord! Weak tea! Cold slops!
I want to live, live out, not wobble through
My life somehow, and then into the dark.
I must have God. this life's too dull without,
Too dull for aught but suicide. What's man
To live for else? I'd murder someone just
To see red blood. I'd drink myself blind drunk,
And see blue snakes if I could not look up
To see blue skies, and hear God speaking through
The silence of the stars. How is it proved?
It isn't proved, you fool, it can't be proved.
How can you prove a victory before
It's won? How can you prove a man who leads,
To be a leader worth the following,
Unless you follow to the death—and out
Beyond mere death, which is not anything
But Satan's lie upon eternal life?
Well—God's my leader, and I hold that He
Is good, and strong enough to work His plan
And purpose out to its appointed end.
I am no fool, I have my reasons for
This faith, but they are not the reasonings,
The coldly calculated formulae
Of thought divorced from feeling. They are true,

Too true for that. There's no such thing as thought
Which does not feel, if it be real thought
And not thought's ghost—all pale and sicklied o'er
With dead conventions—abstract truth—man's lie
Upon this living, loving, suff'ring Truth,
That pleads and pulses in my very veins,
The blue blood of all beauty, and the breath
Of life itself. I see what God has done,
What life in this world is. I see what you
See, this eternal struggle in the dark.
I see the foul disorders, and the filth
Of mind and soul, in which men, wallowing
Like swine, stamp on their brothers till they drown
In puddles of stale blood, and vomitings
Of their corruption. This life stinks in places,
 'Tis true, yet scent of roses and of hay
New mown comes stealing on the evening breeze,
And through the market's din, the bargaining
Of cheats, who make God's world a den of thieves,
The faithful kneeling by the Calvary
Of Christ.   I walk in crowded streets where men
And women, mad with lust, loose-lipped and lewd,
Go promenading down to hell's wide gates;
Yet have I looked into my mother's eyes,
And seen the light that never was on sea,
Or land, the light of Love, pure Love and true,
And on that Love I bet my life. I back
My mother 'gainst a whore when I believe
In God, and can a man do less or more?
I have to choose. I back the scent of life
Against its stink. That's what Faith works out at
Finally. I know not why the Evil,

I know not why the Good, both mysteries
Remain unsolved, and both insoluble.
I know that both are there, the battle set,
And I must fight on this side or on that.
I can't stand shiv'ring on the bank, I plunge
Head first. I bet my life on Beauty, Truth,
And Love, not abstract but incarnate Truth,
Not Beauty's passing shadow but its Self.
Its very self made flesh, Love realized.
I bet my life on Christ—Christ Crucified.
Behold your God! My soul cries out. He hangs,
Serenely patient in His agony,
And turns the soul of darkness into light.
I look upon that body, writhing, pierced
And torn with nails, and see the battlefields
Of time, the mangled dead, the gaping wounds,
The sweating, dazed survivors straggling back,
The widows worn and haggard, still dry-eyed,
Because their weight of sorrow will not lift
And let them weep; I see the ravished maid,
The honest mother in her shame; I see
All history pass by, and through it all
Still shines that face, the Christ Face, like a star
Which pierces drifting clouds, and tells the Truth.
They pass, but it remains and shines untouched,
A pledge of that great hour which surely comes
When storm winds sob to silence, fury spent
To silver silence, and the moon sails calm
And stately through the soundless seas of Peace.
So through the clouds of Calvary—there shines
His face, and I believe that Evil dies,
And Good lives on, loves on, and conquers all—
All War must end in Peace. These clouds are lies.

They cannot last. The blue sky is the Truth.
For God is Love. Such is my Faith, and such
My reasons for it, and I find them strong
Enough. And you? You want to argue? Well,
I can't. It is a choice. I choose the Christ.

(1919)

I Lost My Lord

I lost my Lord and sought Him long,
    I journeyed far, and cried
His name to every wand'ring wind,
    But still my Lord did hide.

I sought Him in the stately shrines,
    Where priest and people pray,
But empty went my spirit in
    And empty turned away.

I sought Him where the Doctors meet
    To turn deep questions o'er,
But every answer tempted me
    To ask one question more.

I sought Him where the hermit kneels
    And tells his beads of pain.
I found Him with some children here
    In this green Devon lane.

(1927)

part four

Getting Christ Out of the Churches

The cry that is often raised, that we are going to secularize religion, and take the clergy away from their "purely spiritual" work, is the cry of the man who dare not face the Cross. He wants to keep his Christ forever standing amid the lilies of the altar, with the sweet incense of worship rising round Him, a weekly refuge from a distraught and vulgar world. He wants to lock Christ up in the Tabernacle, to keep Him in the silence of the secret place, where men must go down on their knees before they touch Him. But Christ wants to come out into the marketplace, and down to the streets; He wants to eat and drink with prostitutes, to be mocked and spit upon by soldiers. He wants to call the dishonest trader from his office desk; to stand at his lathe beside the workman; and to bend with the mother over the washtub in the city of mean streets. He wants to go out into the world, that beauty and goodness and truth—beautiful things, good people, and true thought—may grow up around Him wherever He goes. You cannot keep Christ in your Churches; He will break them into pieces if you try. He will make for the streets in spite of you, and go on with His own work; defying dead authorities, breaking down tyrannies, destroying shams, declaring open war against a Godless world.

(1923)

Herd Church

To [many Christians,] modern problems, politics, industry, economics, are purely secular, they have nothing to do with pure religion and the simple Gospel of eternal life. They do not want them brought into Church or into prayers; they want to have one place upon earth where they will never hear a word about war, wages, housing, unemployment, and all the rest of it.

They have my sympathy, but it will not do. It is only another way of evading responsibility, and refusing the cal of God to come up higher. The religion they want would not be religion at all; it would be a species of entertainment and relaxation. That is what much of our religion is, a substitute for the picture show. We come because we like the service, the music, the preacher, the atmosphere of the place. It soothes us with its sanctity and enables us to sleep and dream.

But this is not religion. These churches are not churches, they are little herds of like-minded people snuggling up to one another for comfort and warmth as animals do. They have their yelps and yowls just like the beasts, their party shibboleths, and common cant, but the life of God is not in them—the mark of the beast is upon them. Their unity does not depend upon their response to the call of God, but upon the primitive instinct of the herd, whereby birds of a feather flock together—Protestant birds and Catholic birds, High Church, Low Church, Free Church birds, but all birds obeying an impulse, not men that hear a call. The world is full of flocks and herds, but what it needs is a society, and a society only exists as every member of it is consciously and intelligently responsive to the call of a higher purpose, and obedient to a higher Will.

(1925)

Community Christians

You can only learn to love God as you learn to love your fellow men. St. John is very blunt about it in his Epistle, and says that if you profess to love God and do not love the Brethren, and he means by that primarily your fellow Christians, you are a liar. "We know that we have passed from death unto life because we love the brethren" (1 John 3:14). The acid test of religious reality is power to produce community life. You cannot have unorganized Christianity, there never has been such a thing, and never will be.

It was upon a company that the Spirit descended at Pentecost, and the first result of that descent was to drive the company out to form a community, which was so filled with the New Life, that they attempted the impossible, and tried to hold all things in common, abolishing private property. And although that sublime and premature effort failed, yet wherever the new life went, there sprang up communities having within them a new power of social unity.

New committees, new rules of life, new red hot propaganda sprang up everywhere. There were conferences at Jerusalem, laws for the Gentile Churches, fiery tracts from St. Peter and St. Paul. There were dissensions and divisions, a wretched sense that the divisions were all wrong, and tremendous efforts to attain to unity. There were all the marks of this dreadful organized Christianity that we have today within twenty years of the Crucifixion. There were Priests that went wrong, Judas was the first, and saints that turned out sinners, as in Corinth. But there never was any doubt that Christian Life was a community life, and that the Will of God was the Unity of mankind in Him. Moreover, the idea that somehow or other Christian men and women should hold their goods in common has never ceased to haunt the minds of those who found new Life in Him. They have never been really satisfied with the idea of absolute property. It has always been foreign to their whole conception of life. If Christian Communism was beyond them, at any rate everyone was to look upon what he possessed as a trust from God to be used for the welfare of the Brethren.

Every fresh revival of the New Life was accompanied by some protest against the system that left untouched extremes of wealth and poverty. Monasticism was an attempt to realize the perfect Christian Community, a life in which men could work and earn their bread to the glory of God, and for the love of the Brethren.

The score of heretical sects that arose in the middle ages, such as the Waldenses, the Albigenses, the Beghards, the Brethren of the Common Lot, were all efforts to maintain a new order of Social life, in which men might live as Brethren, working for the common good. They failed, but then the whole of Christianity is one long record of failure, it will never succeed until we all are one in Him. All Life is a failure, a reaching beyond what we can grasp, an attempt to achieve the apparently impossible—a Birth, a Crucifixion, but a Resurrection, and an Ascension.

They may have failed but apparently whenever Christ touches men they are stirred to try again. *This dream of a new and better social order is as much an essential part of the Christian life as prayer, and communion with God.* Like them it has had its ups and downs. It has been crucified with the life of prayer, all down the ages, but it has risen again to challenge the world, and set men striving after better things. Men cannot meet with Christ in prayer, and remain content to shut Him out of the places where they earn their bread, and live their common life. The Christian life of devotion and the Christian ideal of community life are inextricably bound up with one another, and stand or fall together.

Right at the heart of the Christian Devotional Life there has always been the Breaking of Bread, and when that Sacrament is divorced from the dream of a Christian Social order, it is deprived of its true significance. If we cut off that Bread which is His Body from all connection with our daily bread, and the means whereby we earn it; if we declare that He is present in the Bread of the Sanctuary, but absent from the bread of the street—we deny the Truth of the Incarnation. We deny that "The WORD became flesh—through Whom, all things were made, and without Whom nothing was made that was made" (John 1:3). The Christian Faith demands that we acknowledge a real presence of Christ in the Bread upon the Altar before it is broken and consecrated. We cannot deny that presence without denying that Christ is the Word of God through Whom the worlds were made, and in Whom they find their meaning.

It is this presence of Christ in common bread and His concern with the way we earn it that the world denies emphatically. They are quite willing, the men of the world, to allow that we may find Him, by an act of faith, in that Bread upon the altar, so long as we do not drag Him into the bread of the common street. No body worries about Christ so long as He can be kept shut up in Churches, He is quite safe there, but there is always trouble if you try to let Him out.

The late Bishop of Zanzibar told a great body of Christians that they must "fight for their tabernacles."[1] If that means, as on his lips it did, that we must stand firm for the Truth that the tabernacle of God is with men; if it means that the gates of the little shrine, where men and women come to worship the Christ, are set open wide that He may go out to seek and to save, it is well; but if it means that we confine Him, and seek Him only there among the lilies, it is a dangerous deceit indeed. To confine Christ is to crucify Him. Christ can be crucified in Churches, and the clouds of incense may but serve to hide the sorrow in His eyes.

The first necessity of the Christian Faith is to accept Christ as the meaning of all things, and to see all things only as they are seen in Him. In Him is life, all life, even the life of common bread. Through Him were all those powers given by which men earn and eat today. Through Him were made the monster ships by which the grain is brought to us, through raging storms across three thousand miles of sea. The loaf we break, the wafer that we consecrate, was born, may be, in the golden miles of Canada, America, or the Argentine, and is gathered for us from the ends of the earth, for all the world is one in bread. If it were not for that new worldwide unity in bread, millions who live today would have to die, they could not keep themselves. It is a due development of man. It was the sowing and reaping of a harvest that first turned the nomad hunter, who ranged the forest for his food, like a lion slaying for his cubs, into the settled social tiller of the soil. There never was a harvest until men learned in some measure to work as one. Bread has always been an artificial thing, and is now as artificial as Quaker oats. The throb of the screws, the flames of the blast furnace, the gloom and darkness of the mine, are all in our daily bread. As it lies there upon the altar it is the oblation of our whole intricate and many-sided life, the sweat, and the blood, and the brain of man are in it, men for whom Christ died. The lives of toiling

---

1. Studdert Kennedy is apparently referring to "Our Present Duty," the concluding speech of the 1923 Anglo-Catholic Conference given by Frank Weston (1871–1924), then Bishop of Zanzibar. (The speech has been electronically archived by Project Canterbury at: http://anglicanhistory.org/weston/weston2.html.) Studdert Kennedy attended the conference, and delivered the sermon reprinted in this volume as "Making the World Less Mad, Bad, Inhuman, and Unkind."

million go to make the pure white wafer or the little piece of Bread we hold up before the Lord before the Consecration act, and therefore Christ is in it, or more accurately it is in Christ, and has no meaning apart from Him. *The whole of our Social Order is in the Bread of the Altar which waits the act of the Christian community who lift it up to God.*

We cannot emphasize too strongly the fact that it is the Christian Community that consecrates, it is a corporate act, in which every member of the Church takes part. It is not consecrated by the priest for the people of God, but by the people, the Church which is His Body, through the Priest the Church ordains. It is a corporate act, and that is its very essence. Here then is the Christian community seeking by God's grace to consecrate the Social Order of common life, that it may become the Sacrament of His Presence among men.

What then is the Relation between the presence of Christ in common bread, which the doctrine of the Incarnation compels us to acknowledge, and that Presence which our Christian experience compels us to call, with reverence and gratitude, The Real Presence of the Lord in the Sacrament?

The Presence of Christ in the Bread, and in the present Social Order which is the meaning of the Bread, is *the presence of the Crucified.* Can we doubt that? There never was a time when there was not sin and sorrow in Bread, and there is sin and sorrow in it now—such sin and such sorrow, the sin of slums and the sorrow of the darkened lives that cry for light from the underworld. All sorrow is His sorrow, and, mystery of mysteries, all sin is His sin, who was made sin for us. When, therefore, the Christian community, through its own appointed Priest, holds up the Bread, they hold up the Crucified Lord. They shew forth His death till He come. They identify themselves with Him in His age-long agony of Redemption, and confess with sorrow their part in the sin that mars the winning of our Daily Bread. The lust of power, the faithless fear, the hatred, and the bestial greed which break the worldwide unity of Bread, and make what God wills to be a beautiful and balanced order into a cruel, ugly chaos.

No man can eat alone. The very act of eating brings us into touch with our brothers and with Him. He seeks, it is His eternal nature to seek us in the breaking of all Bread. But the shame of our common life is that we eat and drink not discerning the Lord's Body. We snatch at His gifts like lower animals, seeing only with sensual sight, seeing in the Bread we eat neither the Brethren nor the Christ, but ourselves, and our own lust of life. Thus it is that we eat and drink damnation to our souls, and the Bread of Blessing is turned into a curse. There is the snarl as of dogs in our cities, and the cry of the child in our streets. He seeks us in the common bread, but cannot find us. He could not cease to seek us. If for one millionth part of a second His everlasting search should cease, the stars would fall upon us, and the hills would crumble into dust. For the Life of the Universe is the Love of God. it needs no Church nor Sacrament to secure God's Love for us, or to make it certain that the Eternal Shepherd will come seeking His sheep. That is His Nature, and He could not be false to Himself.

That is the central Truth of the New Testament Revelation. God is not the Eastern Monarch on His Throne waiting for the world to come to Him, He is an ever-active Spirit of Eternally living Love, seeking to Create and to Redeem. God seeks, but before we can be found of Him, there must be from us response. However faint and poor it be, yet there must be some answer to His call. While we are yet a great way off—He runs—but we must first have said, "I will arise and go" (Luke 15:18). The sin that turns the blessing of our Daily Bread, and the means whereby we earn it, into a curse, is that we earn and eat it without a thought of Him. As we have seen, he is seeking us through this New Environment which He has created, the worldwide economic unity, which He has made to be the body of the Brotherhood of man, but we do not answer, we see nothing in it but increased power to gratify our lusts, and so the Body is broken, wounded, torn, it bleeds on battlefields, is diseased in slums, it is covered with festering sores of vulgar luxury, it groans with hunger, and is rent by strife.

This is His Body, in more than a symbolic sense, and it is in the common bread of the oblation before the consecration act. We make too little of the offertory, it is not understood. Money has degraded it, and it has become the collection to pay the verger to stoke the furnace and keep our feet warm while we pray. But in truth we ought to offer up our money too, remembering that money is human flesh and blood, a measure of human energy, physical, mental, and moral in the last analysis. It is not an evil or a sordid thing in itself. There is no greater blessing, nor anything more beautiful than a sound and stable monetary system. The complex network of our modern finance ought to be the healthy nervous system of the Body of Mankind. Contempt of and misuse of money is contempt of and misuse of man, and therefore of God. The sordidness of money is in ourselves, and the kind of shame we have about it is a sign of something wrong deep down within our private and our public life. We always come down to money, we do not lift it up. That is why our very charity has become a curse, a sop to our uneasy consciences, a means whereby we protect ourselves from pain. The offertory has become a joke, and the joke is the sign of the nasty trivial nature of our social life. We snigger about our offering. The perfunctory offering of alms that cost us nothing is a sign of the divorce of the Sacrament from the daily life. It is time we ended that. The alms and the oblations are one—two sides of one thing—which is the Body of the Lord. God is seeking us through money, its power ought to be the power of His Love, and never until it is to us the Sacrament of our unity in Him, can the world find Peace. The misuse of money is the deepest root of War.

In our common life Christ seeks us through Bread and Money, which is another form of Bread, and men do not respond, and therefore He is crucified afresh. *But in the Sacrament we do respond.* The Christian community meets to break the Bread and offer alms in memory and for Love of Him. They are met to plead His Sacrifice, and to identify themselves with His suffering in and for the world. They join in a Confession of our common sin, their part in it, and their sorrow for it. That is the meaning of the General Confession. Men have got it all mixed up with their private confessions and, having but a feeble sense of their own sinfulness, have thought that the solemn words "the burden of them is intolerable" ought to be cut out, because they could not say them with sincerity. But it is not the fact that you lied or evil lusted last week that is intolerable, though it ought to be, it is the procession of prostitutes, the squalor of Bethnal Green, the anguish of children and the torture of women, it is the sin of the world that is intolerable. If you have not begun to feel that, you have not begun to know Him.

Is it not intolerable? O, God in heaven, if you do not know it—go and see. If you still think life is as tidy and neat as your Sunday altar, looking so nice with its lilies and cross, go and see—you must know the tragedy of the altar before you find its Peace. The man whose eyes God has opened sees Christ crucified in the world, and enters into the fellowship of His sufferings, becoming a sin-bearer for His sake.

That is what it means to be a member of a Church. "I fill up in my body what is lacking of the sufferings of Christ for His body's sake, which is the Church" (Colossians 1:24). This is at once the joy and sorrow of the Christian life.

> Gladness be with thee helper of the World,
> Methinks this is the authentic sign and seal
> Of Godship that it ever waxes glad,
> And more glad, until gladness blossoms, bursts
> Into a rage to suffer for mankind
> And recommence at sorrow.[2]

Whenever the Church has been alive with His life it has felt this burden of the world's sin, and this is the very Sacrament of sin-bearing, in which the Brethren acknowledge their part in the world sin, and identify themselves with the suffering of the world's Savior. In it they take the common bread in which they perceive the presence of the Crucified and lift it up, lift it up by a corporate act of honest Love, seeking in it not themselves, but Him, not their will but His Will, not their gain but His glory. *And because they lift it up, and every time it is so lifted up, He can and does take it and use it, as He can use no other Bread,* use it to become in fact His Body, the instrument of a Presence which is a real Presence in a unique and special sense, because it is the Presence of the Christ not merely Born and Crucified as He is in all the world, but Risen and Ascended too—*the Presence of the Christ with Power.* That is why this corporate act, whereby the Bread is lifted up, has ever been the sum and center of the Christian worship, in which they have always found and find the meaning of their lives. In it they pledge themselves, and are endowed with power, to go out and suffer with Him, bearing in Love and striving in prayer against the sin of the world, that men may be led to lift up all bread, and all the means whereby they earn it, seeking in them not themselves but Him, seeking first the Kingdom of God and His Righteousness that all things may be added to them, that so they may eat and drink salvation to their souls and bodies and, living with eyes unveiled, in a Sacramental universe, may everywhere discern the Body of the Lord.

---

2. Browning, *Balaustion's Adventure*, 121.

But where worship is divorced from work, and God's Presence in the Sanctuary from His presence in the street, we run the deadly danger of localizing God, and our Sacraments may be turned into sin. If the Sacrament is to take its proper place as the central act of Christian Worship, Christian men must learn to see in it the whole purpose and meaning of their daily work, and that means that the whole multitude of gifts and powers whereby we earn and eat must be lifted up from the level of use for private profit to the level of use for the Glory of God. Until that is done the Church must continue to suffer and to strive, bearing the sin of the world, she must continue "to show forth the Lord's Death, till He come" (1 Corinthians 11:26), come with the Power of the Risen and Ascended Christ to all men, as He comes to the faithful soul who eats His Body and drinks His Blood.

(1925)

Bread, Work, and Love

Are you afraid of poverty? I am. I have been all my life. I think that if we are honest with ourselves, most of us would confess to a fear of poverty. It is, next perhaps to the fear of death, the most prevalent and powerful of all the fears that haunt and hurt the lives of men and women in the world. Fear has always played a leading part in human life, and the fear of poverty is an ancient enemy. All down the ages men have struggled against it, and human history may well be viewed as the story of that struggle, a tragic and terrible story. That, stated in its simplest and most elementary terms, is what is now called the Materialist Conception of History. Those who take this view of life teach us that if we want to understand ourselves, and the changing history of man, his habits, customs, laws, institutions, his constant wars and his short, uncertain periods of peace, we must go right down to their roots, and there we shall always find one dominant and determining influence at work—daily bread, and the fear of being in want of it, the fear of poverty. It is, they say, the economic factor that is always final. Life, when you strip off the trimmings, is nothing but the struggle for bread.

Now, that seems to be a mean and sordid view of life, and we are tempted to turn from it, and dismiss it with disgust. And yet, if we are honest and courageous in our thought, we cannot help acknowledging that there is much truth in it, and without honesty and courage there is no hope of salvation either for our bodies or our souls. To quote a saying of Professor Huxley's: "There is no alleviation to the sufferings of mankind except through veracity of thought and of action, and the resolute facing of the world as it is when the garment of make-believe with which pious hands have hidden its uglier features has been stripped off."[3] The struggle for bread is a fact, and we must face it and face it naked, stripped of the garments of make-believe that we too often weave in our own minds to hide it.

When we think of ourselves, you and I, and of our daily lives, there is nothing which in reality influences our thoughts and actions so much as the way in which we earn our living, struggle for our daily bread. For many, perhaps for most of us here, the struggle is in part disguised. We are not conscious of struggling with or against anybody else. We apply

3. Huxley, "Autobiography," 16.

for, or are chosen for, a job, and we do it. We may do it for the most part without thinking of what we are to get out of it. It is our duty, and we may find much joy in it. We are paid for our work, but we do not work only, or even mainly, for our pay. We do not consciously struggle for bread. And yet there are facts behind our consciousness. If we lost the job, if the pay were delayed or cut in half, we should become vividly conscious of it. We should be, as we say, brought up against realities. We should become conscious of daily bread.

You applied for and got that job, and you were very pleased. You felt at peace with all the world. You got it. Somebody else did not. But he got something else. Perhaps he did. Perhaps he did not. He may be searching still. You were not conscious of cutting the other out. You did not want to cut him out. But you did. There was a struggle for bread. Sometimes even in these days you can see the struggle naked and without disguise, if you go and stand outside the dock gates at Liverpool and see the foreman come out to get men for a ship's unloading. There is a crowd of men always. More men than jobs. God only knows upon what principle or system they are selected. But watch the faces of those who are not successful, and you see the struggle for bread, naked, and in its nakedness pitiful. Naked or decently disguised, the struggle goes on. It always has gone on. All over the world. Throughout all time. Man with man, tribe with tribe, class with class, nation with nation, there always has been, there is now the struggle for bread, and behind it driving, goading, wounding, the fear of poverty . . .

How are we to reconcile this age-long and worldwide struggle for bread with the picture of our Father's love which is the essence of the Gospel of Jesus Christ? Is the world a home or a battlefield? Is life a struggle or a gift? Is the Gospel picture itself just a golden garment of make-believe with which pious hands have sought to hide the ugliness of the struggle for bread? Must we, if we be honest, tear that garment away and be content to look upon the naked fact? That is a question which, in a thousand different forms, presents itself to Christians of today. Can we face the facts of life and still believe in our Father? God does not give us bread. We have to struggle for it. We must either earn it or steal it; there is no third alternative. If a man will not work, neither shall he eat. That is the law of life. Those who strive to evade that law are thieves. There are the sick, the aged and infirm, and the children, and to them we feel it is right that we should give their daily bread.

But there is something degraded and degrading about giving bread to those who ought to earn it. There is something wrong about begging. Giving away money, or bread for which money stands, is one of the most difficult and dangerous things in the world to do. Even when a brother begs for what he ought to earn, a man might very well hesitate for fear of doing harm. There are men and women we would like to help, and we know they need it, but we dare not offer to give. They are what we call proud. They have a strong conviction that they ought to earn. God does not give us bread. There never was a harvest on the earth until men learned to work together. Men may hunt and kill alone, but they must sow and reap together. It was work that taught us love. That is the other side of the picture. Men have learned to love each other by working together for bread. There is, and there has been, a struggle for bread, but the struggle never made the bread; it has always meant work, and work is the author of love. Husband and wife were first of all workmates. They came together to work for their children, and by working learned to love. The family was a working unit, and is a working unit still.

For thousands of years it was the chief working unit. All labor centered round the home, and the only love there was on earth was found within the home. Men loved their own kith and kin, but outside that narrow circle the world was full of enemies. But slowly the working unit widened as men learned to trade with and work with their neighbors. Then neighbor-love began. It grew very slowly. Men were suspicious of one another and afraid. They distrusted strangers and did not willingly combine. Often they fought one another bitterly before they settled down to work together. But always as they worked together love and friendship grew. And as the working unit widened, wealth increased and the harvest was more plentiful. For the more men work together, the richer the harvest grows. Love is the real source of wealth. It has not been a smooth and easy process this; it has been checked and broken a million times. It is checked and broken still. The old hatreds and suspicions, the old fear of strangers and dislike of foreigners, persist and constantly tend to break the wider working unit up or prevent us making it. But in spite of apparently insurmountable obstacles the majestic process persists. The working unit widens, and with it grows the sweep of neighbor-love. God's plan and purpose for the world are being wrought out through work. He has taken a great step forward in these latter days. The working unit has, with almost dramatic suddenness, widened out until, for the first time in history, it includes the entire world . . .

God has spoken and decreed that from henceforth all men and women, east, west, north, and south, over the length and breadth of the earth, should be workmates, and by working together learn to love. It is in some ways a terrible decree, because we are not ready for it. Our old habits and inherited ways of thought die hard. We still want to be independent and work away at our own little plot. We will try to conquer one another, and pretend that we do not need one another. We break out into squabbles and fights, and the feet of warring armies trample down the golden corn and lay waste the smiling summer lands. We still are savages at heart, suspicious, mistrustful, stubborn, and very much afraid. We wave our flags and beat our drums, and threaten one another at home and abroad. We organize ourselves into independent cliques, classes, and nations, and stand up for our rights. On the surface it would seem as though God's decree were causing more hatred than love. But all this fretting and fuming is vain. God has spoken, and we shall be one. Slowly and painfully, but surely too, we are learning our lesson, the lesson of universal love. We may, like petulant children, beat with our puny fists against the majestic arms of God, but they close, and keep on closing without haste and without hesitancy.

Those who hold to the materialist conception of history and see at the root of all man's life in the struggle for bread are, I believe, right in their facts but wrong in the meaning they give to the facts. They do not overrate the importance of the economic factor in human evolution, but they do misinterpret it. They do not understand the meaning of bread. They think of bread in terms of struggle, whereas it should be thought of in terms of work, and then of love. They think bread means war, when in truth it means peace. This they do because they fall into the special pitfalls which the theory of evolution always contains for careless thinkers. The study of human evolution leads men to concentrate their minds upon the origins of man. They turn back to the past and saturate their thought with pictures of primitive life, primitive habits, customs, and laws. The past tends to become an obsession with them, and they try to explain the present in the light of their obsession. But "if the light that is in thee be darkness, how great is that darkness" (Matthew 6:23).

Used in this way, the historical method becomes a blight and a curse to human thought. It keeps us with our mind's eyes fixed constantly upon the past. It forces us to go upon our way looking where we are coming from. That is fatal. It leads to paralysis of the will. We cannot live, any more than we can walk, looking backwards all the time. We must not keep our mind's eye in the back of our heads. It is not the past which explains the present, it is the present which explains the past. You cannot explain a man by studying a baby; you can only explain a baby by studying a man. This might seem, too, an obvious error, but it is so common as to be almost universal, and it is impossible to overestimate the evil that it does. A great part of the conflict between religion and science is due to the instinctive rebellion of religion against the misuse of the historical method, which keeps the present and the future bound helpless to the past, and seeks to explain and evaluate the higher in terms of the lower, mind in terms of matter, life in terms of mechanism, freedom in terms of necessity, the human in terms of the animal. It is not against Darwinian facts that religion protests, but against Darwinian values or, it would be more accurate to say, pseudo-Darwinian values. Darwin himself was too great a scientist to pretend that he dealt with values at all.

The materialist conception of history, which seeks to explain life in terms of hunger and the struggle for bread, is a particular and pernicious instance of this fallacy. Men are taught to explain the present in terms of the past. Look back, and you see a struggle between tribes, nations, and classes, a constant struggle for bread. The economic factor always has been final and decisive, therefore the struggle must continue and the economic facts always will be final and decisive. The minds of men are concentrated upon and hypnotized by the past, and the blackest features of the past, and thus their faith in the future is paralyzed and perverted. Against this ruinous disease of the mind and spirit, Christian thought protests. It seeks to explain bread in terms of man, and not man in terms of bread. It thinks of human evolution always as an ascension.

That figure of the Perfect Man with wounded hands outstretched to bless ascending to His glory dominates and controls our view of evolution. The hands are wounded, for the struggle was a reality; but they will not always bleed, because love triumphs in the end. He is the true meaning of bread. Bread means work, and work means love, the true love which began and begins at home, but ends by filling all the world and making all mankind a family. It is with our eyes fixed upon the future that we pray, "Give us this day our daily bread"—not merely that we may be fed, but that the Father's name may be hallowed, His Kingdom come, His will be done on earth as it is in heaven. It is with our eyes fixed upon the future that we stretch out our hands and take into them a piece of Bread, which, because in loving fellowship we have offered it up as all bread should be offered up, means Christ, and helps to make that meaning part of the very substance of our souls. For the Kingdom of God comes not by sword or strife, nor yet by sitting still, but as men learn to will and work together in ever-widening fellowship and in the spirit of Him who came not to be ministered unto, but to minister—who is the true meaning of Bread.

(1928)

False Charity

It is impossible to read our Lord's life without gaining the impression that this problem of the people's bread was for ever on His mind. He was no dreamer, He was the greatest realist that ever lived, the most practical person that ever set His hand to any great work in the world; and He knew well, as the Father knows, that we have need of these things. The order of the temptations bears this out. St. Matthew and St. Luke differ in the order of the second and third, but they agree about the first, it was the problem of Bread. To suppose that it was merely the temptation to use His powers to help Himself, is to wrench the whole thing out of context. I am driven inevitably, as I strive, in the light of the gospels, to enter into the mind of my Lord as He sits there in the wilderness, planning, thinking, praying, beset on every side with problems which called for the uttermost thought His finely-trained and beautifully-balanced intellect could give to them, as well as for all the resources of His infinite Love—I am driven to the conclusion that He was thinking out the problem of the people's Bread.

In the dim gray light of the morning, when the rocks and boulders round Him, by natural association of ideas, grew to look like loaves of bread, He was surrounded by an innumerable phantom host of the world's hungry people; for our Lord was never so close to the crowd as He was when He was away from it. He never dreamed of that futile kind of pietism which endeavors to attain communion with God, divorced from His world; He only went away from the world in order to get closer to it. And there, in the dawning light, I believe, He saw stretching out into an endless sea, the millions and millions of the world's hungry men and women; mothers clasping puny children to their shriveled breasts; fathers tearing open their ragged shirts to show the bones beneath their skin, and stretching out lean and skinny arms in supplication; while all around Him, like the moan of the sea, there went up the cry, "Bread! Bread! For God's sake give us Bread. If Thou be the Son of God, command these stones that they may become Bread." And He, seeing the multitude, had compassion upon them, for divers of them had come from afar, so very far, so many weary miles, through so many bitter disappointments, with broken boot soles flapping on their feet, along miles and miles of dirty pavement, miles and miles of filthy streets. Bread, Bread, for God's sake give us Bread! It was the supreme temptation of his life, and how was he to meet it? He felt within Him the pulse of extraordinary powers. He knew that, in some strangely unique and wonderful way, He was the Man, the Son of God; and surely here was the most pressing and crying problem, here was the greatest need, to feed the people. Was it any use giving them God, unless He gave them bread? How could they worship, unless they were fed? Was it not mockery to talk to them of the Father's Love, unless He met their human need? And yet, and yet, He knew man, and needed not that any should tell Him what was in man. He knew that bread alone could never satisfy the hunger they felt ...

Christ's intellectual balance was perfect; and the eagle eye of His Spiritual understanding pierced to the very heart and center of the problem, and perceived the truth which we are painfully and slowly learning—that to feed man is to starve him; he must strive to feed himself. If the man is blest who gives without receiving, the man is cursed who receives without giving. It is our failure to perceive that, which has made Christian charity stink in the nostrils of honest men, and has caused it to become the reproach, rather than the glory and the crown, of His Church. We have been so desperately anxious to secure a moral gymnasium in which the righteous rich could exercise their souls—not by selling all and giving to the poor, but by giving away what they do not really want—that we have failed to remember the effect of their patronage upon the poor. The strong have reserved to themselves the blessing of giving without receiving, and have heaped upon the poor the curse of receiving without giving. By Charity alone can the world be saved, but this is not charity. It tends to obscure rather than to realize the Brotherhood of Man; it is—and thank God we increasingly feel it to be—a put-off, a refusal of the way of the Cross. It is not Christianity; it is an excuse for not being Christian.

We can never feed the people, we can never even satisfy the hunger of their bodies, until bread becomes more than bread and we learn to see it as God sees it, as *the sacrament of the unity of mankind in Him.* The Sacrament of the Altar reveals the truth about Life. In the Blessed Sacrament we reach the Reality of Bread, and that reality is God, who is Love. Christ is the true Bread, *alethinos artos,* the true meaning of all Bread. We there take Bread and consecrate it by a corporate act, and God's answer to that act is the gift of Himself, so that becoming one with Him we are made one with one another. Thus Bread which is the root cause of our divisions becomes in Him the root cause of our unity, and in the Sacrament we live the true life, live it in the sanctuary, that we may learn to live it in the street. The truly social life is the sacramental life, which consecrates to the service of God our daily bread and every means by which we win it. If we fail to perceive the social meaning of the Sacrament, we destroy its whole nature and meaning, and that is where we have failed.

(1923)

Connecting Sacrament and Society

Material poverty is an evil, not because it necessitates simplicity of life; it does not, in itself, necessitate that, it does not produce automatic poverty of spirit, it more frequently produces covetousness and envy; it is an evil, because it is the sacrament of sin, "the outward and visible sign of an inward and spiritual disgrace," which is the best description of the great multitude of mean streets that I have ever heard. Many of those who are most emphatic upon the Sacramental Presence of Our Lord in the Bread which is His Body and the Wine which is His Blood, never seem to have thought out or pondered over the connection between that Presence, and the presence of God in His whole creation. That neglect is a disaster to religion. We must be quite clear, that we go to find Him there, so that we may the better find Him everywhere; that the Sacrament leads us, not to a localization, but to a deeper sense of the Omnipresence, of God.

The connection between the Sacrament and what is loosely called the "Sacramental Principle" of the universe, needs to be perceived and firmly held. He makes Himself known to us in the Breaking of the Bread, that He may more truly and consciously be the honored guest at every meal, and the most living partner in every enterprise whereby we earn our daily bread. That is why the Collection at the Sacrament becomes the Offertory, and the "alms" are one with the "oblations"—our money being united with the Bread and the Wine, that through His Presence in the Bread and Wine He may consecrate our money to be a spiritual bond of Peace throughout the world. To neglect or put in the background this essential connection, is to make sacramental worship quite definitely idolatrous. If Holy Communion does not lead to honest commerce, it fails of its fruit, and "by their fruits ye shall know them." Commerce is communion, and it must either be Holy Communion, or a cursed counterfeit, which leads not to life but to death. Once and for all let us remember, that the sweep of the Sacrament is as wide as the world. If our faith in the real presence of our Lord in the consecrated Bread upon the altar, does not really lead us to perceive His real presence in all bread—if it amounts to anything like the localization of the Presence of God—our sacramental worship has in itself the nature of sin, for sin, at its root, is the denial of the Omnipresence of God. If our love of God's house does not consecrate for us all houses and all homes, if it tends to separate the sanctuary and the street, then our religious observances are literally blasphemous.

In an extraordinarily beautiful passage of his *Confessio Fidei*, Dean Inge confessed: "At times the moving waters at their priest-task seem to have the power which Euripides ascribes to them, of washing away all human ills. At times the mountains speak plainly of the Ancient of Days who was before they began to be; but too often Nature only echoes back my own moods, and seems dark or bright because I am sad or merry. The sweet sanctities of home life, and especially the innocence and affection of young children, more often bring me near to the felt Presence of God."[4]

But, in the Name of God, how are those sweet sanctities to be obtained and preserved, and how is childhood's robe of innocence to be kept white, while many people are housed as they are? Crowded on the top of one another, living under conditions where decent privacy is impossible, playing in streets where evil besets them at every turn. Unless the felt presence of God in your own children makes you long that others too may have that means of grace, it is not God you feel, but a mere creature of your own diseased and super-intellectualized imagination.

If the Church is to be a Church indeed, and not a mere farce—and a peculiarly pernicious farce, a game of sentimental make-believe—she must be filled to overflowing with the fire of the ancient prophets for social righteousness, with the wrath and love of the Christ. Her very existence is bound up with, and dependent upon, an effort, an effort which does not count the cost in any terms of pain, to Christianize the social order under which we live. If I had the tongue of men and of angels, I would use it to plead with the Christian Church, and more especially with those sections of it which profess and call themselves Catholic, to face the real meaning and hope of their calling, and get to grips, as Our Lord from the very beginning got to grips, with the problem of Bread. Unless they do that, no unbroken Apostolic Succession can make their sacraments valid, and no wealth of gorgeous ritual can save their souls alive; for sacrament and ritual alike are mockery, unless they mean the consecration of all things in heaven and earth to the service of the Everlasting God.

---

4. Inge, "Confessio Fidei," 15.

Making the World Less Mad, Bad, Inhuman, and Unkind

"This is a true saying, and worthy of all men to be received, that Christ Jesus came into the world to save sinners" (1 Timothy 1:15). That, I take it, is a point upon which we are all agreed. The Church of Christ exists to save sinners. It is not, and ought never to be considered as an end in itself; it is a means to an end, and that end is the salvation of souls.

If that be granted, then I think that we might take one further step, and assume that whatever else the great word Salvation means—and it would be impossible short of the Beatific Vision to exhaust its meaning—whatever else it means, it does mean and must begin with the unification of the personality. The process of salvation must begin by giving to the human soul some measure of internal unity and peace.

Descartes said that all doubt must end with the fact of his own existence, but, in very truth, that is where all the deepest doubt begins. To say "I am as certain of this as I am of my own existence" is not to claim a very high standard of certainty for a large number of men, for the existence of any settled, united and reliable self is the very thing of which they have no present assurance—no right to be certain—and is exactly what their conduct would lead us to doubt very seriously indeed.

We have to save souls from the world, the flesh, and the devil, and it is not for nothing that the world comes first, because it is through the world that the flesh and the devil make their main attack. The flesh and the devil change not, but the world is ever changing, and in these latter days it has changed rapidly, and has become a patchwork quilt, a tragic and terrible patchwork quilt, stained here and there with blood and tears. It has become an infinitely complex environment which tears and divides human souls. That is ever its way of attack—it divides and so destroys. It damns by division.

We cannot save men from the world by the method of retreat from it—permanent retreat. The practice of periodic retreat is of enormous value, and ought to be an important part of your method of evangelization. But however valuable temporary retreat may be, permanent retreat for most men and women is impossible. They must live in the world and yet not be of it. They must earn their daily bread, and they can only earn it by entering into, and becoming part of, the vast and complex industrial and commercial system by which we all live; they must be members of a nation, they must be citizens of a city, they must be in business, they must work in factories or on farms. They must live in those relationships to other human beings, and, moreover, those relationships must be a part, and a very important part, of them—each one of them. A man is, and ought to be, something more than the sum of his human relationships, and yet his human relationships are and must remain an essential part of himself. An Indian native is more than his caste, and yet his caste is a very important part of him, and is the part which he commonly finds it impossible to reconcile with Christ.

The social system lives in the individual soul. It cannot be too strongly stated that our main business is, always must be, with the individual soul, but it is that main business, once we get to grips with it, which compels us to tackle the question of the social environment, because the social environment lives in the individual and produces in him a conflict with Christ. A man finds himself, as a member of a nation, doing things, and allowing things to be done in his name, which as a Christian individual he revolts from and detests. He finds himself as a citizen of a city obliged to tolerate slums, which are the outward and visible sign of an inward and spiritual disgrace. He finds himself as a business man obliged to accept standards of morality, standards of honesty and uprightness, and ideals of work and its meaning, which as a man he would regard as beneath contempt. He finds that as a worker in a factory he has to submit to conditions and tolerate abuses which his Christian soul abhors. He is, in fact, in a state of internal conflict, and it is largely a conflict of despair; he sees no way out.

Now, I submit that Salvation must begin if not by putting an end to that conflict, certainly by making it a conflict of faith and hope, and no longer a conflict of despair. If he cannot find the right way out in Christ, he will find the wrong way out somewhere else. Nature abhors a conflict of despair as she abhors a vacuum, and she has her own ways out, and one of these ways almost every soul with whom we have to deal finds for himself. All the ways of nature apart from Grace are dangerous, and lead in the end to the disintegration of the personality, which is spiritual death, and which in extreme cases ends in madness.

The first method is that of disassociation. The attempt to live in watertight compartments and settle down to being a permanently divided self—with Dr. Jekyll in the drawing room and Mr. Hyde in the study, and the Prince of Darkness in the cellar.

A very large number of the people who attend our services and partake of the Sacraments are disassociated personalities. They are one person on Sunday and another on Monday. They have one mind for the sanctuary and another for the street. They have one conscience for the Church and another for the cotton factory. Their worship conflicts with their work, but they will not acknowledge the conflict. I want to press home what seems to me to be obvious, that while this unfaced conflict exists, the soul is not on the road to salvation, and while we leave it in that state we are not doing our job. There is a kind of piety about which one would say what the schoolmen said about concupiscence—*rationem habet peccati,* it has of itself the nature of sin. It is this piety of the disassociated personality. The church warden who owns slum property; the devout layman who will not face the problem of war; the earnest brewer who presents a chalice to the church in the suburbs bought with the profits of the drink shops in the town; the Christian workman who helps the vicar, and perhaps serves at Mass, and leaves his mates to strive for an improvement of conditions which he knows is short of justice and humanity, and takes gladly when he gets it, though he will not work for it. Don't you know him? The good, respectable fellow who keeps himself to himself, minds his own business, and is too Christian to be unselfish. All these—and even the pious lady who attends daily Mass and evensong, and draws her dividends from goodness knows (but she doesn't care) where—all these are disassociated personalities and are not on the road to salvation.

The second method is that of rationalization—the conflict ends in compromise, the Christian standard is watered down until it reaches the level of practical politics and practical business. The Christian adapts himself to the world because he cannot adapt the world to himself—and despairs of doing so. He composes a new version of the Sermon on the Mount, which identifies the British Empire with the Kingdom of God and industrialism with the Divine Providence. He does not claim the world for Christ, but is content to stake out a limited claim for Christ in the world. The Church for him is a limited liability company—more limited than liable. But the conflict is not really at an end; it goes on underneath, and from time to time it produces nausea of religion and disgust with its unrealities, a disgust which breaks out into violent criticism of the Church and bitter judgment of fellow Christians. Nothing can save these souls but a social gospel which declares war in the name of Christ upon the world.

The third method is that of repression. And what is repressed is not the world, but the Christ. Men repress and choke back their aspirations and longings for better things. They repress the awkward impression that haunts them that Christ is right; and inasmuch as they do not see how his standard and principles can possibly apply to the world in which they live, they dismiss, or endeavor to dismiss, them as mere ideals worthless for practical men who have to work in the world. The result of this repression is indifference, often tinged with antagonism.

Go back to your parish and do some evening visiting, and you will find specimens in every street. Is there a parish priest who has not beaten his hands in vain at that stone wall, and if he be in earnest, has not beaten till they bleed? Behind that indifference there is a soul in conflict—a conflict of despair. Can we save him? Before you leave London go to the Royal Academy and have a good look at a picture called "The Laborer," by Richard Speed. It is the picture of a workman reading the *Daily Herald*, and all the tragedy of the modern factory hand is in it. I would like to put that picture in church underneath a Crucifix. "Inasmuch as ye have done it unto the least of these, ye have done it unto Me" (Matthew 25:40). There is a light of hope in the workman's eyes, as though he saw a way out. I heard a Christian who went to see it, and remarked that no man ever got that look in his face through reading the *Daily Herald*. I have been wondering what we would put in its place—*The Church Times? The Record? The Guardian?* I do not sneer—this is no time for cheap sneers—I am not sneering, I am asking, can we bring hope into the laborer's face?

It is not only matrimonial divorce which issues in moral disaster. It is always disastrous for man to attempt to put asunder those whom God has made one, and there is no divorce more morally disastrous than that between the reformer and the revivalist—the divorce between the men who, through Christ, are endeavoring to pour new life into the world, and those who are endeavoring to change the world so as to make it a fitting environment for and expression of that life. Each is poverty-stricken and powerless without the other. A divorce between the secular and the sacred means the death of real religion. The secular without the sacred is a body without a soul, and that can do nothing but stink and foster parasites. The sacred without the secular is a soul without a body, and whatever that may be it is not human. It is neither what man is nor what he is meant to be. There is a natural body and there is a spiritual body, and the idea that we are meant to be bodiless spirits is neither Christian nor true. I believe in the resurrection of the body and the life everlasting.

We come, then, to this practical issue. If we are to succeed in the re-evangelization of England and of the world, we must definitely recognize that what is often called the social message of Jesus Christ is an essential part of the Gospel. It is not an addendum to it, it is not something which follows conversion; it is that to which men need to be converted.

At present the overworked parish priest tends to be so absorbed in the saving of individuals that the social message fades into the background or becomes non-existent, while those who are alive to the necessity of Christian reform become so engrossed in the problems of the mass that they forget the individual problem. This divorce is fatal. As long as it continues the priest does not really save individuals and the reformer fails to help the world. There must be a union of forces. Every individual is in some form a walking, talking, suffering social problem. It is not enough to make the devotional life our main concern, and allow an occasional lecture or preachment on social matters to be added on as a make-weight. The social life must be brought right into the heart of our devotion, and our devotion right into the heart of our social life. There is only one spiritual life, and that is the sacramental life—sacramental in its fullest, its widest, and its deepest sense, which means the consecration of the whole man and all his human relationships to God. There must be free and open passage between the sanctuary and the street. We must destroy within ourselves our present feeling that we descend to a lower level when we leave the song of the angels and the archangels and begin to study economic conditions, questions of wages, hours and housing. It is hard, it is very hard, but it must be done. It must be done not only for the sake of the street, but for the sake of the sanctuary, too. If the Real Presence of Christ in the Sacrament obscures the Omnipresence of God in the world, then the Sacrament is idolatrous, and our worship is actual sin, for all sin at its roots is a denial of the Omnipresence of God. And this is no sensational bogey, but a real danger. I have been to Mass in churches where I felt it was sinful, sinful because there was no passion for social righteousness behind it. *When ye spread forth your hands I will hide mine eyes from you; yea when ye make long prayers I will not hear you; your hands are full of blood. . . . Cease to do evil, learn to do well. Seek judgment. Relieve the oppressed. Judge the fatherless, plead for the widow. Little children, keep yourselves from idols. (Isaiah 1:15, 17; 1 John 5:21)*

Remember that medieval ritual was a natural expression of medieval life which, at any rate, tried to consecrate all things to God—tried to build the Kingdom of God on earth, and dedicated all arts and crafts, all human activities to him. In that setting it meant much; apart from that setting it means nothing, and worse than nothing—it is a hollow mockery, the way out is not to destroy ritual, but to restore righteousness, and make our flaming colors the banners of a Church militant here upon earth.

What have we got to do?

1. *Teach.* Teach the social implications of the Gospel and the social meaning of the Sacraments. If Christian social teaching were not so rotten we would not have Socialist Sunday schools.

2. *Preach.* Preach without fear and without respect of persons the Christian Gospel of service and humility. Lift the whole social question above party and above prejudice; bow down neither to one side nor the other; recognize neither class nor party, but seek the truth.

3. *Pray.* Bring the whole world into your prayers. Pray as members of the worldwide Church.

4. *Demonstrate.* Demonstrate that in the Catholic Church there is a power which can knit together in a strong and stable unity men and women of different nations, different classes, different temperaments and interests. Demonstrate beyond doubt that the fellowship of the Catholic Church is different from and superior to, anything that claims the name of fellowship in the world. Different from the unity of nations, the unity of unions, the unity of parties.

If we fail to do that, if we split asunder into sections more numerous than those that already exist, especially if we split on anything even remotely connected with the Sacrament—have you sat down and faced the awful possibility which lies on the other side? The possibility that there is nothing either in heaven or earth which can unify men and make them one, the possibility that a Catholic Church is just a beautiful dream which can never come true.

That is the possibility that faces the man in the street today as he watches our party bickerings and sectional divisions. Dumbly he is asking today, "Have you anything to give us which can make the world in which I live less mad, less bad, less inhuman and unkind?" What is the answer of this great assembly going to be? Are we going to make another division in an already divided and helpless world, or are we, through the tender mercy of our God whereby the dayspring from on high hath visited us—are we going to give light to them that sit in darkness and in the shadow of death—and guide the feet of this poor, worn, and weary world into the path of lasting peace? Is our Lord of the Sacrament strong enough to enable us to keep our tempers, conquer our prejudices, and overcome our fear, our lethargy and mental sloth? Can he make all business the Father's business, and the only way a holy way against the common enemies of all mankind? If the Christ our Movement worships cannot do this, then may the Christ of the ages destroy our Movement and scatter its futilities on the wings of the wind to the seven seas, and give us the glorious Christ who can—and will!

(1923)

Force Is Weakness, Love Is Power

Would it not be enough, you say, to state that God is Love? No; that may mean anything or nothing apart from Him; it is a universal that is not concrete, and therefore does not bite and sting. But in Jesus it becomes distinct and powerful. In Him it means, first of all, that God is not force, that God is unarmed; that He is, from the world's point of view, helpless, as helpless as the babe in the manger, or the Christ upon the cross. That He has no weapons wherewith to drive men to His will. That He is for ever persuading, and not compelling.

This is the first tremendous fact about God that the life of Christ reveals. It is a fact so far-reaching and revolutionary in its effect, that it has taken us years to recognize it. Men simply could not bear it. They had always worshipped an armed God, a God with weapons in His hand and instruments of dreadful punishment, and they simply could not understand this revelation of the humility of God. The whole history of Christian theology is largely made up of strenuous efforts to reconcile the armed with the unarmed God.

Here and there men have caught glimpses of the truth, and have known that force is not an attribute of God; but for the most part they have been unable to accept it. They simply could not worship what they did not fear. And yet that is redemption in a nutshell, as St. John perceived. "Perfect Love casteth out fear, because fear hath torment" (1 John 4:18). Men, like children, are never really saved, never really become personalities, until they live righteously, not because they fear punishment for wrongdoing, but because they love the good life.

Here in this perfect Life, in almost every scene of it, we find revealed the meaning of the power of God, and are startled to find that, from the world's point of view, it looks like weakness. And yet, as we go deeper, we perceive how true it is, and begin to understand that force is always, and everywhere, a sign of fear—that is, a sign of weakness. Behind the vast armies and navies which we call the great powers of the world, there is fear. Fear it is that drives us out to war. Fear is the father of ferocity, and the forger of the sword. From the Creative point of view, which is God's point of view, force is weakness, and only Love is power.

This is the truth which, becoming concrete in Christ, challenges the world, bidding men see that they can never be saved until they are brave enough to disarm. If the Church takes up this challenge, she will be brought into inevitable conflict with the world, and her children will be called upon to suffer for their faith. It means that she can have no more to do with Nationalisms and Imperialisms that find their final sanction in force. That she cannot bless national guns and consecrate national Colors. It is going to be the greatest struggle in history, this is. From the modern battlefields the Christ has come forth vindicated at every point, with a new note of challenge in His voice, proclaiming to mankind that they must either gird themselves to follow Him, or suffer the sorrows of the damned. Not that He wills those sorrows, not that they come from him, but that apart from Him they are inevitable. This is the first truth that is born of the name of God. It may be objected that . . . if a criminal or a lunatic runs amok with a revolver, someone must stop him by force, before anyone can attempt to heal or redeem him. Thus it has been sought to reduce pacifism to an absurdity. But this argument leads us to two clear conclusions:

1. That force is negative in its results and, in itself, adds nothing to mankind. It is not a glorious victory to stop a lunatic; it is an awful necessity.
2. That force can only be used, with reluctance, to protect *mankind as a whole* from criminals and madmen.

From those two conclusions we arrive at the position, that the only form of force which Christians can tolerate or support is a police force—an international police force to protect the world from criminal and lunatic national mobs. This is the real practical alternative with which we are faced. It is not an immediate choice between our present conditions and immediate disarmament. It is a choice between National Armaments and International Police. That will come in time, but we are miles from it yet, and we certainly shall not be borne to that rational haven on the crest of an emotional reaction from war. Before it comes to pass, there will have to be martyrdom for it on a pretty large scale. Martyrdom for the principle of International Police, which now seems an absurdity, must become a reality. There will come to the conscience of the world a testing-time, and the Church must be prepared to produce her martyrs if she is to remain a Church at all. It is not a pleasant prospect. I do not want to be a martyr in that way at all. It is morbid to seek martyrdom, and the Church has rightly discouraged it in the past. It will be a beastly business. So many good men will be on the other side. They will have their ideals. There is no ideal which war fever cannot take, and twist to its own purpose. The great words Freedom, Honor, Peace, Justice, will boom out their thrilling challenge, and, reaching down beneath the reason, will wake the ancient instincts from their sleep and send men out to slay their brothers in an ecstasy of sacrifice. Only when the river of blood has swollen to a sea, and the nations reel back weary from the slaughter, will reason wake again; and that awakening will be torture, torture of complete disillusion; but from that torture, please God, will spring to life the Spirit of Triumphant Peace. That will come. I see no escape, and I dare not be confident that I shall survive the ordeal; the temptation will be terrific. Not plain choice between good and evil—temptation is seldom if ever that—but confusion—with a babel of conflicting voices, and apparent right on both sides. Those who refuse to take the sword from sloth, cowardice, self-interest, or pride, will damn their souls. Those who take it with a good conscience will be saved through the bitterness of disillusion—and those who refuse to take it out of honest Love for God and Man, will be crucified, but will rise again, to see of the travail of their souls and be satisfied. So I believe it will be.

(1923)

What Can *I* Do to Save?

We should remember constantly that our first duty, the only *raison d'etre* of our existence, is that "through the tender mercy of our God whereby the day spring from on high hath visited us, we may give light to them that sit in darkness, and in the shadow of death, and guide their feet into the way of Peace" (Luke 1:78–79).

If all that our religion does for us is to save us from the great abyss, if we are deaf to the cry of those who are reeling over the edge, clinging wildly to some last hope, or lying in the depths; if it does not fill us with the longing to save others, it is a fraud, it will not last. Life will get us yet. "Let him that thinketh he standeth take heed lest he fall" (1 Corinthians 10:12). If you feel no longing to right wrongs, to war against injustice and cruelty, to defy tyrannies, to abolish ugliness and dirt, look out! You are standing on a rotten piece of ground; it will give way beneath you when the hour comes, and you will do down. No rites, no ceremonies, no soft music and stately ritual will avail to save you. They will go down with you, and you will stand by a broken altar with filth upon the fair linen cloth and cry in vain for your comfortable Christ. I tell you I have been there, and I know. You cannot stop at crying: "What shall I do to be saved?" You must go out into the world, crying: "What can I do to save?"

All around you there are men and women who are well-nigh desperate. You must learn to hear them cry. They do not all speak plainly of their need. They do not know what they want. Some curse and swear, some laugh, some sneer, some dance defiance of despair; all but the weakest wear some pitiful disguise to hide their secret sorrow from the mockery of men. If you take men and women as you find them, and have no eyes to see them as they are, you walk in the world through a land of dreams, and never reach reality at all. Whatever else this odd world is, it is neither conventional nor commonplace. As usual, extremes meet, the cynic who sneers and the theoretical idealist who smugly smiles, carry on their warfare in a phantom universe that centres round themselves. One gleam of God's reality would lay them both stark dead.

Three months ago [at] Paddington Station one dreary Sunday night, I was accosted by a young man, who touched his hat to me, and asked if he could carry my bag. The touching of his hat made me sick to start with. You see he did not do it because he really respected me, or thought me worthy of it. He was crawling for a job. That is disgusting. I felt ashamed all over. My very bones blushed . . . It was servility. I do not and did not blame him. Necessity knows no law. But I was ashamed, and am ashamed. If any man touches his hat to me, not because he respects me, but because necessity puts him in my power, he degrades himself and me. Both slaves and slave-drivers are an abomination to the Lord. If you really like that sort of thing your soul is in danger.

I let him carry my bag, not that I really wanted it—I could have carried it myself—but because I wanted to talk with him. We went down the street, and talked of many things. At last I asked him whether he believed in God, or went to a place of worship. There came into his face a look which was in itself the most dreadful reply to such a question—a grin that was half a sneer, and he poured out at me his philosophy of life. It was just bitter, naked, disillusioned cynicism. The War and the Peace had finished all that for him. Every man for himself and the devil take the hindmost was the truth about life. There was no room in the world for Gentle Jesus, and that sort of stuff . . . He did not believe that the ultimate reality was reasonable, or that there was any meaning in life. Peace—or what we called Peace—has as many victims as War, it damns as many souls to the outer darkness of despair. It is the task of the Christian Church to save them.

We are often told that the Church has nothing to do with social questions; that there is no social Gospel; and that we should stick to our real business of saving individual souls. There is truth in the warning, but in the way it is often put it is just the half-truth which is the most dangerous sort of lie. It is perfectly true that we must not mistake the Kingdom of Comfort for the Kingdom of Christ, and suppose that if we could secure adequate wages and decent conditions of life for everyone our work would be done, but the souls we have to save are incarnate not disembodied souls, and there are conditions of life which are soul-destroying, not merely because they are painful, but because they are essentially degrading, inhuman, and wrong. All poverty is not degrading. There is a poverty which, as Christian saints have often shown, can set men free, and endow them with real wealth, the wealth of joy in simple things. But there is a degrading and destructive poverty which starves and stunts the human soul and makes for death, not fullness of life. Against that the Church, if she be true to herself, and true to her Lord, must wage ceaseless and unremitting war.

The poverty of men such as this one whom I met, and there are millions of them, is prostitution of the human personality. It is a branch of the white slave traffic, and it is our duty to stamp it out of the world, not merely by rescuing individuals who are compelled to prostitute themselves by crawling for employment as this man was compelled to do for the sake of his wife and children, whom the dole could not keep, but by devoting ourselves to the reform of those conditions which force him into this position. There are miles and miles of our modern cities and villages, too, which in the eyes of Christ are as beastly as a brothel, and for the same reason, they are the symbol and the sign of wholesale traffic in human souls... Living and working under such conditions it is well-nigh impossible for many to cling to their first act of faith, and believe that at the heart of things there is a Person expressing a reasonable purpose that they can in some measure understand. They see no evidence of it, and it is difficult to show them any, either.

(1925)

The Spirit of Prayer Can Overcome War

They ruined it all for me as a child; they told me that God's will was the Cross. God wished Christ to be crucified; He wished Judas to be a traitor, Pilate a coward, the priests to be fiends, and the crowd to be cruel and fickle-hearted. It was all part of His plan. Of course that is impossible. God cannot plan treachery and murder. They told me that when Christ realized that His prayer could not be answered, He meekly bowed His head to God's plan, and said, "Thy will be done." The cry of agony was the prayer, and "Thy will be done" an act of meek submission. It is the topsy-turvy kind of interpretation that arises from the Almighty-Monarch-on-the-Throne idea of God, Who wills both good and evil.

But it is madness. God could not will the Cross. It must have been utterly abhorrent to Him. God's will for Christ was that He should live the perfect life, bear witness to the final truth, and bear the torch of perfect love undimmed through everything. That was God's will, and Christ's work; and if it was to be done, it must mean that the Cross be carried, and all it meant endured, to the very end. That was necessary because of sin. So in His agony Christ prays, "Thy will be done." The prayer is immediately answered. The angel of God appears to comfort Him. Terror dies within His soul, hesitation disappears, and with His battle prayer upon His lips, "Thy will be done," He goes out from the garden in the majesty of manhood to bear such witness to His truth, to live in death so fine a life, that He becomes the light in darkness of every age, and the deathless hope of a dying world.

Too often we model our prayers upon the false interpretation of Gethsemane. Our prayers are too often either a wail of agony or a kind of indent upon God for supplies to meet our needs, with "Thy will be done" put in at the end in case God cannot take away the pain we plead against or grant us the supplies we need. "Thy will be done" ceases to be the great prayer, and becomes the necessary apology for praying.

. . . We [parsons] have taught our people to use prayer too much as a means of comfort. Not in the original and heroic sense of uplifting, inspiring, strengthening, but in the more modern and baser sense of soothing sorrow, dulling pain, and drying tears. The comfort of the cushion, not the comfort of the Cross. Because we have failed in prayer to bear the Cross, we have also failed to win the crown.

From the soldier's point of view the condemnation of such prayers begins with the conviction, bought by bitter experience, that they do not work. Religion as an insurance policy against accident in the day of battle is discredited in the army. The men have lost what faith in it they ever had. Just as the rain descends upon the just and the unjust, so do the shells, and good and bad, praying and prayerless, are shattered into bits. It is terrible, but it is true; as terrible and as true as life. The flying shell that shrieks in a shell is as impartial as an avalanche or a volcano. It is as inevitable as the Cross. Though in their agony men cry to God if it be possible to let it pass, it will not pass if the laws by which it flies must bring it to your feet. As God did not quench the fires that burned the martyrs or close the lions' mouths before they tore them limb from limb, so God does not turn aside the shell that flies shrieking out the call to martyrdom for me or for my son. Even as I pray now I may be blown to bits, as Christ, still praying, suffered on the Cross, and as His followers all down the ages have died the death with prayers upon their lips. Christ never promised to those who prayed immunity from suffering and death.

Well, then, what use is praying? What answers do we win? We win the only answer worth having, the power to pass through danger and through death with a spirit still unbroken and a manhood still unstained.

In all these things we can be more than conquerors through Him Who loves us, because through prayer He can pour into us the gift of the splendid spirit. And it does not end there, for having poured it into us, He can, through our prayers for others, pour it through us into them. The splendid spirit can run through the men who really pray, like a stream of living fire, out into the world of men and women who need just that, and only that, for with that comes all that's best worth having in this world.

A shell is just an iron sin, like the nail that pierced His feet. It is just sin wrought into metal. Sin can be worked into any form. It is just a gift of God misused. Sin takes form and substance in a million ways: it pours forth in speech, it is painted in colors, it is built into bricks and mortar, it is carved into marble. Wherever a gift of God is misused sin takes form. It took the form of a wooden cross and crucified the Son of God; it takes the form of an iron shell and kills God's children by the score. War is just sin in a million forms, in a million of God's gifts misused. God cannot deal with war in any other way than that by which He deals with sin. He cannot save us from war except by saving us from sin.

How does God deal with sin? By what way does He conquer it? By the way of the Cross, the way of love. He suffers for it; He takes it upon Himself, and He calls on us to share His burden, to partake of His suffering. He makes an army of the Cross, an army of men and women who pledge themselves to fight with sin and gladly suffer in the fight, that by their strife and suffering the power of evil may be broken and the world redeemed.

Prayer is the means of communication by which the suffering and triumphant God meets His band of volunteers and pours His Spirit into them, and sends them out to fight, to suffer, and to conquer in the end.

Prayer will not turn away the shell from my body; it will not change the flight of the bullet; but it will ensure that neither shell nor bullet can touch me, the real me. Prayer cannot save me from sorrow, but can draw the sting of sorrow by saving me from sin. And in the end, through prayer and the army of those that pray, God will reach down to the roots of war and tear them from the world. When at last through prayer the stream of the Spirit has flowed out to all, men will look upon their guns, their bombs, their gas cylinders as mad monstrosities, and will take the metal from the earth to mould and beat it, not into engines of death, but into means of beauty and of life.

Prayer, true prayer, will bring us victory. For victory comes at last to those who are willing to make the greatest venture of faith, and the supremest sacrifice. By prayer we can conquer war itself, and march at last into the New Jerusalem of God.

(1918)

This Good Samaritan Business

Of all the stories told by the Nazarene there is no one that has held the human imagination more powerfully than the story of the Good Samaritan, the picture of the poor fellow lying wounded and bleeding on the road from Jerusalem to Jericho. There is the exquisite character touch of the one man who hurries by in deadly fear without even looking at him, and the other who, while he goes to the length of stopping to see what's up and half wanting to help, starts thinking of himself, and, remembering that there might be other thieves knocking around, immediately turns away with terror in his face and pelts down the road as fast as his legs will carry him so as to get to Jericho before dark. And finally, the decent old Samaritan on his donkey coming along in the gloaming and doing the necessary kindness, despite the fact that the man was a Jew and he was a Samaritan, and the Jews felt towards the Samaritans very much what the English felt for the Germans immediately after the sinking of the *Lusitania*.

It is a wonderful picture drawn by a master hand and by one who, as St. John says, knew men and needed not that any should tell Him what was in men. And there is no human conscience not completely dead, that does not answer, for a moment at any rate, to the command "Go and do thou likewise." Many would say in fact that in this command, honestly and earnestly obeyed, lies all that really matters about the Christian faith. But if you set out to obey it in earnest you begin to find that it isn't as easy as it looks, this Good Samaritan business.

To start with, what you find in life is that there isn't only one road from Jerusalem to Jericho that is infested by thieves. Men can go to Jericho in all sorts of ways and women too, and this old world of ours is plagued with an infinite variety of sharks going around seeking what they can pick up. The first problem that hits the man who sets out to be a good Samaritan is just the problem of numbers.

You see, the Good Samaritan in the story was lucky, he only struck one man that had been knocked out, and he had all that was necessary—a donkey, some oil and wine, and twopence. But when I go out on that tack I don't find one man, I find processions of them, and I have not got all that is necessary. If I am to do it properly I seem to need a bottomless pocket, infinite wisdom, a fleet of motor cars and a general hospital, and even that would not be enough, because an enormous number of these poor devils that lie beside the roads to Jericho have not merely been knocked about bodily, they have lost their characters, they have lost their power of will, they are without hope in the world and without faith in themselves or in anything else. And it's when you get up against a proposition like that that you begin to realize your own limitations and to feel the need of some power greater than yourself. Giving money away is a ticklish business and as likely to do harm as good, and anyhow, when you get a fellow who has lost himself so to speak, money is no good at all.

The truth is that playing the Good Samaritan if you do it square and honest, drives you back to the necessity of a Savior and of a Gospel of salvation. If there is no such thing as the Love of God and His redeeming Power, the endeavor to play the Good Samaritan on the million roads that in this world lead downward from Jerusalem to Jericho would break the heart of the bravest and burst the brain of the cleverest that ever lived on earth. I guess that's partly what the Gospel story means. There was once One who tried to play Good Samaritan to us all, and He lay in a garden and cried in pain and broke out into bloody sweat.

And there is another side to it. It was all right for the Good Samaritan in the story picking up the chap by the roadside, but he did not own the road; if he had owned the road, his duty would have been to get it cleared of thieves, and not to keep trotting along with a donkey picking up men that had been knocked out.

And that brings you up with a bump against the whole social problem, because you and I are part owners at any rate of these roads to Jericho that are infested by sharks and thieves, and it doesn't do for us to think that our duty ends in helping to supply endless charitable funds, and financing innumerable societies to save the underdog. We cannot stop short of an earnest endeavor to clear out the thieves, and so to strengthen the travelers on the road that they may be able to defend themselves against those we cannot clear out.

And that is the double way the Good Samaritan story hits me. First of all, that if I am to be any good I need to look after my own soul, I need God, I want to have an extra store of faith and hope, of vigor and vitality with which to inspire and uplift those who fall out by the way. Men are always thinking of a parson as a pious sort of bloke who goes about holding up his hands in horror and cursing people for their sins. But that's not the way I look at it at all. My job really is doctoring people that doctors are no good to, and helping people that nothing on earth but only God can help, and striving all I know to give people faith and hope and power to be happy. There are more sins committed because men and women are bored and miserable and hopeless than for any other cause whatsoever, and if by preaching or teaching or talking or just by being friends with them I can give them faith and hope and the Love of God, then I am doing my job. And it isn't only a parson's job, it is the job of every man and woman in the world so far as they can do it. A parson has to try and do it for lots of people—everyone can do it for some.

It's right enough that if you really go and do likewise you won't be far from the Kingdom of God, but it's no easy task, and if you set about it honestly you will be on your knees in a fortnight asking God for help. If that is not true, I am a Dutchman. People are always saying to me, "I need not go to Church and I need not say any prayers, I can be perfectly good without either." If you mean by being good, not running away with your neighbor's wife, paying your debts and speaking the truth more or less, you may manage all right, but not if you mean by being good the Good Samaritan touch. If you are going to do that you must have a spring-cleaning inside and you must go on seeking hope in the hopeless, power to love the unlovely, to see beauty in the unbeautiful and give strength to the weak and wobbly, or you will inevitably find yourself unequal to the task. When a man comes in and sits down before you and tells you that he has made a complete muddle of his life and has nothing left to live for and care for in the world and might as well go to the devil quick, you may be as rich as Croesus and as clever as Winston Churchill, but he would have you beat to the wide unless you had something more.

Jesus of Nazareth knew what he was about, and before He said to this fellow who was trying to catch him out and to whom he told the immortal story "Go and do thou likewise," He told him solemnly, "The first and greatest commandment is, "Thou shalt love the Lord thy God with all thy Heart, with all thy soul, with all thy mind and with all thy strength, and then comes the second, thou shalt love thy neighbor as thyself."

A man has never been up against ultimate reality until he has stood beside a fellow man knocked out on the road down to Jericho and, looking at him, realized with horror that he had no donkey, no wine or oil, and not a sou to bless himself with, and nothing to give but himself. Then it is that a man asks "What am I worth?" and cries on his God for help. I have been there many a time and have known, God help me, that I am not worth much.

(1932; posthumous)

Work

Close by the careless worker's side,
    Still patient stands
The Carpenter of Nazareth,
    With pierced hands
Outstretched to plead unceasingly,
    His Love's demands.

Longing to pick the hammer up
    And strike a blow,
Longing to feel His plane swing out,
    Steady and slow,
The fragrant shavings falling down,
    Silent as snow.

Because this is my Work, O Lord,
    It must be Thine,
Because it is a human task
    It is divine.
Take me, and brand me with Thy Cross,
    Thy slave's proud sign.

(1927)

If I Had a Million Pounds

I would buy me a perfect island home,
    Sweet set in a southern sea,
And there would I build me a paradise
    For the heart o' my Love and me.

I would plant me a perfect garden there,
    The one that my dream soul knows,
And the years would flow as the petals grow,
    That flame to a perfect rose.

I would build me a perfect temple there,
    A shrine where my Christ might dwell,
And then would I wake to behold my soul
    Damned deep in a perfect Hell.

(1927)

It's Hard to Be a Carpenter

I wonder what He charged for chairs
At Nazareth.
And did men try to beat Him down,
And boast about it in the town,
"I bought it cheap for half a crown
From that mad carpenter"?
And did they promise and not pay,
Put it off to another day,
O did they break His heart that way,
My Lord the Carpenter?
I wonder did He have bad debts,
And did He know my fears and frets?
The Gospel writer here forgets
To tell about the Carpenter.
But that's just what I want to know.
Ah! Christ in glory, here below
Men cheat and lie to one another so
It's hard to be a carpenter.

(1927)

Sources

Part I

"Broken Dreams," *Food for the Fed Up*, 273.
"What Is God Like?" *The Hardest Part*, xi–xii, xiv–xv.
"What Is God Up To?" *The Hardest Part*, 1–7.
"Mad Misery," *The Hardest Part*, 10–11.
"In a Shell Hole," *The Hardest Part*, 15–16.
"Glory of War," *The Hardest Part*, 31–33.
"Preserve Thy Body," *The Hardest Part*, 18.
"Burying the Dead," *The Hardest Part*, 161–64.
"Running," *Lies!* 198–99.
"W-A-R," *Lies!* 4–5.
"Fed Up," *Food for the Fed Up*, 7–8.
"Facing Facts," *The Hardest Part*, 191.
"Waste," *Rhymes*, 25.
"A Song of the Desert," *Rhymes*, 52.
"The Sniper," *Rhymes*, 97.
"The Pensioner," *Rhymes*, 118–19.

Part II

"A Suffering and Triumphant God," *Food for the Fed Up*, 261–62.
"Christ Crucified Everywhere," *The Word and the Work*, 57–58.
"After War, Is Faith Possible?" *Lies!* 117–28.
"Why Does God Permit War?" originally published as "The Religious Difficulties of the Private Soldier," in *The Church in the Furnace*, 378–91.
"God is Powerful But Not Almighty," *Food for the Fed Up*, 49–68.
"God Suffers But Overcomes," *Lies!*, 149–53.
"The Messianic Passion," *Food for the Fed Up*, 95–116.
"In God's Heart," *Food for the Fed Up*, 260–62.
"Facing Up to Suffering," *Food for the Fed Up*, 175–204.

"The Sorrow of God," *Rhymes*, 81–85.
"Indifference," *Rhymes*, 27.

Part III

"The Plain Bread of Religion," *The Wicket Gate*, 27, 30.
"Four Great Certainties," *The Wicket Gate*, 31–56.
"Master Passion and Neighbor Love," *Lies!*, 107–115.
"The Three Temptations," *The New Man in Christ*, 191–213.
"Sin Is No Private Matter," *The Wicket Gate*, 179–83.
"Community, Suggestion, and Salvation," *The Wicket Gate*, 183–93.
"A Sin-Bearing Community," *The Wicket Gate*, 196–204.
"Faith," *Rhymes*, 12–14.
"I Lost My Lord," *The Unutterable Beauty*, 108.

Part IV

"Getting Christ Out of the Churches," *The Wicket Gate*, 211.
"Herd Churches," *The Word and the Work*, 32.
"Community Christians," *The Word and the Work*, 64–72.
"Bread, Work, and Love," in *If I Had Only One Sermon to Preach*, 261–69.
"False Charity," *The Wicket Gate*, 148–53.
"Connecting Sacrament and Society," *The Wicket Gate*, 166–69.
"Making the World Less Mad, Bad, Inhuman, and Unkind," originally published as "Salvation," in *Report of the Second Anglo-Catholic Congress*, 143–50.
"Force is Weakness, Love is Power," *The Wicket Gate*, 85–88.
"What Can *I* Do to Save?" *The Word and the Work*, 4–7.
"The Spirit of Prayer Can Overcome War," *The Hardest Part*, 107–16.
"This Good Samaritan Business," *The New Man in Christ*, 232–36.
"Work," *The Unutterable Beauty*, 110.
"If I Had a Million Pounds," *The Unutterable Beauty*, 113.
"It's Hard to Be a Carpenter," *The Unutterable Beauty*, 116.

Bibliography

Works by Studdert Kennedy
(publication dates indicate first printings)

The Hardest Part. London: Hodder & Stoughton, 1918.
Rough Talks by a Padre. London: Hodder & Stoughton, 1918.
Rough Rhymes of a Padre. London: Hodder & Stoughton, 1918.
Why Aren't All the Best Chaps Christians? London: Hodder & Stoughton, 1919.
Lies! London: Hodder & Stoughton, 1919.
"The Religious Difficulties of the Private Soldier." In *The Church in the Furnace: Essays by Seventeen Temporary Church of England Chaplains on Active Service in France and Flanders,* edited by Frederick B. MacNutt, 378–91. London: Macmillan, 1919.
More Rough Rhymes of a Padre. London: Hodder & Stoughton, 1920.
Peace Rhymes of a Padre. London: Hodder & Stoughton, 1920.
Democracy and the Dog Collar. London: Hodder & Stoughton, 1921.
Food for the Fed Up. London: Hodder & Stoughton, 1921.
The Sorrows of God, and Other Poems. London: Hodder & Stoughton, 1921.
Songs of Faith and Doubt. London: Hodder & Stoughton, 1922.
"Salvation." In *Report of the Second Anglo-Catholic Congress, London, July 1923—"The Gospel of God,"* edited by Francis Underhill and Charles Scott Gillett, 143–50. London: Society of SS. Peter & Paul, 1923.
The Wicket Gate; or, Plain Bread. London: Hodder & Stoughton, 1923.
Lighten Our Darkness: Some Rough Rhymes of a Padre. London: Hodder & Stoughton, 1925.
The Word and the Work. London: Longmans, Green, 1925.
I Pronounce Them. London: Hodder & Stoughton, 1927.
Religion: A Blessing or a Curse? London: P. S. King & Son, 1927.
The Unutterable Beauty. London: Hodder & Stoughton, 1927.
"Bread, Work, and Love." In *If I Had Only One Sermon to Preach,* edited by James Marchant, 261–69. New York: Harper & Brothers, 1928.
Environment. London: Ernest Benn, 1928.
The Woman, the Warrior, and the Christ. London: Hodder & Stoughton, 1928.

Rhymes. London: Hodder & Stoughton, 1929.
The Unutterable Beauty. London: Hodder & Stoughton, 1931.
The New Man in Christ. London: Hodder & Stoughton, 1932.
Bread. London: Industrial Christian Fellowship, 1934.
What Did Christ Mean? London: Industrial Christian Fellowship, n.d.

Other

Browning, Preston Mercer, Jr. "G. A. Studdert Kennedy: Poet and Priest." MA thesis, University of North Carolina at Chapel Hill, 1957.

Browning, Robert. *Balaustion's Adventure: Including a Transcript from Euripides*. London: Smith, Elder, 1871.

Carey, D. F. "Studdert Kennedy: War Padre." In Mozley, *G. A. Studdert Kennedy*, 115-61.

Carpenter, Edward. *Pagan and Christian Creed, their Origin and Meaning*. NY: Harcourt, Brace, 1920.

Chapman, Mark D. "King and Kennedy: Two Visions of Ministry for 8 March." *The Expository Times*, n.s., 110 (1999): 141-43.

Desenis, Philip A. "The Concept of a Suffering God as Found in H. Wheeler Robinson and G.A. Studdert Kennedy." BD thesis, Eden Theological Seminary, 1953.

Ede, W. Moore. "Studdert Kennedy: His Life in Worcester." In Mozley, *G. A. Studdert Kennedy*, 87-111.

Ellis, Robert A. "Geoffrey Studdert Kennedy: The Pastor and the Suffering God," *Transformation* 22, no. 3 (2005): 166-75.

Grundy, William. *A Fiery Glow in the Darkness: Woodbine Willie, Padre and Priest*. Worcester, UK: Orborne, 1997.

Huxley, Thomas Henry. "Autobiography." In *Method and Results: Essays*, 1-18. New York: D. Appelton, 1896.

Inge, William Ralph. "Confessio Fidei." In *Outspoken Essays* (Second Series), 1-59. London: Longmans, Green, 1923.

Jeffs, Ernest H. "G.A. Studdert Kennedy." In *Princes of the Modern Pulpit*, 152-82. London: Sampson Low, Marston, 1944.

Kirk, P. T. R. "Studdert Kennedy: ICF Crusader." In Mozley, *G. A. Studdert Kennedy*, 165-91.

Mozley, J. K., editor. *G. A. Studdert Kennedy, By His Friends*. London: Hodder & Stoughton, 1929.

———. "Home Life and early Years of His Ministry." In Mozley, *G. A. Studdert Kennedy*, 13-83.

Purcell, William. *Woodbine Willie: An Anglican Incident. Being Some Account of the Life and Times of Geoffrey Anketell Studdert Kennedy, Poet, Prophet, Seeker After Truth, 1883-1929*. London: Hodder & Stoughton, 1962.

Rodd, Cyril S. "Four Settings of the Passion." *The Expository Times*, n.s., 109 (1998): 134–38.

Sinclair, Ronald Sutherland Brook. *When We Pray: A Method of Prayer Taught by G. A. Studdert Kennedy*. London: Hodder & Stoughton, 1932.

Strachan, Kenneth. "Studdert Kennedy on Evangelism." *Theology* 96 (1993): 260–69.

Studdert Kennedy, Gerald. *Dog-Collar Democracy: The Industrial Christian Fellowship 1919–1939*. London: Macmillan, 1982.

———. "'Woodbine Willie': Religion and Politics After the Great War." *History Today* 36 (1986): 40–45.

Temple, William. "Studdert Kennedy: The Man and His Message." In Mozley, *G. A. Studdert Kennedy*, 205–37.

Vines, Maxwell L. "The Theological Struggle of Woodbine Willie." *Foundations* 22 (1979): 261–72.

Wells, H. G. *Mr. Britling Sees It Through*. London: Macmillan, 1916.

Weston, Frank. "Our Present Duty." In *Report of the Second Anglo-Catholic Congress, London, July 1923—"The Gospel of God,"* edited by Francis Underhill and Charles Scott Gillett. London: Society of SS. Peter & Paul, 1923.

White, C. Douglas. "A Study of Preaching as a Force for Social Change as Reflected in the Ministry of G.A. Studdert Kennedy." PhD diss., Southwestern Baptist Theological Seminary, 1978.

Wilkinson, Alan. "Searching for Memory in Time of War: Theological Themes in First World War Literature." *The Modern Churchman*, n.s., 27 (1985): 13–21.